NASTY, BRUTISH, AND SHORT

THE LIVES OF GANG MEMBERS IN CANADA

MARK TOTTEN
WITH THE ASSISTANCE OF DANIEL TOTTEN

JAMES LORIMER & COMPANY LTD., PUBLISHERS
TORONTO

James Lorimer & Company Ltd., Publishers, acknowledges the support of the Ontario Arts Council. We acknowledge the financial support of the Government of Canada through the Canada Book Fund for our publishing activities. We acknowledge the support of the Canada Council for the Arts, which last year invested $24.3 million in writing and publishing throughout Canada. We acknowledge the Government of Ontario through the Ontario Media Development Corporation's Ontario Book Initiative.

The Canada Council | Le Conseil des Arts
for the Arts | du Canada

ONTARIO ARTS COUNCIL
CONSEIL DES ARTS DE L'ONTARIO

Library and Archives Canada Cataloguing in Publication

Totten, Mark Douglas, 1962-
    Nasty, brutish, and short : the lives of gang members in Canada / Mark Totten with Daniel Totten.

Includes bibliographical references and index.
Issued also in electronic formats.
ISBN 978-1-4594-0038-2

    1. Gangs--Canada. 2. Gang members--Canada--Biography.
3. Gang prevention--Canada. 4. Juvenile delinquents--Canada-- Biography. 5. Juvenile delinquency--Canada--Prevention.
I. Totten, Daniel II. Title.

HV6439.C3T68 2012   364.106'60971   C2011-908185-

James Lorimer & Company Ltd., Publishers
317 Adelaide Street West, Suite 1002
Toronto, ON, Canada
M5V 1P9
www.lorimer.ca

Printed and bound in Canada

This book is dedicated to the memories of the many young people who have died from suicide, homicide, or accident. You demonstrated incredible courage and strength while confronting adversity. May you all rest in peace.

ACKNOWLEDGEMENTS

There are many persons, groups, and organizations I would like to thank.

This book would not have been possible without the generous financial support of the Ontario Arts Council, Writer's Reserve Grant. Diane Young, my tireless editor at Lorimer, deserves a long holiday far away from me. I am quite certain that she will join a gang if she ever sees me again.

I am indebted to the following persons for their expertise, time, support, and kind words of encouragement: Dr. Craig Bennell, Department of Psychology, Carleton University; Erin Wolksi and Irene Goodwin, Native Women's Association of Canada; Jacqui Wasacase and the Regina Anti-Gang Services program staff, North Central Community Association; Barb Rawluk and Brian Lunde, National Crime Prevention Centre, Public Safety Canada; Stuart Amyotte, Elder, WonSka Cultural School; Peggy Rubin and her staff team, Prince Albert Outreach Program, Inc.; Inspector Bob Mills, Sergeant Rob Lockhart, and Constable Denise Perret, Royal Canadian Mounted Police; Sergeant Shinder Kirk, Combined Forces Special Enforcement Unit, BC (retired); Patrol Sergeant Cecil Sveinson, Winnipeg Police Service, a.k.a. Nisotay Muskwa (Two Heart Bear), Sundance Helper, Lodge

Conductor, Pipe Carrier, and member of the Spruce Woods Sundance Family; Rob Rai, Assistant Manager, Surrey School District Safe Schools Dept.; and Kim Pate, Executive Director, Canadian Association of Elizabeth Fry Societies.

To the young people and families across the country whose voices form the body of this book, I thank you all. This book is a reflection of your suffering, challenges, and incredible strength.

Finally, I owe special thanks to my family. Sharon Dunn, you have been my rock and a fearless leader for far too many years to count. Words cannot adequately describe your unwavering support and compassion. You are my hero. Kaila and Leah, you have put up with Daniel and me, the only men in your family (sorry, Shadow doesn't count) for what probably seems a century. Daniel, you continue to amaze me with your dedication and hard work. Wasn't it just yesterday I learned how to change your diaper? Carol McLurg (a.k.a. Nanny and great-grandmother), you have always been there. I love you all.

TABLE OF CONTENTS

✳ CHAPTER 1 ✳

PUTTING A HUMAN FACE ON GANGS

Sylvie,[1] twenty-three, a "maximum security risk," has been living in a ten-foot by ten-foot cell in an all-female correctional facility for four years. Although her cell was designed for one, because of overcrowding she has been double-bunking (sharing her cell with another inmate) for the past two years. The cell is the size of a typical bathroom, with a toilet and bunk bed. Sylvie is serving a lengthy sentence for violent offences and institutional infractions, and has spent time in segregation—"the hole." She has been isolated for serious infractions and prolonged periods of suicidal behavior. She has been caught smuggling drugs, selling contraband tobacco, having sexual relations with other women, and stabbing members of rival gangs. Though she leads an all-female prison gang, she has been trying to get out of the gang for the past year. On the outside, she was a member of a male-dominated, violent street gang. Some of her offences came during the invasion of a rival gang's house.

Sylvie has two young children whom she sees monthly during

supervised visits at the prison. A social worker brings them for the visits. She is frequently suicidal and hurts herself at least once or twice every week, usually by cutting her arms with just about anything sharp enough—pens, pencils, staples, paper clips, kitchen utensils. Sometimes she butts her head against the concrete wall of her cell. She sees life as hopeless and she sees no end to her misery. She is conflicted about seeing her children because she feels like a bad mother. Her children, both girls, are wards of the child welfare system. Sylvie is angry at her social worker for having begun an adoption process.

Sylvie endured years of abuse and spent most of her childhood and adolescence in foster homes and group homes—twenty-five of them. Her mother and stepfather were both intravenous drug users—crack cocaine and morphine, by choice. Sylvie describes a mother who was unable to protect her from six years of sexual abuse by a male family member, that started when Sylvie was five. Her mother first denied the abuse happened, then acknowledged that, yes, she had been aware of it but felt helpless because of her addictions and her love for her husband. Even when Sylvie was in care, this man would abuse her during visits with her mother and stepfather.

Both Sylvie's mother and stepfather also grew up in care, in "too many foster homes and group homes to count." Both suffered chronic physical and sexual abuse, in care and in their families of origin. Both had parents who were addicted to alcohol and drugs, and both had some family members who were gang-involved. Her stepfather never held a job for more than a couple of months, because of his drug use. Her mother suffered from borderline personality disorder and bipolar disorder, but hated the side effects of the medication her doctor prescribed, saying it made her feel like a vegetable. She self-medicated with illicit drugs instead.

Sylvie told me she felt abandoned and rejected. She never

wanted to go to foster homes or group homes. It felt like a revolving door, around and around from home to child welfare placements and back. She believed that her mother blamed her for being "out of control," when she just wanted her mother to acknowledge the sexual abuse she had experienced and confront her abuser. She also wanted her mother and stepfather to quit the drugs. She told me she would run away from the foster homes where she was placed to go back to her mother because Sylvie felt she needed to take care of her mother, to make sure there were groceries in the house, and that her younger siblings got to school.

Intelligent and resilient, Sylvie loved reading and did exceptionally well at school until she dropped out after grade eight. Her grandmother had introduced her to books, and read to her frequently. But then, while she was in foster care, back on a home visit she tried to hang herself with a skipping rope from a ceiling joist in the basement. Her grandmother found her in time. She had neck injuries, but recovered after a one-month stay in the psychiatric unit of the local children's hospital. She never disclosed the sexual abuse to anyone at school, in the hospital, or at the foster home. Her mother's refusal to stop the abuse was humiliating enough. She did not need to have people thinking she was a liar.

Entering adolescence, Sylvie evaded child welfare workers and increasingly lived on the streets, engaging in survival crimes such as shoplifting, selling stolen goods, and trading sex with friends for food and a place to stay. She resorted to violence to defend herself on many occasions. She was incarcerated four times, in secure and in open young offender facilities, for a total of two years.

She searched for a family, for a sense of identity, and for protection from the violence on the streets. She thought she had found true love with a man in his mid-twenties. For about a month, Peter bought her clothes and gave her cocaine and marijuana. He offered her a place to stay. They had sex often and she believed that this meant Peter, a member of an African gang, loved her. Suddenly, after four weeks of bliss, he demanded money for the drugs, clothes, and rent. Sylvie was shocked. She had never had a job. She offered to work at a drive-through restaurant, but Peter told her minimum wage was not good enough. He told her she would have to work the streets to pay him back. Although she tried to quit drugs, it was too late—by now she was addicted to weed, cocaine, and morphine. It was a vicious cycle. Her body craved the drugs, Peter had a steady supply, and she had no way to pay him back. He told her he would kill her if she was not paid up within two weeks. He began to beat her and force sex on her. She had flashbacks to the sexual abuse she experienced as a child. Her cutting escalated out of control. She used razors and a hunting knife to slice her arms.

Throughout her adolescence, Sylvie was sent to see psychologists and psychiatrists, usually after she had attempted suicide or had beaten somebody up. Sylvie estimates that she slashed her wrists, tried to hang herself, and overdosed at least twenty times. A string of labels was attached to her—Attention Deficit, Oppositional Defiant Disorder, Conduct Disorder, Anti-Social Personality Disorder, Depression, Bipolar Disorder, and Borderline Personality Disorder. They made her feel blamed for being abused and rejected. The doctors prescribed medications, but she could not tolerate them. When she was twelve and on a home visit, her stepfather flushed all her medication down the toilet, saying, "You don't need that shit." By then Sylvie had reached the same conclusion; she was stockpiling her pills and selling them at school and to other kids in care.

Sylvie's grandmother was one of her few positive adult role models. A recovering alcoholic, her grandmother said she saw Sylvie as a second chance—a chance to erase all the mistakes she had made with Sylvie's mother. Sylvie often found comfort at her grandmother's apartment. She was never judged and could always count on a safe place to sleep, shower, and get fed.

Partly, she admired Peter and his role in the gang. He was a take-charge kind of guy, giving out orders to his soldiers and new recruits. He was also highly respected, because of his violence. She had seen him beat younger gang members when they tried to rip him off or when he believed they were flirting with her. But another part of her was confused and afraid. Although she had become accustomed to selling her body on the streets, she felt ashamed and wished she did not have to do it. She became increasingly violent with other young women in the gang, using her status as Peter's girlfriend to get what she needed.

After a while, Sylvie developed a plan. She asked Peter if she could run her own group of girls on the street and turn over the profits to him. In return, she would not have to sell herself. Much to her surprise, Peter agreed. Sylvie had a keen business sense and soon was making hundreds of dollars a night for the gang. Then, one night when the gang was partying, word arrived that a rival gang was having a house party a couple of blocks away. It seemed a good time to carry out a home invasion, steal the rival gang's drug money, and beat them up. Peter handed Sylvie a gun he had bought from a Hells Angels member. Five of them stormed the rival gang's house. Peter handed Sylvie the gun. She had never held a gun, let alone fired one, and started shooting wildly. Peter, Sylvie, and the rest promptly ran home. She threw the gun in some bushes on the way. Later that night, the police came knocking and arrested her, Peter, and the others. They were held without bail and, eventually, she was convicted of attempted murder. Peter and the others were convicted of weapons offences and assault.

By the time I interviewed her, she had been leading a prison gang since shortly after her incarceration began. She had discovered that the centre was a violent place and that she needed to develop a network of women for her own protection. She also needed a constant supply of drugs to feed her addiction. Her gang was different from Peter's. Hers had a sense of companionship, support, and equality. The sex she had with other women was not forced, and it felt good. Many women inside had same-sex relationships while incarcerated, yet also had boyfriends on the outside. She was not allowed any contact with Peter—in fact, she had no idea where he was doing his prison time.

Sylvie's situation illustrates one of the key messages of this book: Gang members are not born bad. Instead, they are trained by the adults around them. Each gang member in Canada has a human face. Each is someone's son or daughter, sister or brother, nephew or niece. Many, like Sylvie, are parents of young children. They arrive in this world innocent and sweet, just children themselves. They leave in body bags, or are incarcerated deep in the bowels of correctional centres for most of their adult lives; they are outcasts. Given the nature of their traumatic lives, it is hardly surprising that they become involved in gangs. It should be no surprise when they kill others, or die violent deaths themselves.

NOT A NEW PHENOMENON

Gangs are not a new phenomenon. Organized groups of criminals have been around for centuries—pirates, smugglers, bootleggers, cattle rustlers, horse thieves, currency counterfeiters, hooligans. It is hard to know if gang membership and gang activity are on the rise in Canada because there has been little scientific research on the topic. Academics started to investigate the phenomenon of gangs seriously only in the 1990s, and there still has not been a comprehensive, Canada-wide study on the subject of gangs, based on accounts of themselves. Media and law enforcement reports are often the most authoritative sources available. A number of reports, however, suggest that there are an increasing number of large and small cities, rural areas, and reserves where gangs have taken root. These reports also suggest that some types of gangs are becoming increasingly sophisticated and better organized. Correctional Service Canada also reports that the number of gang-involved inmates has increased over the past couple of decades.

Much of what is known about the history of gangs comes from other countries—the USA, Britain, and France, among others. In North America and parts of Europe, we can trace the history of gangs back to the Industrial Revolution. In North America, the immigration of European settlers brought class divisions based on race and ethnicity. Street gangs took root as a response to discrimination and poverty. Gangs rebelled against inequality, but they were also an important source of economic profit. As early as the middle of the eighteenth century, there were gangs such as the Long Bridge Boys and the Fly Boys in New York City, looking for identity, status, and pure economic survival. These gangs were not as involved in crime as modern-day gangs, but are thought to have been predatory fun seekers.[2] The Forty Thieves, an Irish-American New York City gang, were identified in the 1820s as a serious concern. During the nineteenth century, gangs quickly took root in cities such as Philadelphia and in parts of California, primarily in response to entrenched poverty and racism. By 1865, New York probably had the most gangs in North America, with Jewish, Italian, African, and Irish organized criminal groups.

In the twentieth century, gangs in America tended to evolve in impoverished areas, with economic differences taking priority over ethnic and racial problems. The Mafia also landed in the USA in the 1920s, having originated in Italy in the nineteenth century. The Great Depression brought more gang activity, primarily among Mexican and African groups, in cities such as Chicago, Los Angeles, Detroit, and Boston. After World War II, motorcycle and prison gangs emerged as new threats.

American prison gangs emerged in the 1960s and 1970s in California, including such groups as the Aryan Brotherhood, the Black Guerilla Family, and La Nuestra Familia. The Crips gang was founded in Los Angeles in the 1960s, the Bloods gang formed in the 1970s in response to the Crips, and both expanded into the greater California area.

In Britain, criminal gangs can be traced back to the 1890s in London. The Scuttlers gang members were referred to as "hooligans." In the 1930s, Glasgow was reported to be Britain's most violent city, with gangs such as the Bee Hive Boys. Gang activity was also reported in other countries, including Germany, France, and Switzerland.[3]

THE RISE OF GANGS IN CANADA

The history of gangs in Canada has not been investigated in a comprehensive manner. Stephen Schneider provides one of the few historical accounts of gangs in Canada in *Iced: The Story of Organized Crime in Canada*. He traces the roots of these groups back to the sixteenth century, when pirates attacked fishing boats off the Grand Banks in Newfoundland. He then documents smuggling in the nineteenth century, by such groups as the Whisky Traders in Western Canada in the 1860s. In the late 1800s, criminal groups were involved in currency counterfeiting, cattle and horse stealing, opium smuggling, and the smuggling of Chinese nationals into the USA. In the late 1800s and early 1900s, British Columbia was a main importer, exporter, and producer of opium (which could be smoked). Bootlegging in alcohol followed in the 1920s. From the 1950s to the 1980s, Quebec was a main stopover point for heroin smuggling from Europe to North America. Biker gangs such as the Hells Angels originated after World War II.

The emergence of Canadian gangs can be traced to poverty and racism, proliferating under conditions of social inequality.

Criminal youth groups gained a foothold following World War II when the focus was on the reintegration of veterans, and youth issues were not high on the social policy agenda. Starting in the 1970s, Canadian gangs were documented in large urban centres, including Haitian gangs in Montreal, Jamaican posses in Toronto and southern Ontario, Warrior gangs in Winnipeg, and Asian gangs in Vancouver.[4]

One of the first street gangs in Canada was Winnipeg's Dew Drop Gang, which endured briefly from 1949 to 1950. Winnipeg had a number of other adult criminal groups after World War II, including some that robbed banks and jewellery stores. Criminal youth groups were also evident, primarily engaging in assaults and break and enters. *The Winnipeg Free Press* referred to them as "hooligans."[5] In the mid 1980s, local media reported that active youth gangs in Winnipeg included the Rattlers, Maidens, Native Warriors, and the Rockers. In Toronto, the Beanery Boys Gang was active in the 1940s. Members were reported to be violent.

By now, there are pockets of youth gang violence across Canada. The rate at which young Aboriginal gang members are killing each other and committing suicide far exceeds the levels of such extreme violence in any other group in Canada. We cannot assume that gang activity is a "reserve problem," out of sight and out of mind. Aboriginal young people are rapidly exiting their reserves because of intolerable living conditions. Young people from sub-Saharan Africa and from other war-torn countries are also over-represented in gangs in Canada. These war-affected young people who have experienced atrocities and been forced into child soldiering arrive in Canada trained to violence and well suited to gang life. Gang leaders can spot these traumatized kids a mile away.

The Aboriginal birth rate is rapidly increasing—the child and youth population in many cities and rural areas will grow substantially within the next decade. The birth rate of many new

Canadian groups is likewise much higher than that of the main-stream population. This is critical information because young men in these groups are so over-represented in gangs.

The situation of gang-involved young women in Canada is not often considered. Often, these women are portrayed as cunning, manipulative, and "wannabe men." There is a common myth that all-female gangs are abundant and that their violence is escalating out of control. In fact, this is not true. Comparatively speaking, male gang members far outnumber gang-involved young women. Those women who are gang-involved play very different roles than their male counterparts do, and their pathways into gang life are not the same. There are hundreds of missing and sexually trafficked Aboriginal girls and women in Canada, and every year some of them end up murdered. We do not need to look any farther than the Highway of Tears in northern British Columbia or the Downtown Eastside of Vancouver. Commercial sexual exploitation, the modern-day version of sexual slavery, is a common way for gangs to generate income in Canada. What kind of a country allows its children to be disposed of in this manner? Would things be different if it were white girls and women who were being killed? This is a complex issue that I shall explore in detail in Chapter Four.

Many people believe that the gang problem can be best understood by examining the individual characteristics of members. Statements like "he came from a good family," "she was trouble from day one," and "he always hung out with a bad crowd" abound. Why are these "explanations" so popular? Could it be because they let us off the hook? When the focus is on individual agency or pathology, social factors such as poverty, racism, and the impact of cultural violence are ignored. Families, schools, communities, and governments are not held account-able. Deplorable social conditions are ignored. Instead, we can lull ourselves by saying, "He was just a bad seed." If only it were so simple. There are far too many gangs and gang members to explain away the phenomenon in such a simplistic way. The gang problem does have an individual aspect, but social factors are just as important.

The vast majority of young gang members have survived severe child maltreatment and trauma. The vast majority suffer from serious mental health problems. Many youth become gang members as a result of being institutionalized in the very programs set up to help them—foster homes, group homes, and secure youth justice facilities. Aboriginal youth are at particularly high risk, given that one in ten is taken into the care of the child welfare system and many more end up incarcerated.

In fact, one of the best ways to become a gang member or become head of a gang is to be incarcerated. There is little rehabilitation in Canadian jails and prisons; instead, inmates become proficient, more hardened criminals and more sophisticated gang leaders. Getting the "bad guys" off the street is a short term solution. For every bad guy incarcerated, two more take his place in the 'hood. Many gang members come from what I call "super gang families." They have parents as well as brothers, sisters, uncles, and aunts involved in the same gang or in rival gangs. Members of these families are responsible for a disproportionate number of homicides and other acts of extreme violence. Other young people form gangs with best friends they meet in elementary or high school.

When one takes the time to sit down with gang members and hear their stories—what life has been like for them in early childhood, adolescence, and young adulthood—a clear picture emerges. Instead of just seeing them as "gang members," I see that these young people have endured tremendous suffering; yet many have hidden talents and skills. Some are talented singers and rappers; others are poets and writers. Many have highly developed business skills that could be applied in the business world outside of gang life. Many are parents, struggling to raise children in impoverished and marginalized circumstances. Finally, most have serious health problems—brain damage, developmental delays, learning disabilities—or terminal illnesses, such as AIDS. If we could finally acknowledge the human face of gang-involved young people, we should find it easier to develop truly effective strategies for preventing gang involvement, for supporting the exit from gangs, and for implementing effective criminal justice system responses.

A FEW WORDS ABOUT MY RESEARCH

I have spent the past twenty-five years in the world of violent young criminals and gang members. As a certified social worker, I have counselled high risk children, youth, and families in the justice, social services, and child welfare fields. As an expert witness in gang trials, I have testified on issues related to gang culture and homicide. As an educator, I have delivered hundreds of keynote addresses and workshops for community members, corrections and policing professionals, policy makers, and school officials. As an evaluator, along with Sharon Dunn I have conducted multi-year projects investigating the outcomes of gang intervention and prevention programs. As a sociologist, I have conducted six studies across the country with young people, investigating various aspects of gang life.[6] These experiences provide the foundation for this book.

In this book, I draw upon my in-depth interviews with 519 gang members over the past 17 years, 380 of which were male. The average age of these young people was 18 years (ranging from 14 to 30 years) and 24 per cent (127) had been convicted of murder or manslaughter. Sixty-nine per cent (360) had been incarcerated[7] and 39 per cent (202) had grown up in the care of child welfare group homes and foster homes. The total sample size is representative of those gang members in large and medium-sized cities and small rural communities in Canada[8] and is many times larger than the average sample size used in previous Canadian studies.

It is important to understand that I use the term "youth gang" to refer to young people aged twelve to thirty years. I do not want to leave you with the impression that I am only concerned about teenagers.

In most of these studies, I spent time with gangs, getting to know the members, and building trust.[9] After doing this for some time, I asked members if they would consent to participate in confidential, audio-taped, in-depth interviews, the purpose of which was to explore the meaning of various activities and gang culture.[10] I wanted to understand gang members' use of violence and involvement in crime from their perspective. Another primary goal was to trace the lives of gang members, from infancy to adulthood. Semi-structured interview questionnaires were developed for each of the six qualitative studies and structured surveys were used in the two evaluation studies. The interview questions were modified from existing questionnaires used in a variety of studies having a focus on gang culture, severe violence, offending, and other aspects of gang life. Some modified scales were replicated in the qualitative studies.[11] Both evaluation studies used modified versions of existing surveys and scales used in other North American and European gang studies.[12] The average interview time in the qualitative studies was approximately five hours.[13]

The method I used to analyze the in-depth interview data was based upon the techniques of ethnographic data analysis.[14] This is an approach that generates theory from observation.[15] The quantitative data for the remaining 229 cases (those involved in gang project evaluations) were coded and entered into a database.[16] Rigorous methods for assessing truth status have been previously described and were utilized in my studies; they include triangulation of data sources[17] and investigative discourse analysis.[18] Twenty-four cases were excluded from the analysis because of concerns about accuracy and consistency (these cases were not included in the sample of 519 cases).

Ethics is a central part of any study involving young people who engage in criminal activities and high-risk behavior. In my studies, I had to make sure that participants were not harmed by virtue of being involved in studies, and that they did not harm others. This meant that I had to protect the anonymity and confidentiality of those involved in my research, yet at the same time make it clear that I had legal and moral obligations to inform the relevant authorities should I find out about serious crimes they were involved in or serious harm they had perpetrated on others. Child welfare officials had to be informed if I discovered that children were being abused. Mental health professionals had to be contacted if participants were suicidal or had indicators of serious mental illness. The police had to be informed if participants had engaged or were engaging in serious offending, such as carrying guns, home invasions, or assaults leaving victims with significant injuries. In cases where I had to report concerns to relevant agencies, I was surprised to find that the participants were often relieved to get these issues addressed. They did not want more children to suffer harm. They did not want anyone to commit suicide. They wanted to deal with their legal problems.

With the permission of the young gang members who participated in my studies, I have reproduced their narratives—their spoken words—to highlight key points. I have also included some of their poetry and other written work. In all cases, I have protected their identities. Each has a fictitious name. Because many have been involved in high-profile gang crimes, I have altered their stories in minor ways to protect them. Many of these young people have developmental problems, brain damage, or low levels of literacy. In order to improve comprehension for you, the reader, I have slightly revised their accounts and enhanced the grammatical structure. It is important, however, to understand that these narratives remain as the voices of young gang members. They are not fictitious. Some are raw, violent, and explicit. The reader will find some of them disturbing, no doubt. The reader is not alone. I am haunted by many of their stories, and I have been immersed in their world for many years.

✳ CHAPTER 2 ✳

UNDERSTANDING THE BIG PICTURE

Charlie, twenty-four, is an Aboriginal gang member in Western Canada. His long, black hair is pulled back in a ponytail. He is about my height (five feet eleven inches) and slim, not more than 130 pounds. He is wearing a muscle shirt and has many gang-related tattoos on his hands and upper arms. He looks awkward in his shirt because he is so thin. He has been in and out of provincial and federal correctional centres since the age of eighteen. He was released two days ago and is homeless. We are sitting at a picnic table in a park. He wants to get back into a counselling program for gang members, but is not allowed back because he tried to recruit young people into his gang on two previous occasions when he was in it. He rolls up his sleeves and says to me, *"Look, Mark, my arms are clean."* He is proud that he has not injected crack or morphine for the past three months. Although illicit drugs are readily available inside the correctional centre, he claims that he was able to resist the temptation during his last stint inside. I ask him if his health is okay, and he looks downward. He tells me *"Not so good, Mark."* He is HIV positive and has hepatitis C, both contracted from sharing needles while he was incarcerated.

He spent most of his adolescence on the streets of a small northern city and in young offender facilities. When he was only ten, he ran away from home with his sister to escape the violence and drinking. His sister was seven. They were apprehended by social services and placed in separate foster homes. They were allowed to talk over the phone every week and had monthly visits. Both were unhappy, having been placed with white foster parents and non-Aboriginal children. Soon, by the time his sister was eight, they had made a plan to run away. On a cold February night, they met at a set of railway tracks, walked the short distance to the automated teller machine enclosure at a Toronto Dominion bank branch, and spent the night inside. Charlie had enough money to pay for two bus tickets to Winnipeg, a much larger city with a sizeable street population, where they intended to blend in, and "fly below the radar" of child welfare workers.

Things went fairly well in Winnipeg until Charlie was arrested for breaking into cars, looking for money to spend on food. When he was put into a young offender facility awaiting his trial, his sister was again placed in a foster home. Charlie was convicted of multiple break and enters and sentenced to six months secure. After serving this time, he was placed into another foster home. He ran away after three weeks and again found himself on the streets of Winnipeg. He met some friends he had made in prison, who invited him to "go down" or join their gang—the Indian Posse. They told him how much money they made every night dealing methamphetamine and cocaine. Charlie, needing money and protection, agreed. His friends told him that he would have to do his "minutes" before becoming a member, and also do a "mission," as directed by their higher-ups. Charlie's mission was to beat up a drug dealer from a rival gang, steal his drugs and money, and give them to his friends' bosses.

The next evening, Charlie's friends pointed out the rival gang member he was to assault. They watched as Charlie punched this young man, kicked him repeatedly with his steel-toed boots, then took his drugs and money while he lay bleeding in the alley. After Charlie and his friends turned over the drugs and money to their superior, he was astonished to find his friends starting to beat him viciously. It lasted two minutes. Charlie thought he was going to die. They hit him with a two-by-four, punched him, and kicked him while he was lying on the ground. Then, the beating abruptly stopped. His friends helped him up and congratulated him on being accepted into the gang. Charlie, in shock, thought he should go to the hospital but they said that was not allowed. Instead, they gave him a baggie of cocaine and told him to snort it. Charlie had never done coke before, so they showed him how to scoop the cocaine out of the baggie with a knife and snort it. Charlie liked the rush. He felt like he was flying and forgot about the pain. Within a day or two, he was hooked.

Charlie's story is not that unusual. Many young men who become involved in gangs are first bounced around foster homes, the streets, and young offender facilities, then get recruited into low-level, disorganized street gangs that have fluid membership. The young men see their gang as their family, their protection on the streets, and a source of steady income. Drug abuse is common, as is violence. Typically, the young men are in poor health.

Gangs can be found throughout Canada and their level of activity and membership varies by region. There are three major categories: street gangs, mid-level gangs, and organized crime groups.

The multi-dimensional frameworks that I[1] and others[2] have developed highlight the different types of Canadian gangs involving young adults.[3] Street gangs are visible, hard-core groups that come together for profit-driven criminal activity and severe violence. In Canada, most street gangs are based in ethnically marginalized neighbourhoods and reserves and do not expand outside their turf or province, though a few gangs with higher levels of sophistication have expanded to other parts of Canada or to the United States. Gang-related communication rituals and public displays of gang-like attributes are common, including tattoos.[4] Gang involvement in Canada exists on a continuum, and there are different types of gangs. The degree of organization in the gang is defined by its structure and hierarchy; its connection to larger, more serious organized crime groups; its sophistication and permanence; the existence of a specific code of conduct or set of formal rules; initiation practices; and the level of integration, cohesion, and solidarity among the gang's members.[5] Types of gangs include African-Canadian, Aboriginal, Asian, Hispanic, posse, crew, motorcycle, prison, skinhead/neo-Nazi, occult, party crew, club, Folk Nation, and People Nation.

This integrated Canadian model allows for a general typology that can be applied and adapted to identify specific types of gangs. The common structure is very similar to that identified in the USA,[6] Europe,[7] and other countries.[8] The continuum includes *street gangs,* such as Malvern Crew (Toronto), Galloway Boys (Toronto), Jamestown Crips (Toronto), Driftwood Crips (Toronto), Redd Alert (Prairies), Mad Cowz (Winnipeg), Jamaican Posse (Montreal), Native Syndicate (Manitoba and Saskatchewan), Native Syndicate Killers (Manitoba and Saskatchewan), Fresh Off the Boat (Calgary), and Fresh Off the Boat Killers (Calgary); *mid-level gangs,* such as United Nations, Independent Soldiers, the Red Scorpions (all in BC), and Les Bleus (Montreal); and *organized crime groups,* such as the Hells Angels, Triads, Italian Mafia, and Russian Mafia.

STREET GANGS
Almost all youth gang members in Canada belong to street gangs. Street gangs are involved in serious crime and violence many

times every week—this differentiates gangs from non-criminal youth groups.

Street gangs have some stability over time, lasting at least one year or more. Membership is fluid.

Typically, they claim an area (their "turf"), which they protect from rival gangs. This may be a housing project or an area they claim to be their own for drug distribution. Members identify themselves through a common name, symbols, colours, signs, graffiti, clothing styles, bandanas, and hats. They rely on violent entry and exit rituals to protect the gang from outsiders.

Ethnic and racial minorities, including Aboriginals, dominate membership of Canada's youth gangs. While some gangs have members mainly from a single ethnic group, an increasing number are multi-ethnic.

Many youth who join gangs have already been identified as drug users and have been involved in serious and violent crime.

The majority of youth gang members are male, although there are a significant number of female gang members in Canada.

Compared to mid-level gangs and organized crime groups, street gangs have lower levels of sophistication and engage in less serious crimes. They are much less structured and relatively non-hierarchical. Members are younger, and the gangs tend to be based out of schools, reserves, or neighbourhoods.

MID-LEVEL GANGS

Mid-level gangs have characteristics of both street gangs and organized crime groups.

Mid-level gangs can be multi-ethnic, although some groups in the Prairie provinces are exclusively Aboriginal. Members may come from different socio-economic backgrounds, but most Aboriginal and African gang members have lived in extreme poverty. These gangs are frequently rooted in school, justice, and child welfare settings—family blood lines and neighbourhoods are important.

Compared to organized crime groups, mid-level gangs are made up of unstructured, smaller groups or cells. Like street gangs, relationships with other groups are fluid and opportunistic—often organized around lucrative criminal opportunities. Mid-level gangs are involved in serious crimes: extortion, kidnapping, drug dealing, smuggling, homicides and extreme violence, and trafficking. Violence is often initiated in response to perceived threats from other groups, whether real or not. Members rely on violent entry and exit rituals to protect the gang from outsiders. They are frequently sophisticated and disciplined.

ORGANIZED CRIME GROUPS
Organized crime groups are highly structured and hierarchical—often modelled after successful companies. These organizations have flourished over time and are recognized, feared, and respected.

They typically have exclusive membership based on family, race, and ethnicity. They are complex enterprises with rules, bylaws, and constitutions.

STREET GANG MEMBERSHIP AND ROLES
Youth gang membership can be modelled as concentric circles: wannabes/posers are on the outside, new recruits are in the outermost ring, and leaders are in the innermost ring (see Figure 1). Most gang leaders require new recruits to meet certain criteria and perform serious crimes of violence before they are allowed membership.

The leadership structure is made up of the founder and core members who started the gang. Membership ranking can be hierarchical.[9] Often, there is no one person who directs all other members, although older members have more influence than young members. Leaders (also called bosses or presidents) actively promote and participate in serious criminal activity. These males are generally in their mid-twenties or early thirties. Veterans (also called "higher-ups") decide which criminal activities the gang will participate in and their loyalty to the gang cannot be questioned. Along with the leaders, they are responsible for settling internal conflicts. These conflicts typically arise from members' having friendships with rival gang members; members having sexual relations with girlfriends of fellow gang members without their expressed consent; and members stealing either money from criminal profits or chemicals such as crack cocaine, crystal methamphetamine, and ecstasy. Punishments range from severe beatings to death. Core members usually have been with the gang since it started, and are experienced, proven members.

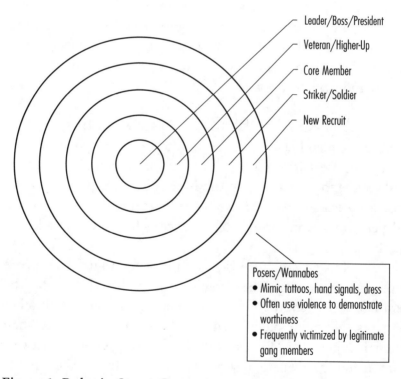

Figure 1: Roles in Street Gangs

RECRUITMENT

There are a handful of different routes into gang involvement. Some members are "born in," others are jumped in, some are actively recruited, some get "sexxed in" or raped in, and yet others form their own gang (original gangster). Some of these routes are characterized by a high degree of motivation and choice; others involve no choice. Fred Mathews, a psychologist with Central Toronto Youth Services, distinguishes between "push" and "pull" factors that lead to youth involvement in gangs. "Push factors" come from within the individual, such as the desire for a sense of belonging or identity. "Pull factors" include the need for protection or the lure of making large sums of money.[10] Motivational factors vary considerably by geographic location, socioeconomic factors, ethno-cultural origin, age, and the involvement of other family members in a gang lifestyle.[11]

The recruitment process is different depending on gang type. (By "recruitment" I mean the process whereby youth are brought into a gang or how they gain access to gangs.) Recruitment can be formal, often taking place in young offender or adult facilities, with gang members directly sponsoring young adult prospects. Joining a gang is seen as a normal thing to do for some family members who have been exposed to the gang by brothers, uncles, or fathers.

In other instances, street gangs and criminal organizations require recruits to perform specific tasks. This is active recruitment, and follows a standard process in each gang. Most gang leaders require prospective recruits to meet certain criteria before they are allowed membership.[12] These youth have to prove themselves to rise through the ranks; they often earn serious money for their gangs. To gain entry, a new recruit generally requires sponsorship and will have to "do minutes"—survive a beating. Younger gang members are most likely to be involved in the most serious crimes of violence, since they are in the recruitment process. These members have their loyalty tested often by gang members, and are "put in work" to undertake criminal activities when directed by leaders.[13] This is called "crime-in," and can involve armed robberies, aggravated assaults, murders (in which the candidate is referred to as being "murdered-in," and involves killing a rival when ordered to do so by a higher-up), drug dealing, and pimping.[14]

New recruits are required to commit a series of criminal acts, called strikes, or missions, at the direction of their superiors to prove loyalty. Many of the gang-related crimes in Canada are strikes committed by new members trying to increase their gang status. They must also produce a copy of their criminal record. The greater the number of convictions, the more respect the recruit achieves in the gang. Strikers (sometimes called soldiers) are likely to engage in serious acts of violence.[15]

Wannabes (or posers) are at particularly high risk of being victimized by violence at the hands of legitimate gang members. These youth are looking for a sense of belonging and family, and will go to great lengths to mimic gang membership through tattoos, dress, display of colours, and hand signals.

A man named Junior told me how he was actively recruited into his gang. It was in a young offender centre, at the age of fourteen. By the time I interviewed him, he had spent most of his life in correctional facilities: *"In total I did fuckin' sixteen–seventeen years, pretty much half my life in the pen. The correctional, first time, got sent there from [a young offender centre]. I was fourteen, that's when I got involved in gangs. I was with them from '98 up to '04."* He went on to say that things were different back then: *"It's not like it is now. I made more money. People were not strung out on coke as they are now. It was fun then because of all the money."* As a new recruit, he followed orders: *"When I was in that gang, it was a little bit of everything. I knew where to get guns when I needed them, drugs when I needed them. I did what I was told to do. You could rely on me, no questions. I got involved because people could rely on me—to stash guns and drugs. People did that for me, too."* As he moved up in the gang, his role changed. Because he was trusted by gang leaders to hand over money, he ran the girls on the street, even though he said that he did not like doing that: *"I felt bad about putting girls on the street. That bothered me the most. I always had in the back of my mind if that was my little sister, how would I feel. I would get mad and beat up another guy for that. I didn't think of it too much of the time. I was partying, I'd have the whole day to chill then start drinking at night."* He also was involved in home invasions and attacking other gang members: *"If I was rushing someone's house, it was probably a drug dealer, so I didn't feel too bad. If it was rollin' someone it was probably another gang."*

Eventually, though, he got tired of doing the time for the crimes of his higher-ups. A good part of the time he spent incarcerated was not even for things he had done. Getting older, he came to the conclusion that he had to move on with his life. He got beaten out of his gang for refusing to do more time for the leaders, but he felt the beating was worth it. Now when he does time, it is for his own crimes.

> *I realized that ten–twelve years, I think that's how long it's been, I wasted all that time doing fuck all. The minute you get picked up, it's like they don't know you [the leaders for whom you are doing time]. I've done that to a few people too, gone to jail. I'd try to help them out if they were going to jail, in trouble. Doing something I was told to do. I just got fed up with doing years for someone else. The past couple of times in jail have been for stuff I've done—I can blame myself, past two or three times. I still have a temper, that attitude. I am still involved somewhat in*

that lifestyle, I'm still, if someone disses [disrespects]
someone I'm with, I want to attack him.

Gender plays a crucial role in determining routes into gang
involvement. Many female gang members get "sexxed in" or
raped in; have a boyfriend, husband, or partner who is gang-
involved; associate with the gang through partying and drugs; or
associate through the sex trade. Sexxing/raping in occurs when
young women are forced to endure sexual assaults by multiple
gang members. Two case examples may illustrate.

From the age of fifteen to nineteen, Kitty was the only female
in an all-male street gang. She had to show the male gang members that she was deserving of their respect and that she was
tough. She also needed a strategy to avoid being forced into the
sex trade to bring money into the gang. Over a three-year period, she resorted to pimping out a stable of anywhere from six
to ten fifteen- to seventeen-year-old girls. She was widely feared
on the streets because of her propensity for severe violence. She
continued this lucrative operation until she was apprehended,
charged, and incarcerated for four years in both youth and adult
facilities. She told me how treatment by her childhood caregivers
had set the stage for gang membership:

> *My dad is old now and probably isn't going to be*
> *around for much longer. He's probably sick. He's*
> *done needles for as long as I can remember. Coke*
> *and mo [morphine]. That's what I remember when*
> *I was young. Always lots of people coming and*
> *going, lots of girls and needles and alcohol. They all*
> *were slammin' [shooting up]. My dad was a dealer*
> *and a pimp—that's why there were always lots*
> *of girls and drugs around. That's how they [child*
> *protection] took me. I brought a friend home when*

I was like five or six and my dad and all those people were doing needles and then my friend went home and told her mom and child welfare came to get me later that day. The cops picked my dad up.

The second case involves Susan, twelve, who began running drugs for male members of an established street gang after resisting their demands for a couple of months. Her mom, aged twenty-seven, had called a program asking for help with her daughter. Susan was already on probation for assaulting a thirteen-year-old girl at school. Susan, living with her mom and a new baby sister, was feeling extremely bitter and angry at her mom for spending so much time with her baby sister. She rarely made curfew, skipped school regularly, and associated with older male teens at night. She refused all of her mom's attempts to get her into counselling and recreational programs.

Her mother was white, and her father was Cree. She had never met her father, although she carried a picture of him, and had many of his physical features. Susan said she experienced discrimination because she looked native. The night before I interviewed her the exterior and windows of their home had been covered with red spray paint, with Indian Posse graffiti and slurs like "Susan is a slut," "Skank lives here," and worse. She began running drugs for the Indian Posse gang the next day. She told me she had no choice. She would have been gang-raped in if she had continued to refuse.

GANG CULTURE

There is an abundance of research on gang culture.[16] Gang culture includes things like hand signals, dress, and tattoos. In general, it encompasses the various forms of communication within and between gangs.

There are some common indicators of membership. The more indicators there are, the greater the likelihood that a young person is gang-involved. These indicators include stylized dress and haircuts; jewellery; tattoos; gang slang; graffiti and drawings; letters and personal writings; weapons; monikers or nicknames; hand signs; substance abuse; claiming or repping (representing a gang using their dress, hand signals, graffiti, etc.); association with known gang members; burns and scars, particularly those which are stylized (such as cigarette burns in the form of a triangle); branding (including burning a gang tattoo off); gang photos on social media sites; and money.

In general, there are two different gang nations or alliances, with many different gangs affiliated with each nation.[17] For example, the Bloods are affiliated with the People nation and the Crips are associated with the Folk nation. This is important, because it helps explain the Bloods' and the Crips' communication rituals. People Nation groups use *left identifiers*, such as forming their hand signs with the left hand; wearing their hats tilted to the left; rolling up the left pant leg; resting their hand in the left pocket; and wearing jewellery to the left. Folk Nation group members use *right identifiers* to distinguish themselves, wearing articles of clothing to the right (hats, bandanas, belt buckles), wearing jewellery to the right, and rolling up the right pant leg, and so on.

HAND SIGNALS AND DRESS

The Bloods and Crips are two good examples, each having adopted specific cultural forms and public presentations. Bloods identifiers and symbols include the colour red, red bandanas ("rags"), the letter *C* crossed out in words as disrespect for Crips, and disrespectful anti-Crips graffiti. Crips identifiers and symbols include the colour blue; blue bandanas; using the letter *C* in place of *B* in writing, in disrespect for Bloods; and calling themselves "Blood Killas" (BK).

Most Blood gangs, for example, use one hand to form a variation of the lower-case letter b to represent or lay claim to their territory or faction. "Repping" with hand signals is used in many situations where other gang identifiers (such as graffiti) may not be possible or appropriate, and can also show that a gang member is in the area to conduct gang business as opposed to just passing through. Usually these signs are made by formation of the fingers on one or both hands to make some sort of symbol or letter. It can also serve to relay more specific information, such as what faction they represent within a larger gang or in which activities they are currently engaged. Individual letters can be used to tell stories when flashed in rapid succession, each representing a word beginning with that letter. Because hand signals are only displayed when wanted (compared to dress or graffiti), they are usually the most consistent signifier of gang affiliation across geographical areas. Some gang-related hand signals, unfortunately, are similar to other common hand signs. This can result in confusion between gang members as well as with individuals who are not affiliated with gangs. Sometimes the result is violent victimization.

GRAFFITI

Gangs use graffiti to communicate with rival gangs and community residents. Graffiti may mark a geographic turf or a drug turf, threaten and disrespect rival gangs and their members, remember a fellow gang member who has been killed, or facilitate business transactions.

Gangs commonly claim a turf by "tagging" public spaces such as walls on buildings, fences, or other surfaces. Individual members also tag their own names on public spaces. For example, the African Mafia Killers tag "AMK" is painted on conspicuous places to demonstrate to rivals that they "own" a specific turf. When members of the African Mafia Killers want to disrespect the African Mafia gang, they write over or cross out the African Mafia tag. In so doing, the African Mafia Killers are openly disrespecting the African Mafia. African Mafia

Killers also disrespect the African Mafia by writing the name "African Mafia" upside down or on its side. Gangs will also use graffiti to communicate a specific message to rivals, most often in the form of a threat. For example, if the Bloods gang intends to shoot or kill a specific Crips gang member, the Bloods will often tag the rival gang member's name with other words or numbers indicating violence. Young Canadian gang members may use the number 187 (the California Penal Code number for murder), draw a gun pointed at the name, or write "die" beside the name. Graffiti is also used to indicate gangs that affiliate with each other. It is common for gangs to cooperate in the distribution of large amounts of illicit drugs, the goal being for each gang to make as much money as possible. Often, the affiliation is temporary and ends when the criminal project is completed.

When a gang wants to pay homage to a member who has been killed, the gang often paints a mural on the side of a building, with the phrases "In memory of" or "Rest in Peace," along with the name of the deceased. Individual gang members write their own names on the mural. Although these murals are a way of memorializing members who have been killed, they also serve to increase the gang's visibility and its status.

Graffiti is also used to facilitate criminal activities, such as drug dealing and selling stolen goods. For example, it is common for gang members who sell drugs to paint an arrow on a building or fence indicating the location of where they are dealing. Historically, the United Nations gang stamped their initials (UN) on the bricks of cocaine they were selling.

TATTOOS

Street gang members use tattoos for several reasons, leading to most gang members having numerous tattoos, particularly if they have spent time in young offender facilities, jail, or prison.

Tattoos are of symbols that the gang has adopted, and are worn and used for intimidation. Members of violent gangs usually wear their tattooed gang name in large bold letters. Wearing an unauthorized tattoo typically results in the wearer being severely beaten or killed.

Crosses between the knuckles on both hands are meant to signify the number of years served in federal facilities (one cross is equivalent to one year served). Three dots or cigarette burn marks forming a triangle (usually near the thumb or wrist or next to one eye) signifies *"mi vida loca"* ("my crazy life").[18] My research, along with a small number of studies using samples of adult men, suggests that the tear drop tattoo can have specific meanings depending on its shape and location.[19] As an expert witness in gang homicide trials, I have testified that this tattoo can signify one or more of the following: the wearer has killed a member of a rival gang; the wearer has spent time in prison; or the wearer is memorializing the death of a fellow gang member or family member.

PRIMARY ACTIVITIES OF STREET GANGS

Contrary to popular belief, gang members spend the majority of their time hanging out, meeting basic needs such as food and shelter, partying, and being incarcerated. It is not a glamorous lifestyle, and most street gang members live in poverty. They generally withdraw from society, and use drugs and alcohol heavily. Because of the drugs, gang members may commit property crimes and crimes of violence, often on an impulse.[20] The case of Lillian, a twenty-one-year-old female gang member, is illustrative. She is homeless and preoccupied with getting high and finding her next meal. She sleeps on couches at friend's places when she can, and trades sex or drugs for places to stay when friends will no longer take her in. She cannot stay at the local women's shelter because she is strung out on methamphetamine. Residents are not permitted to show up high. Although she makes more than enough money every night to support herself and pay for her drugs, she has to give almost all of it to her captain in the gang. Lillian is in poor health. She has "meth mouth" (advanced tooth decay that results from prolonged methamphetamine drug use), numerous open abscesses, and weighs only ninety-five pounds.

Lillian has been convicted of numerous property crimes, including break and enters and shoplifting, stealing mainly food and money. When she is not dealing or taking care of her basic needs, she hangs out with her gang-involved friends in drop-in centres or on the streets. She finds the constant search for meals, for a roof over her head, and for her next fix monotonous and boring. She uses drugs to escape and to forget.

My research indicates that many ex-gang members, when asked to reflect on their gang life, say it has been meaningless and a waste of time. Despite the thrills from periodic violence (home invasions and gang fights, for example), members say that gang life is mostly boring and monotonous. Yet, many young gang members also indicate that their gang is a haven from violence and discrimination in their families and communities.

CREATING MEANING

How do gang members find meaning in hopeless and meaningless lives? How, say, do gang members recreate the psychological thrills and the rush of doing street crimes after they have been incarcerated? The jailbreak is one way. Leading police on a manhunt for weeks, and taunting them along the way, can give meaning to otherwise hopeless lives. Giving the finger to the correctional system makes heroes out of otherwise marginalized and downtrodden gang members. The Regina Correctional Centre jailbreak is a good example.

On August 24, 2008, six Aboriginal young men, all believed

to be Indian Posse gang members, broke out of the Regina Correctional Centre: Ryan John Agecoutay, twenty-five; Preston Clarence Buffalocalf, twenty-two; Cody Dillon Keenatch, nineteen; James Joseph Pewean, twenty-five; Daniel Richard Wolfe, thirty-two; and Kenneth Lee Iron, twenty-three. They were being held in Unit 3D but were able to break through a wall. Built in the 1960s as a medium-security area, Unit 3 had been modified into a secure remand unit four years prior to the jailbreak. The escape was well thought out, relying on the building's poor-quality infrastructure and the help of other inmates. Police described the escapees as very dangerous and likely armed.

These men were being detained in the Regina Correctional Centre on charges ranging from murder to aggravated assault. It is likely that they had been enthralled by *Prison Break*, a hit television show.

All six had histories very similar to those in my studies. All had been beaten and battered throughout childhood and early adolescence. Some had been abandoned on the streets by parents, others were apprehended and placed in a revolving cycle of group and foster homes. Some had fetal alcohol spectrum disorder, others had mental health disorders and developmental impairments. Some had children of their own. All were searching for meaning.

One, Daniel Wolfe, a founding member of the Indian Posse street gang, was in the Correctional Centre on two counts of first-degree murder and three counts of attempted murder after a violent home invasion in Fort Qu'Appelle, Saskatchewan. Even before that incident, though, he had had a large following in Western Canada. The media reported on his crimes regularly, but he was also an occasional media commentator, and was viewed by some as a strong supporter of Aboriginal culture, a "warrior" with the goal of taking back land for his people and defending Aboriginal rights. The jailbreak gave him folk hero status among some groups, particularly marginalized young Aboriginal men looking for adult role models. He has since been murdered.

MAKING PROFITS FROM SERIOUS CRIME

Steve, twenty-three years old, had been out of his gang for thirty-seven weeks. He was in a halfway house and addicted to drugs. He was HIV positive. Although he had exited his gang, he was still engaged in drug dealing. He came by it naturally—his father had led a drug crew for many years. He told me about the money he made dealing drugs, both when he was in the gang and after he left it. Steve estimated that, on a good night, he could gross a thousand dollars, about two-thirds of which he had to turn over to his higher-up in the gang. Like many of the other young people I interviewed, he talked about the perils of gang life—perpetration of and victimization by violence, time spent incarcerated, and the rollercoaster of emotions:

> In grade eight, I dropped out. I started getting into heavy drug use at age thirteen. I was doing jobs, selling drugs to support my drugs. Friends were cool, okay, kind. Not really friends but associates. So you have cash, dope, that was the main thing. When I was getting high, thirteen, fourteen, fifteen, I was never in a gang. I got initiated, I was down, a gangster. I sold drugs for my homies, got high with them. It [was a] group thing, not missions. Ever since that I've been hanging with [name of gang], selling dope and stuff. I could stab people, bear spray, mace, pepper spray, club them wrong, shoot somebody...Since I was born I got involved in gangs. Since age fifteen, in and out of jail. Correctional [name of jail], penitentiary, group homes when I was old enough to get charged, then Juvie. I have mixed feelings, everything. There was

no medium [mood]—happy, sad, really happy, really sad. It is not even a lifestyle. Gang life is sickening, it leads nowhere. Down, like lockdown in jail, or up, like heaven.

Making money through serious crime may be episodic for disorganized street gangs, but it usually involves complex relationships and an organized division of labour for higher level gangs. As street level robberies and violent confrontations between rival gangs increase, victims are made aware of a "turf war" as gangs establish their territory. It is common for rival gangs to take control of separate high-rise apartment buildings in social housing communities and use them as bases for dealing drugs, pimping young women, selling and storing firearms, and shooting at rival gang members from upper floor apartments. Often, members charge a fee for protection from external intruders from housing community residents. As members become entrenched in violence and crime, the complexity of their behaviour increases and they assume a permanent place in specific geographic spaces. They come to acquire a steady supply of chemicals to sell, such as crack cocaine, crystal methamphetamine, ecstasy, and heroin, and an arsenal of guns to protect themselves and kill off rivals. The frequency and seriousness of violence and crime escalate. Because of their extreme use of violence and their large profits from crime, street gang members are afforded great respect and status within the social housing community. The reputation and status of gang members grows with the intimidation of any witnesses to their criminal activities. Both community residents and rivals are impressed.

ENGAGING IN EXTREME VIOLENCE

Street gangs generally use threats, violence, and intimidation to gain respect and fear in the neighbourhood. Billy's case is typical.

He told me about his role as a soldier in his gang. He was ordered to be the "muscle" in his gang—essentially a violent debt collector. He discussed the downside of this lifestyle, and how he was able to deal drugs and steal cars as a way out of the enforcement role.

> *I was an enforcer, a short little guy like me, I was their muscle, a force to be reckoned with. What I did was I made well sure everybody paid. If you did not, there were going to be problems. I just was just like the collector. If you had problems with this guy, hurt my bros, I was the one who dealt with it. It's a mixture because I did do muscle. I was the muscle for a while then I was kinda sick of it. I did not want to keep on breaking people's arms and legs, smashing their heads. So I started dealing. I was numb, I had no feelings. I did not feel anything. I was doing more things. When someone needed a car I would steal it. I was using. I had no remorse or pity. It was business, nothing personal.*

Violence within and between gangs is associated with gaining social status and reputation. There are emphases on honour, personal integrity, and territoriality. Issues of self-esteem, gender identity, and self-protection are involved.

Violence often occurs over seemingly insignificant incidents that are perceived as disrespectful by rival gang members, including the crossing out of a rival's graffiti or painting it upside down, or showing a rival's hand signs upside down, or crossing out a rival's hand signs with another finger. Acts of disrespect for a gang member's reputation by someone outside of the gang can result in violent retribution. In street gangs, the violence is often irrational, undertaken in response to perceived threats by rival gangs or threats within gangs. It is common for gang members to be victimized by their "higher-ups" if they contravene specific norms. Having unauthorized sex with a girlfriend of another gang member or ripping off gang leaders are worthy of severe beatings.

WHY ARE ABORIGINALS, POOR MINORITIES, AND YOUNG IMMIGRANTS FROM WAR-TORN COUNTRIES OVER-REPRESENTED IN GANGS?

Youth from racialized groups (non-dominant ethno-racial communities who, through the process of racialization, experience race as a key factor in their identity[21]) have higher levels of social and economic disadvantages and are at increased risk for social exclusion, negative physical and mental health outcomes, and gang membership.[22] Discrimination and social exclusion are a part of daily life for many newcomers (that is, immigrants and refugees arriving less than five years ago) and ethno-racial youth.[23] Canada has roughly five million immigrants, half of whom are youth, living in large urban centres.[24] These youth face multiple barriers and challenges in settling in Canada, including stress related to the immigration and resettlement process, exposure to atrocities during the time they were interned in refugee camps, lack of access to vital services, language barriers, intergenerational and gender differences, and adolescent developmental transitions.[25] To make matters worse, thirty percent of immigrant children and youth live in families whose total income falls below the official poverty line.[26]

Until the 1990s, traditional refugees to Canada were often Eastern Europeans escaping Cold War oppression. In general, these refugees integrated well into Canadian society because they had high levels of education and employability and resembled Canadians, both ethnically and culturally.[27] However, the makeup of refugees coming to Canada since then has changed. Most are fleeing violence from war-torn countries in

Sub-Saharan Africa, Afghanistan, and in the Middle East. Most do not have the levels of education and employability of the traditional refugees to Canada (i.e., Eastern Europeans). Many are black Africans with varied cultural, ethnic, and socioeconomic histories who have difficulty speaking English or French. Many are Muslims who face racism because of Westerners' unfounded fears of terrorism and because of the stereotyping of religious and cultural traditions (such as fasting, wearing the hijab, or daily prayers).[28]

The involvement of minority males as victims and offenders through gang violence leads to the perception that gangs are an "imported" immigration issue.[29] This is a myth. Canadian-born youth are more likely to report membership in gangs than are youth born in other countries. Immigrant gang members are no more likely to be involved in crime—as offenders or victims—than their Canadian-born counterparts. In fact, recent immigrants are least likely to report gang membership. Immigrants who have been in Canada for more than ten years are more likely to report gang affiliation.[30] Serious gang activity is most common among poor people and disadvantaged minority groups: This is racialized poverty. Poverty rates are very high for recent immigrants, visible minorities, and Aboriginals, making their children especially vulnerable. There are, however, exceptions to this, including Indo-Canadian gangs such as the Independent Soldiers in BC, many members of which have middle-class backgrounds.

Immigrant youth with strong academic aspirations and positive family backgrounds are unlikely to become involved in gangs. But, the more immigrants suffer from economic and social marginalization, the greater the risk of gang recruitment. The greater the suffering of new immigrant parents, the greater the risk their Canadian-born children will engage in gang activity.

Socio-economic challenges lead some parents to take on

more than one job—which often results in children going unsupervised.

The situation of Canada's Aboriginal population deserves special attention, particularly because of their proportionally high rate of gang involvement and incarceration. First Nations, Métis, and Inuit peoples comprise 4 per cent of the population of Canada, or approximately 1,325,000 people.[31] The majority live in Manitoba, Saskatchewan, Alberta, and the Northern Territories, and almost half the Aboriginal population now lives in urban areas. The proportion of Aboriginal peoples is increasing rapidly compared to every other group in Canadian society, and their average age is much younger than that of the rest of the population.

Although most Aboriginal communities are strong and resilient, far too many have a high burden of suffering. High rates of psycho-social problems include entrenched and severe poverty, overcrowded and substandard housing,[32] ill-health and suicide,[33] alcohol and drug abuse, involvement with the justice system,[34] family violence, community violence, homicide involving Aboriginals as both perpetrators and victims (on-reserve violent crime rates are especially high),[35] missing and murdered girls and women,[36] involvement in the sex trade,[37] school dropout and unemployment,[38] and institutionalization.[39]

Data on the ethno-racial backgrounds of Canadian gang members are very limited. A handful of studies have been based on urban gangs in various parts of the country. There are provincial estimates by police,[40] and a few studies have focused on incarcerated gang members. These data in urban areas suggest that the vast majority of gang members are visible minorities. Aboriginals, African-Canadians, and Asians make up the highest proportion of members, followed by Caucasians, Latinos, Middle Eastern members, and members from other backgrounds. Estimates on provincial composition of gangs suggest that 37 per cent of BC gang members are Asian, almost all Saskatchewan gang members are Aboriginal, just under 60 per cent of both Manitoba and Alberta gang members are Aboriginal, approximately one-third of Ontario gang members are African-Canadian, and roughly 50 per cent of Nova Scotia and Quebec gang members are African-Canadian.[41] Studies of federally incarcerated gang members suggest that most are African-Canadian (37 per cent), followed by Caucasian (29 per cent), Aboriginal (20 per cent), and Asian (3 per cent). Those from other backgrounds account for 11 per cent.[42]

There has been an evolution from ethnically homogeneous to more multi-ethnic gangs since the 1980s. Roughly one-third of gangs in Canada are composed of two or more ethno-racial groups (these are called hybrid gangs). Street gangs in Saskatchewan appear to be the most homogeneous (Aboriginal). British Columbia is an interesting example. South Asian street gangs evident in the 1990s have evolved into ethnically diverse gangs. Current examples of multi-ethnic gangs in the Lower Mainland include the Independent Soldiers and the United Nations. These gangs tend to be single-generational, less territorial than others, and do not emphasize traditional gang rights and rituals. On the other hand, ethnically homogeneous gangs tend to be intergenerational, highly structured and territorial, use identifiable means of communication, and rely on violent entry and exit rituals to protect the gang from outsiders. Current examples in Canada include the Chinese Big Circle Boys and Fresh Off the Boat; the Vietnamese Viet Ching; the Aboriginal Native Syndicate, Redd Alert, and Indian Posse; the African Mad Cowz and African Mafia, and the Latino Mara Salvatrucha 13. Many of these gangs operate independently in small cells. The Hells Angels motorcycle gang, which is almost exclusively Caucasian, poses a significant threat in many parts of Canada because of its size and the sophistication of its criminal business operations, but it rarely involves young people.

For marginalized, abused, and vulnerable youth, there are many positive aspects to gang life. Many Aboriginal and minority gang members speak of a sense of family and belonging in their gangs, a safe place to hang out with friends, an identity, and a good source of income. For many youth who grow up in communities characterized by high unemployment, entrenched poverty, and violence, gang involvement is a rational choice—a way to find employment and protection. Gangs can also provide a shelter for young people who have suffered from racism, war atrocities, and the adverse effects of colonization (including having dysfunctional parents who suffered abuse in residential schools). Members believe they can fight back against social injustice. Kim told me that when she was a gang member "*I was beating up white girls who were being mean to me. They called me squaw. They were racist.*" Kitty, twenty-one, talked about how being the only Aboriginal girl in her all-white school led her to "act out" and get incarcerated. She was convicted of a string of assaults on Caucasian females: "*My real mom I don't like. She could never take care of me or my brother or sister. She's an addict. That day they picked up my dad, I got put in foster care. I've been everywhere—I've stayed in different places—until I went to jail— pretty much all my life...They took me from the ghetto and put me into a rich neighbourhood. I was the only Indian in an all-white school...Then I started to act out and went to [secure custody facility] lots.*"

There are still many gangs in Canada that are racially segregated. What follows are brief descriptions of some ethno-racial minority groups and the gangs associated with these groups. I also discuss biker gangs and prison gangs in this section.

ASIAN GANGS

East Asian (including Chinese, Japanese, Korean, Vietnamese, and Taiwanese) and South Asian (Punjabi, Fijian, Pakistani, Indian, Sri Lankan, Bangladeshi, Iranian, Afghani, and Filipino) male youth are over-represented in gangs, particularly in BC.

More than one-third of British Columbian youth gang members are Asian. Asian organized crime includes Chinese groups like the Triads, loose criminal affiliations, migrant smuggling organizations, Vietnamese street gangs, Korean groups, and the Japanese Boryokudan (Yakuza). Asian organized crime groups place high priority on ethnicity for membership. Common criminal activities include extortion and protection rackets, home invasions, sophisticated credit card fraud, counterfeiting, and thefts of high-tech components (computer chips, for example). Drug trafficking is a major source of revenue. In Canada, Chinese organized crime groups import chemicals from Asia for the production of ecstasy. The Lower Mainland of British Columbia is a primary base for Asian organized crime.[43]

Most Asian organized crime is based on guanxi relationships (the connections or networks that are the foundation of Chinese culture). Guanxi is a social system, based on the ties between people related by blood or marriage. These complex social relations make it very difficult to refuse a request of any kind from a family member, a friend, or even an acquaintance. If an individual has already requested a favour, she or he must honour any future requests in return. Should he or she be unable to return a favour made by someone with whom there is a guanxi relationship, the individual must find another person who can. A chain reaction is commonly triggered, and the ensuing honour-based code of silence makes it exceedingly hard for police to solve gang crimes. Contrary to Western ideals of familial blood ties, the extended family in most Asian cultures includes people bound by these social relations. Highly structured gangs and triads provide members with a sense of family, which is particularly appealing for immigrants without blood family members in Canada. Asian youth gangs, on the other hand, act as "storm troopers" on the front line for these more established organized crime groups and get a small share of the criminal proceeds. Within these complicated social relations, disrespecting another individual is not permitted. Showing disrespect (that is, causing someone to lose face) usually results in the aggressor's being shamed and socially excluded.[44]

Historically, South Asian gang violence has been extreme, sporadic, and triggered by pride and honour, the saving of face, and hyper-masculine posturing about young women. Compared to the highly structured and low profile murders by outlaw motorcycle gangs and Asian organized crime groups, South Asian youth gang violence has been very public and high profile, particularly in BC.[45] Until recently, in BC there were, on average, ten murders per year involving eighteen- to thirty-five-year-old South Asian young men as either victims or perpetrators. Codes of secrecy and intimidation of witnesses have made solving gang crimes problematic in these closed communities.

The 2004 Group of Ten Report on South Asian group crime in British Columbia attributed the extreme violence to a conflict between the patriarchal and authoritarian values of the parents and the more liberal Western values of their sons. But most gang members do not have healthy adult role models, because of a lack of parental engagement. Some immigrant parents have to work long hours to support their families, making them unavailable to help their children, many of whom struggle with racism and social acceptance. They are absent parents.

It is important, however, to understand that these gang members are not representative of the overwhelming majority of South Asian boys and young men in Canada. We are speaking only of those who become gang members.

Extreme definitions of violent masculinity compensate for the crises of alienation and identity experienced by these second-generation South Asian young men. Many have deep-rooted feelings of inadequacy. They desperately want to belong to mainstream Canada, yet they are caught between two worlds: they are not white like Caucasian youth, nor are they black like African-Canadian youth. They feel emotionally separated from their families because their parents adhere to a belief system that does not apply to Canadian youth culture. Deep-rooted parent-child schisms result in some young men defining their identity upon reputation, pride, and "eye for an eye" patterns of retribution and revenge. Extreme violence and gang activities can be alternative means of achieving power, money, and status. What are often portrayed in the media as trivial acts of disrespect or of looking at someone the "wrong way" are, to South Asian gang members, acts that trigger a deep-rooted resentment at being devalued in Canadian society.

ABORIGINAL GANGS

The development of Aboriginal gang culture must be contextualized through the historical lens of the destruction of Aboriginal identity and culture. The intergenerational mark of colonization and forced assimilation is found in the minority of youth who join gangs. The grandparents and parents of today's Aboriginal gang members were stripped of their parenting capacity. A sheer will to survive—and achieve a sense of family, an identity, protection, steady income—explains why Aboriginal youth join gangs. School bonding and family attachment cannot prevent gang involvement for these youth. Many adopt an African-American hyper-sexualized violent masculinity, copied from rap artists and US gangs. In a cruel twist, they become alienated from their communities and lose their identity as a Cree, Blackfoot, Lakota, Dene, or Métis (for example). It is the modern version of forced assimilation, with the gangs doing the work of assimilation instead of the Canadian government.

Most Aboriginal young people who grow up in high-risk environments do not become gang-involved. They have positive school and community supports, and particular individual attributes (such as perseverance and determination). Yet, Aboriginals do experience a disproportionate burden of suffering, and this does help explain their participation in gangs. Racism, colonization, marginalization, and dispossession; the loss of land, traditional culture, spirituality, and values; and the breakdown of community kinship systems and Aboriginal law are all factors. Girls and women are particularly vulnerable to gang recruitment, partly because of sexist and misogynistic values and practices in many Aboriginal and non-Aboriginal communities.

AFRICAN-CANADIAN GANGS

Although there are likely more African gang members in Canada than of any other racial group,[46] there is very little research on African-Canadian street gangs. These gangs seem to be based on the Bloods and Crips gangs in the United States, although it is rare for American and Canadian Blood or Crips gangs to have formal ties. The Bo-Gars and Crack Down Posse gangs are amongst the most senior African-Canadian gangs in Canada. They have been based out of the Montreal area since the late 1980s. The Crack Down Posse was the original Crips gang in Montreal, whereas the Bo-Gars are believed to be the founding Bloods gang in that city. They have been sworn enemies for decades. Bloods and Crips gangs have been active in Toronto for approximately twenty-five years, as well. Various factions of these gangs have been located in social housing projects, including Jamestown-Rexdale and Jane-Finch. Jamaican Posses have also been around for decades in Canada in some cities, such as Toronto and Montreal.

Like most other gangs in Canada, black gangs have emerged in conditions of entrenched poverty and racial inequality. With the arrival of crack on the streets as a relatively cheap alternative to powder cocaine, African gangs took root in Canada to fight for control over this lucrative market. As with other racially based gangs in Canada, African-Canadian gang violence is most often directed at other African-Canadian gang members. The overwhelming majority of perpetrators and victims of black gang homicides are black.

WAR-AFFECTED YOUTH GANGS

Discrimination and social exclusion are a part of daily life in Canada for many immigrants and refugees from war-torn countries. Barriers and challenges include stress related to the immigration and resettlement process, dealing with exposure to atrocities in refugee camps, lack of access to vital services, language barriers, intergenerational and gender differences, adolescent developmental transitions, and acculturation (the change in an individual or a culturally similar group that results from contact with a different culture).

Although all war-affected refugees have suffered multiple traumatic experiences, East African refugee youth (those from Somalia, Eritrea, Sudan, and Sierra Leone) are more likely to have been forced into child soldiering or sexual slavery. Memories of committing or experiencing atrocities permanently mark these youth. These young people are more likely to have spent long periods (up to eight years, in some cases) in refugee camps, where they received extremely poor support and lived in conditions conducive to serious and chronic health problems.

The Lost Boys of Sudan, for example, are the tens of thousands of Sudanese children who became orphans when their families were killed in the civil war. In order to survive, they had to cross Sudan to reach Ethiopian and Kenyan refugee camps—a distance of 1,600 kilometres. It is estimated that a couple of hundred of these youth have ended up in Winnipeg.

It is no coincidence that Winnipeg is the Canadian city most affected by gangs made up of youth from war-torn countries.

The Mad Cowz formed there around 2000, becoming involved in low-level cocaine trafficking. Members were primarily from Somalia, Ethiopia, Eritrea, Sudan, and areas north of the Sahara (Iraq, Yemen, Saudi Arabia, Egypt, and Libya). By 2004, they had well-established drug lines in the city and were actively recruiting war-affected young men. Their primary rival was the Aboriginal B-Side Boys gang, with whom they fought for control of local drug trade. In August of 2004, fourteen-year-old Sirak "Shaggy" Okbazion was dealing cocaine for the Mad Cowz. He was shot dead, a casualty of the gang war. When he was six years old, Shirak and his family had left war-torn Eritrea, and they had landed in Canada four years later. His parents said that they were powerless to prevent his descent into gang life.

Following an internal conflict over what to do about Okbazion's murder, the African Mafia split from the Mad Cowz in the summer of 2005. Like the Mad Cowz, the African Mafia core membership was composed of highly traumatized youth who had experienced severe violence in their homeland. On October 10, 2005, Phillipe Haiart, an innocent bystander and the son of a local doctor, was gunned down at the corner of Sargent Avenue and Sherbrook Street. He took bullets intended for the Mad Cowz gang.

In Canada, faced with poverty, school failure, the threats of the streets, the availability of drugs and weapons, and mental health issues, traumatized young men are easy prey for gang leaders on the lookout for new soldiers.

WHITE SUPREMACIST GANGS

The skinheads emerged in Canada in the late 1970s in Montreal, Calgary, Vancouver, Ottawa, Edmonton, and Toronto. Since that time, they have operated in unorganized individual groups such as Aryan Resistance Movement Skins, Northern Hammerskins, and Final Solution Skinheads. Canadian skins were modeled after the

USA and UK movements, adopting the shaved head or cropped hair, suspenders, Doc Martens boots, and bomber jackets. Boot laces and suspenders were used as signals. The colour red indicated that the wearer had spilled blood in the race war. Currently, most skins are careful not to attract too much attention, often sporting longer hair and refraining from the coloured suspenders and boot laces. Although their political objectives are disjointed and unclear, they focus on protecting the white race and engage in violence directed against sexual, racial, and ethnic minorities.

Not all skinheads are racist. The Skinheads Against Racial Prejudice group has been involved in battles with racist skins. Most Canadian skinheads have Dutch, German, British, or Scandinavian origins. Many have backgrounds in other youth subcultures, such as skaters and punks. It is debatable whether or not the skinheads are an actual gang. Most of their behavior is deviant, not criminal. The context of skinhead activity is important. These groups have tended to emerge in Canada, or to escalate their activities, in response to unemployment and poverty. Immigrants are blamed for economic problems.[47]

The Aryan Resistance is an international gang that has had a presence in prisons and on the streets in Alberta, Toronto, and Montreal. Restrictions were imposed on inmates of the Edmonton Remand Centre in 2003 after a full-blown war between Redd Alert and Aryan Resistance. The White Boy Posse, an Edmonton-based white supremacist gang, had between fifty and a hundred members in its prime. Although still active, its membership has been considerably reduced. It is involved in trafficking cocaine and other drugs. It often uses the swastika in tattoos and other gang paraphernalia. It has ties with the Hells Angels and is a sworn enemy of the Bandidos biker gang, the Manitoba Warriors, Alberta Warriors, Indian Posse, and Redd Alert. In March 2008, police targeted the White Boy Posse in a large investigation called Project Goliath.

Like many other Canadian street gangs, skinheads are unorganized, membership is fluid and unstable, and they operate independently in cells. There is no identifiable leadership structure. Their members' backgrounds are not unlike those found in many other Canadian street gangs, typically characterized by severe domestic violence, entrenched poverty, homelessness, school drop-out, and drug and alcohol abuse. Although there are similarities between skins and street gangs, there are differences as well: skins are motivated by ideology and use violence as a mechanism to advocate for political change, their activities are not profit-driven, and most skinhead groups do not share the gangs' concept of having a neighbourhood turf.[48]

Then there are the biker gangs and prison gangs.

BIKER GANGS

Biker gangs, or outlaw motorcycle gangs, are identifiable by: showing colours in public (wearing jackets and other attire to represent the gang); use of violence to defend and grow their territory; and an identifiable hierarchical structure, wherein new recruits commit the bulk of crimes and violence, and higher-ups are relatively privileged to do as they wish. Often, biker gangs get street gangs to commit violence on their behalf. The Hells Angels are by far the largest outlaw motorcycle gang in Canada, with the Nomads being an elite branch of the Hells Angels. They engage in crimes such as prostitution, fraud, extortion, and drug trafficking.

Turf wars between rivals are common, such as the public war in the late 1990s between the Hells Angels and the Rock Machine in Quebec. Turf rivalry has resulted in roughly 150 deaths in Canada. Some members admit to having carried out a high number of murders. Gerald Gallant, for example, told police he had murdered twenty-seven people during the Quebec conflict. In 2009, police largely dismantled the Quebec chapters of the Hells Angels, arresting roughly 150 members in Quebec, New

Brunswick, France, and the Dominican Republic.

The Criminal Intelligence Service Canada reported that as of April 2009, there were 34 Hells Angels chapters across Canada, with roughly 460 full-fledged members. Ontario had the highest number of chapters (fifteen), followed by BC (eight), Quebec (five), Alberta (three), Saskatchewan (two), and Manitoba (one). After the Hells Angels moved into Ontario in 2000, they quickly took over the Para Dice Riders, Satan's Choice, and Last Chance. Toronto has the highest proportion of Hells Angels members in the world.

The Bandidos are the next most powerful outlaw motorcycle gang in the world and are expanding their presence in Canada. They are not afraid to kill their own. Eight Bandidos members and associates were found murdered in a small Ontario town outside of London in 2006, part of an internal cleansing of the Canadian chapters. The USA head office had ordered the Winnipeg chapter to carry out the hits.

There are other outlaw motorcycle gangs active in Canada. The Outlaws were first reported in Canada in 1978, when a couple of Satan's Choice chapters in Quebec decided to form the Outlaws. They are sworn enemies of the Hells Angels. Satan's Choice, once very active in Ontario, was taken over by the Hells Angels in 2000. The Rock Machine formed chapters in Ontario after the war with the Hells Angels in Quebec; they cooperate with the Bandidos. The Para Dice Riders were once strongly entrenched in Toronto, but were taken over by the Hells Angels in 2001. The Last Chance was a small gang in Ontario until it was also taken over by the Hells Angels in 2000–2001. The Lobos gang merged with the Hells Angels in that same period. The Loners had a small presence in Ontario in the late 1990s, resisted a merger with the Hells Angels, and subsequently formed chapters in the USA and Europe. The Vagabonds were also taken over by the Hells Angels when the Angels moved into Ontario. Finally, the Red Devils have a small presence in the Hamilton area.

PRISON GANGS

Unfortunately, many of Canada's jails, prisons, and secure young offender centres are gang-infested. It is common for facility administrators to ask new inmates if they are gang-involved. If the answer is yes, a discussion about safety should ensue. There are three options: the inmate can be placed on a "gang range," a specific area where members of the same gang are housed; the inmate can be placed in segregation (commonly referred to as the "hole") for his or her own protection; or the inmate can be transferred to another institution. The two latter options often happen if an inmate wishes to exit the gang or has already done so, or there is no specific range dedicated to his or her gang in that facility.

It is important to understand that gang activity in correctional facilities does not necessarily reflect gang activity on the streets. Certain facilities are well known for the emergence of gangs inside, which often have no relationship to gangs in the regions surrounding those institutions. As well, inmates who have exited their gangs on the outside, or those who have never been a member of a gang, may join gangs on the inside for protection.

Correctional Service of Canada has been slow to acknowledge the seriousness of the gang problem inside its facilities. Provincial governments, likewise, have been reluctant to admit to gang problems in their young offender centres. In April 2007, the federal government established an independent panel to review the system. The panel's report, published that December, set out a vision for transforming the federal correctional system. It recommended, among other things, increased emphasis on eliminating drugs from prisons, and effective management of the growing number of offenders with gang affiliations. Correctional Service of Canada reports that more than one out of six adult male offenders has gang affiliations, and the ratio has been increasing since 1997 (from 12 per cent to 16 per cent). One out of ten adult women offenders in federal custody has gang affiliations. This also has been increasing over the same period (from 7 per cent to 12 per cent). Roughly one-quarter of major incidents in institutions and 14 per cent of major incidents involving convicted individuals in the community (i.e., offenders on parole) involve gang members. Correctional Service of Canada reports that, in general, gang-affiliated offenders tend to pose higher risks in its institutions. Incarcerated gang members are more likely to be involved in violence and contraband offences and are usually less responsive to institutional programming.

* * *

To sum up, then, street gangs have lower levels of sophistication, engage in less serious crimes, and are much less structured than mid-level gangs and organized crime groups. They are relatively non-hierarchical, members tend to be younger in age, and most are based out of schools, reserves, or neighbourhoods. Roles in gangs include wannabes or posers (who are outside of gangs), new recruits, strikers or soldiers, core members, veterans or higher-ups, and leaders (also called presidents). Gang culture includes specific hand signals, dress, and tattoos. In general, it encompasses various forms of communication within and between gangs. Gang life is not glamorous: hanging out, drug and alcohol use, and meeting basic needs are the common activities. Making profits from serious crimes and engaging in severe violence help to create meaning in what seem to be hopeless lives. Death is an ever-present theme, whether it involves suicide, homicide, or various forms of accidental death. Finally, Aboriginals, poor minorities, and young immigrants from war-torn countries are over-represented—because young people who endure immense suffering are most likely to become gang-involved.

✳ CHAPTER 3 ✳

GANG ACTIVITY ACROSS CANADA

It is difficult to find accurate data on the number of gangs in Canada. Police-based estimates are likely inflated: there is no commonly accepted definition of a gang, and levels of funding depend partly on how large the gang problem is. If police report high gang activity, they are likely to get more money to fight it. In addition, there is little academic research focusing on gangs across the country; most studies have focused on specific regions.[1] As well, it is difficult to come up with a list of gang names and members because low-level street gangs are in a state of constant flux. Names and membership frequently change.

Criminal Intelligence Service Canada (CISC) estimates vary widely. In 2006, CISC identified 344 street gangs with 11,900 members. Three per cent of the identified gangs were organized crime groups. Most street gang members were between twenty-one and thirty years of age, and almost all gangs had both youth and adult members. Roughly 6 per cent of gangs were youth only (eighteen years and younger), and gangs were active in 166 urban, rural, and Aboriginal reserve areas. By 2010, CISC estimated that the total number of gangs of all kinds could be as high as 900. Although this may seem like a large increase, figures should be interpreted with caution. It could be that new gangs are forming, but it could also be that police are counting gangs differently (organized crime groups could be identified as street gangs, for example, and cells from larger gangs could be identified as new gangs). As well, street gangs could break apart, forming smaller groups, and gangs could be changing names.

Gangs are active in all parts of the country except PEI, Yukon, and Nunavut. (Nunavut and Yukon have rates of violent crime that far exceed those of anywhere else in the country, but gang activity is not part of the problem.)[2] Western Canada has consistently had higher violent crime rates and gang activity than central and eastern Canada, probably because of pockets of high crime in cities such as Vancouver (the Downtown East Side), Winnipeg (the West End, West Broadway, Centennial, and North End neighbourhoods), Regina (the North Central neighbourhood), and Saskatoon (including Pleasant Hill and Riversdale communities). These areas are characterized by transient young men who are high school drop-outs, single-parent families with high rates of violence and abuse, addicts, high poverty, poor housing, and drug dealing.

It is important to remember that street gangs in Canada are in a constant state of flux: membership is fluid; gangs often come together to make large profits from criminal activity and then disband. It is a slippery matter, therefore, to identify street gangs by name, because the names change constantly. All that being said, there are benefits to identifying gangs in various geographical areas of Canada. Here are some examples.[3]

BRITISH COLUMBIA

An RCMP briefing note written in June 2010 estimates that BC had 133 organized crime groups, with a total of 800 members, and an additional thirty street gangs.[4] Many are loosely organized and are centred upon manufacturing and selling drugs, with the related violence. Gangs have migrated from the Lower Mainland to northern cities and smaller regions, resulting in battles over the drug trade between traditional criminals in those areas and the newer gangs. Prince George, for example, has experienced a sharp increase in home invasions and severe assaults, activities gangs use for intimidation and to collect drug debts. This small city now has one of the highest per capita rates of violent crime and gang activity in the country. Gangs that have migrated from the lower mainland up to Prince George include the Independent Soldiers and the Game Tight Soldiers. Until recently, Abbotsford had the highest rate of murders in Canada, well above the national average. Most of these killings were gang or drug-related. Some were associated with the Red Scorpions gang.

Once dubbed the "murder capital of Canada,"[5] Abbotsford has experienced a marked decline in gang related crime and murders recently, most likely due to the formation of a gang suppression unit in May 2010. Gang members have been locked up or chased out of town, and the Abbotsford Police Youth Squad has stepped up its efforts in local schools to educate young students about the perils of gang life.

Victoria has also encountered gang activity and violence, most likely related to its large homeless population, many of whom are addicts. However, most gangs (including 18th Street, Bloods, Crazy Dragons, Crips, and MS 13) have been based in the Lower Mainland. Aboriginal gangs are active on some reserves and in the Downtown East Side of Vancouver. The most sophisticated gangs include the United Nations Gang, Independent Soldiers, and Red Scorpions. Many low-level gangs buy drugs from organized crime groups such as those that are Asian and the Hells Angels. In Vancouver, the most prominent gangs include the Hells Angels and the United Nations Gang. Chinese triads and

Eastern European mafia groups are known to be active in the Lower Mainland. Other gangs in the Vancouver area include the Big Circle Boys and the Independent Soldiers.

The Red Scorpions were formed in 2000 by Michael Le and Konaam Shirzad while they were incarcerated at a young offender facility. They created the gang to run drug trafficking operations—the so-called dial-a-dope lines. These are drug trafficking operations set up to sell drugs such as cocaine, heroin, or ecstasy by way of a phone call. Buyers request a product, a meeting location is chosen, and drugs are exchanged for money with a drug runner. The meetings are usually held in public places. In 2007 Le and Shirzad formed an alliance with Jamie Bacon of the infamous Bacon Brothers, with Le providing the drug network and Bacon providing the muscle. Following Jamie's involvement, his two brothers joined the gang, all three having been high school bullies in Abbotsford.

Members of the Red Scorpions have "RS" tattoos on their arms and necks, and they are known to have been at war with the United Nations gang—a rivalry heightened after the Bacons left the United Nations for the Red Scorpions. The Scorpions have been linked to many shootings and were involved in the killing of six people in a Whalley condominium in 2007. Dennis Karbovanec, a close friend of Jonathan Bacon, pleaded guilty to three of the murders in 2009. Within the past two years the influence of the Red Scorpions has waned, primarily because of the incarceration of Jamie and Jerrod Bacon and the emergence of the Duhre Brothers (Balraj and Paul), who taxed and partially took over the Bacons' trafficking network in Abbotsford. Jonathan Bacon was murdered in August 2011.

Founded in the late 1990s in Abbotsford by a group of high school friends, the United Nations gang is based in the Fraser Valley. Membership is based on high school relationships, and the name refers to the multi-ethnic nature of the gang. Currently it also has cells in the Vancouver area. Historically, it has had control of the Downtown East Side drug market and has operated trafficking lines throughout the Lower Mainland. It has had connections to Mexico and California and has developed trafficking networks across Canada. Its leader, Clayton Roueche, is now imprisoned in the USA on a thirty-year sentence. He was instrumental in setting up a sophisticated drug-running enterprise using helicopters to ferry marijuana from BC and cocaine from the USA. The gang has also been involved in arms trafficking, extortion, home invasions, illegal immigration, kidnapping, money laundering, passport fraud, and people smuggling.

The gang was a rival of the Hells Angels until recently, but they are now known to be cooperating with them. Many of the United Nations leaders have been taken off the streets and are now serving lengthy prison sentences. They include Jong Ca, John Lee, Daryl Johnson, Douglas Vanalstine, and Barzan Tilli-Choli. The United Nations gang is believed to be responsible for many attempts on the lives of the Bacon Brothers.

The Independent Soldiers, founded in 2005, is also based in BC. They are a multi-ethnic, cell-based gang primarily involved in trafficking cocaine. They have fluid membership and leadership. Most of the higher ranking positions are occupied by Indo-Canadians of Punjabi origin. It is active in Vancouver, Kamloops, Kelowna, Chilliwack, Abottsford, Prince George, Surrey, Calgary, Edmonton, and Montreal. The Soldiers are involved in drug distribution, money laundering, and violence. Enemies include the United Nations and Hells Angels, among others, and this has led to many unsolved shootings and murders. They wear red and black colours and have the initials "IS" on jackets and hats. The leader, Sukhvinder Dosanjh, died in 2005 in a car accident. Peter Adiwal assumed leadership and was shot by Red Scorpions members in 2009. He is now a paraplegic.

Other small, loosely knit street gangs have come and gone over the recent past in BC, although the Empire Gang, for example, has evolved over the years to become more sophisticated. Its primary activities are kidnappings, extortion, and dial-a-dope operations in Langley and Surrey.

Since the early 1990s, roughly one hundred Indo-Canadian young men have been murdered in BC, primarily in the Lower Mainland. Most of these murders have been gang-related.

ALBERTA AND NORTHWEST TERRITORIES

The 2009 Provincial Threat Assessment on Organized Crime in Alberta and Northwest Territories, published by the Criminal Intelligence Service Alberta, identified eighty-three criminal organizations and gangs. The Crazy Dragons were among the most sophisticated, with many cells across Alberta, in other provinces, and in the Northwest Territories. The Independent Soldiers had also migrated east from BC. Most other gangs were either Asian-based (such as Fresh Off the Boat and Fresh Off the Boat Killers) or Aboriginal (including Indian Posse, Redd Alert, and Alberta Warriors).

Seven organized gangs were identified in Grande Prairie, including the Crazy Dragons and the Hells Angels. These groups were involved in dial-a-dope operations, street level trafficking, and fortified crack houses, "re-vinning" of vehicles (replacing the previous vehicle identification number with a new, fraudulent number), fraud, debit and credit card skimming, extortion, theft, prostitution, and Internet pornography. They were linked to other gangs in Alberta and Western Canada.

Entrepreneurial crime groups and gangs have migrated to Fort McMurray, Calgary, and Edmonton over the past decade. The economic boom, largely fuelled by the oil and gas industry, attracted the lucrative drug trade. A transient pool of workers from Eastern Africa (including Somalis who fled the civil war) and Eastern Canada, along with Aboriginal young men, has been making big money. However, since 2005, more than thirty young Somali men have been murdered in the province, mostly in Fort McMurray, Edmonton, and Calgary. Most cases remain unsolved. Although most of these young men are not believed to have been gang members, they did belong to low level drug trafficking groups in Ottawa and Toronto. A few were loosely affiliated with Toronto's Jamestown Crips gang. Some Calgary and Edmonton gangs migrating to Fort McMurray have used young Somalis as small-time dealers, so the government has begun supporting programs for young Somali men. An integrated policing team has also been established across the province (ALERT, the Alberta Law Enforcement Response Teams).

Hobbema, Alberta, likely has one of the highest rates of gang activity in all of Canada. Although there have been at least thirteen reported gangs in the area, the most sophisticated and active are the Indian Posse, Samson True Soldiers, Alberta Warriors, East Side Players, D-Block (formerly Ghetto Boys Crew and West Side Players), and Redd Alert.

There are roughly six gangs active in the Saddle Lake area. Gang activity revolves around the drug trade, and property crime involves the theft of guns.

Enoch has approximately four active gangs. Violence and drug trafficking are their main activities.

Many Edmonton gangs are organized along ethnic divisions, including Central-East African, Persian, Chinese, Middle Eastern, and Central European alignments. African gangs are connected to the Dixon Blood Crew and Jamestown Crew in Toronto.

The Crazy Dragons have surpassed the Hells Angels as the top gang in Alberta. The Crazy Dragons are primarily Asian based, although with many white members as well. They originate out of Edmonton but have cells throughout Alberta. The Crazy Dragons have been linked to supplying Calgary's Asian gangs with guns.

Calgary gangs over the recent past include Fresh Off the Boat,

Fresh Off the Boat Killers, Crazy Dragons, Lebanese Mafia, Brown Town, Clippers, Galloway Boys, Independent Soldiers, Pinky Crew, and Redd Alert. Most homicides in Calgary are gang-related. In 2008, there was a gang war between Fresh Off the Boat and Fresh Off the Boat Killers. Minh Tri Truong (now dead) and Brandon Boychuk were leaders of the two gangs at the time. Many shootings, stabbings, and murders were linked to these two gangs, both of which depended on drug trafficking for their primary source of income. They have also migrated to other towns and cities, including Brooks, Medicine Hat, Lethbridge, Red Deer, Canmore, Edmonton, Banff, Regina, Toronto, and Vancouver, and to the Fraser Valley. Fresh Off the Boat has been aligned with the Independent Soldiers and 403 Soldiers gangs, whereas Fresh Off the Boat Killers has been aligned with the United Nations and the Crazy Dragons.

The Fresh Off the Boat–Fresh Off the Boat Killers war has resulted in the deaths of over two dozen people in Calgary since 2002. The Fresh Off the Boat gang was formed first, when a group of high school friends set up a dial-a-dope business. A schism developed, resulting in rival Fresh Off the Boat Killers.

The Independent Soldiers cells migrated to Alberta starting in 2008. Calgary, Edmonton, and Grande Prairie have reported Independent Soldiers activity. They are known to cooperate with both the Hells Angels and Fresh Off the Boat.

There is very little gang activity in the Northwest Territories. Cells of the Crazy Dragons, Indian Posse, Alberta Warriors, and Redd Alert have been active in Yellowknife. These gangs are primarily based in Alberta but have migrated north because of the drug trade.

SASKATCHEWAN

Saskatchewan has historically had the highest concentration of gang membership of all provinces. There are roughly twenty street gangs in this province, almost all Aboriginal. Indian Posse and Native Syndicate are the most sophisticated, with cells in Manitoba and Northern Ontario in addition to those in Saskatchewan. The Hells Angels and their puppet club, the Freewheelers, have been in conflict with Native Syndicate over the drug trade. Saskatoon, Regina, and Prince Albert have the highest number of active gangs, including Brown Premise, Crazy Cree, Redd Alert, Crazy Dragons, Indian Mafia, Crips, Tribal Brotherz, Scorpion Brothers, North Central Rough Riderz, Hill Side Warriors, and several others. Fort Qu'Apelle, Yorkton, and many reserves also have gang activity. Regina and Saskatoon have traditionally had very high rates of violent crime and gang activity, most of which happens in highly marginalized neighbourhoods.

MANITOBA

There are roughly twenty-five street gangs in Manitoba, with about one-third being made up primarily of youth. A majority are Aboriginal, along with smaller numbers of African and Asian-based groups. These latter gangs are primarily active in the Winnipeg area (including the Mad Cowz, African Mafia, and Asian Bomb Squad), whereas Aboriginal gangs are based in Winnipeg (such as Native Syndicate and Indian Posse) and in rural areas and reserves (including Manitoba Warriors, Indian Posse, Native Syndicate, and Native Syndicate Killers).

Winnipeg has had one of the highest per capita rates of violent crime and gang activity in Canada for many years. Already having one of the highest levels of policing in the country, Manitoba added a Gang Response and Suppression Plan (GRASP) in January 2010.

A significant number of youth gang members reside in Winnipeg's West End, West Broadway, Centennial, and North End neighbourhoods. These neighbourhoods are also known to have high rates of drug offences, break and enters, sexual exploitation, and sex trade activity.

Over the past decade, Winnipeg has experienced a significant increase in the number of refugee and war-affected youth immigration. Most come from African and Middle Eastern countries. These young people are over-represented in gangs such as the Mad Cowz and African Mafia. Some of these youth have been recruited in a local young offender centre.

A mostly white gang known as the Zig Zags or Zig Zag Crew cooperates closely with the Hells Angels and is active mainly in the Fort Rouge and Osborne Village neighbourhoods.

One-per-center motorcycle gangs (which are criminal gangs, as opposed to the 99 per cent of motorcycle clubs that are law-abiding) are known to operate in the city, including the Hells Angels and the Bandidos.

ONTARIO

There are approximately 180 gangs in Ontario, with roughly 80 in the Greater Toronto area and 95 in other regions of the province (York, Peel, Waterloo/Kitchener, Thunder Bay, Ottawa), including northern reserves. Of these gangs, a handful are criminally sophisticated, highly organized, and linked to groups in other parts of Canada. They include the Slingers (Waterloo), the Quebec-based Crack Down Posse and the Bo-Gars (Niagara Falls), Jamestown Crips, the V.V.T. (named after Valvettithurai, the birthplace of the Tamil Tigers, and active in Montreal, Hamilton, Ottawa, and Waterloo),[6] the Malvern Crew (Toronto), and the Ledbury-Banff Crips (Ottawa).

Toronto has had the highest number of active gangs in the province for many years. The city experienced a peak in gang-related gun violence in 2005, that has gradually been decreasing ever since. The most high-profile incident was a Boxing Day, 2005, shooting on downtown Yonge Street that resulted in the death of fifteen-year-old bystander Jane Creba. The incident was a shootout between rival gangs. Although almost all victims of gang violence have been gang-involved young black men, the local media does not devote much coverage to their cases. Arguably, the Jane Creba murder got so much coverage because she was Caucasian.

The Toronto Police have initiated various projects targeting street gangs, all in neighbourhoods characterized by poverty, social exclusion, and a lack of social services. Project Corral, initiated in 2009, descended on the Falstaff Crips and the Five Point Generals in May 2010. Both gangs were linked to the Shower Posse, a Jamaican organized crime group. The project also involved the Ontario Provincial Police, Peel Regional Police Service, Hamilton Police Service, Canada Border Services Agency, and the Ministry of Community Safety and Correctional Services. Other countries involved in the gangs' drug distribution ring included Panama and the Dominican Republic, with the Shower Posse supplying both the Crips and the Generals with drugs. Project Kryptic aimed to dismantle the Driftwood Crips in the Jane and Finch community. Project XXX targeted the Rexdale public-housing-based gang the Jamestown Crew. Project Flicker targeted the Ardwick Bloods around Islington and Finch. Project Impact took place in the city's northeast neighbourhood of Malvern. Finally, Project Pathfinder focused on the Galloway Boys gang in the neighbourhood of Kingston and Galloway.

The Ledbury-Banff Crips and the West Side Bloods are the two most organized gangs in Ottawa. The former are based in a south end social housing project bearing the same name and have been involved in drug trafficking, fraud, gun crimes, and prostitution. Some members have been active in Alberta (Calgary and Fort McMurray), trying to muscle into the drug trade. Some members have been deported back to their home countries (Rwanda and Ethiopia). The Westside Bloods are based in a number of west end social housing projects, including Ritchie, Ramsey, Dumaurier, and Michele Heights. They have a significant influence over the drug trade in the west end. There are other smaller Ottawa gangs, some of which have ties to the Ledbury-Banff Crips and the West Side Bloods.[7]

The Hamilton police report that there are twenty-two active gangs in that city, primarily involved in drug trafficking and prostitution. They include the Original Blood Brothers (also known as the Oriental Blood Brothers), Oriole Crescent Crips, Front Line Bloods, Trethewey Gangsta Killaz, Cutthroat Bloods, Driftwood Crips, Hamilton Blood Soldiers, Get Money Squad, Red Dragons, Downtown Crips, and the Assyrian Kings. Some cooperate with more sophisticated organized crime groups, such as the Musitano crime family. Other Italian Mafia families, such as the Papalias and the Luppinos, are active in Southern Ontario and parts of Toronto.

QUEBEC

There are roughly fifty known gangs in Quebec, most being Haitian, Jamaican, or Hispanic-based. Most gangs are ethnically homogenous and tend to be aligned with Red or Blue factions. Gangs with a high degree of criminal sophistication and linked to outlaw motorcycle gangs (such as the Hells Angels) or the Italian mafia include the Bo-Gars, Crack Down Posse, the Syndicate, and the Wolf Pack. Most gangs in Quebec are in the Montreal area, with the remainder based in Gatineau, Laval, Longueil, and Quebec City. Smaller street gangs, made up mostly of youth, are pocketed in different areas of Montreal, particularly the Côte-des-Neiges–Notre-Dame-de-Grâce, Sud-Ouest, Villeray–Saint-Michel–Parc-Extension, and Montréal-Nord neighbourhoods. Some are modelled after the Crips and Bloods gangs in the USA.

Traditional organized crime has had a presence in the city since the early 1900s, mainly in the form of the Irish West End Gang and Vito Rizzuto's 6th Family. The Rizzuto family was part of the Montreal Cotroni family but became independent after an internal struggle for power. Vic Cotroni founded the older family in the 1940s. Strife between the Calabrians and Sicilians led to a Mafia war in the late 1970s in Montreal. The mafia was involved in racketeering, conspiracy, loan sharking, money laundering, murder, drug trafficking, pornography, and gambling. It has been allied with the Hells Angels, West End Gang, and the Bonanno and Gambino crime families. The Rizzoto family's influence has gone into decline with the recent murders of Nick Rizutto Jr. (December 2009) and Nicolo Rizutto (November 2010).

Conflict between the Montreal mafia and the street gangs over the drug trade erupted in 2010, with firebombings of cafés in Montreal, in one of which Ducarme Joseph, former head of the 67s gang, survived an attempt on his life. Two of his associates were killed in that March 2010 incident.

MARITIMES

In Nova Scotia there are roughly ten gangs, including the Gaston Road Gang, G-Lock, Murda Squad, North End Dartmouth, Money Over Bitches, Wolf Pack, and the Woodside Gang. A small number of gangs have connections to other parts of Canada (such as North Preston's Finest), primarily in the sex trade. The most well-known Halifax street gang is North Preston's Finest, which recruits its members mainly from the black community of North Preston in Dartmouth. Primarily involved in prostitution and commercial sexual exploitation, gang members have coerced Nova Scotian women into going to Toronto to work the streets. Other gangs include the Spry-Town Mafia, based in the Spryfield area, and Bloods and Crips gangs based throughout Halifax and Dartmouth. Biker gangs such as the Hells Angels also play a key role in Halifax's gang world, but recent arrests have limited their power.

There are roughly seven gangs in New Brunswick, with four in Moncton and the rest in the northern part of the province. They include various factions of the Crips and the Bloods. Some have links to gangs in other parts of Canada, including Ontario and Quebec. Again, prostitution and the trafficking of young women are the main criminal activities.

One of the few active gangs in Newfoundland and Labrador is Street Fame.

Gangs with interprovincial connections include Indian Posse, Native Syndicate, Crazy Dragons, United Nations, Independent Soldiers, Bo-Gars, and North Preston's Finest. Transnational gangs identified in Canada include MS 13 and the 18th Street Gang.

✶ CHAPTER 4 ✶

WOMEN'S INVOLVEMENT IN GANGS

My baby daddy and a couple of other boyfriends were gang members. All were part of [name of their gang]. I wouldn't fuck with anybody who was not [a member of the gang]—I'd get a minute. They are family. I will never leave. My best friends are in the gang. My sisses and friends. I have never got a minute from [name of gang she was associated with]. I am affiliated, that's all. Lots of people say that I am, some are my best friends. I have easy access to money, drugs, anything I need for people who are looking. I am always the connection person. My mom started bringing her buddies around [to abuse me] when I was very young.

Loretta, aged twenty-one years and the mother of a three year-old son, told me that she would never stop being involved with a gang. Like most other gang-involved women in Canada, she was "affiliated" with the gang through her best friends. She made the distinction between being a member of the gang and dealing drugs. Why did she deny being a gang member? She likely denied her membership because child welfare would have taken her child away if she had admitted belonging to the gang. She herself had grown up in many foster and group homes, having been sexually abused by her mom's "buddies." When she said "*I wouldn't fuck with anybody who was not—I'd get a minute,*" she meant she would get beaten for one minute if she dared associate with any-one from a rival gang.

BACKGROUNDS OF GANG-INVOLVED YOUNG WOMEN

Although there are no hard data in Canada, it is likely that young women make up a small percentage of all gang members. Historically, Canada has had few all-female gangs. Most youth gangs are male dominated, with a minority of female members. Gang-involved young women have unique and special risks compared to male gang members. Typically, their backgrounds include a history of severe victimization (mainly physical and sexual abuse); repeated running away (from home and child welfare facilities) and prostitution; a history of unhealthy, dependent relationships, primarily with older males; and mental health issues. Young women's gang activity is most closely related to abuse and trauma suffered at home.[1]

Sylvie talked about the connection between child sexual abuse, growing up in care, and gang involvement. Her narra-tive typifies the sexual trauma young gang-involved women suffer in their own gangs as well as during their childhood. Her initiation into her gang consisted of a severe beating. When she wanted to exit, she was again beaten and then gang-raped by three men:

I was raised in what you would call an abusive, dysfunctional home. In and out of foster homes and since the age of twelve in and out of jail. Eleven years of my life incarcerated—I'm sick of it. Since the age I can remember of my childhood days, my mother was in a common-law relationship with my stepfather—he was really good to me. They were together for 18 years. But when I was a child [an older male family member] used to molest me every chance he got. I was about five, six years old when he first started doing things to me 'til I was about eleven. My family travelled a lot and my mom and stepdad partied a lot as well as used I.V. drugs all the time. Instead of trying to kill myself I was introduced to a new clique called [name of gang].

There are important gender differences in the process by which young women are charged, the context of their criminal behaviour, and the types of offences they commit. Males and females differ in levels of participation, motivation, and degree of harm caused by their offences. Violence committed by young women usually occurs in self-defence or in anticipation of victimization by physical or sexual assault. Girls are much less likely to engage in serious, violent crime, and are much more likely to engage in non-violent property and drug offences. Girls are far more likely to enter the justice system from the child welfare system or from engaging in status offences (running away, prostitution, underage drinking, truancy, curfew violations), administrative breaches, and shoplifting. Child sexual abuse is strongly associated with self-destructive behaviour and it can lead to other criminal activities (such as solicitation and substance abuse), which in turn lead to increased violent offending. A majority of these young women have a history of running from

abusive homes, child welfare facilities, and mental health centres—acts that are criminalized.[2]

CATEGORIES OF GANG-INVOLVED YOUNG WOMEN

There are at least three categories of young women involved in
gangs: female members of all-women street gangs, women who
are affiliated with male-dominated gangs, and street women in
the sex trade.[3] The level of peer support is an important distin-
guishing factor. Members of all-female gangs differ from young
women who are affiliated with male-dominated gangs, and street
women, likewise, are different from gang-involved women.[4]

Young women who are members of all-female gangs are not
as vulnerable as the girlfriends, wives, and partners of male gang
members. The affiliation and status of this second group of
women is defined by their "men"—husbands, boyfriends, and
common-law partners. These women are likely to experience
extreme physical and sexual violence from their male partners
and are dominated by them. Called "missuses," they are frequently beaten into subservient roles. If these women get rejected
by their partners, they become the property of other male gang
members. Carolyn told me, "*I was his property. He would give me
to them [pass her around to other gang members for sex].*" Often,
these women monitor the behaviours of other affiliated women,
ensuring that they are not intimate or flirting with their "man."
While women involved in all-female gangs often experience a
sense of belonging and family, women affiliated with male gangs
are in a position of dependency and often feel very isolated. Yet,
because of the code of silence, they must demonstrate loyalty and
cannot talk about their violent victimization. The unwritten rule
is that they don't betray their men under any circumstance.

Women who are in relationships with ex-gang members also
experience extreme violence from their men. The cases of Ricky

(aged twenty-six) and Steve (aged thirty) are illustrative. Both men had been convicted of assault against their girlfriends on numerous occasions. Both had been incarcerated for these crimes. Sixteen-year-old Susan reflected on the violence perpetrated by her man: *"I was defending myself with my baby daddy. I used a baseball bat on him. He is in jail now because he beat me up."* Kim was twenty-two and had been homeless on and off for five years. She spoke about her boyfriend, who is currently in jail for assaulting her. She fears for her life when he gets out: *"One of my boyfriends went to jail. He pulled my hair out, ripped off my clothes. Since November 2010 he has been in jail. My cousins beat him up in jail. Stole his canteen money, hit him with [a weapon]. I don't know what to do when he gets out."* Finally, Christine, aged twenty-three, wrote about how her daughter was taken away by social services because of her boyfriend's violence and gang involvement. She also added that her brother was recently killed by his gang for attempting to exit it. Violence seemed to be omnipresent in her young life:

> *He used to beat me and [my daughter] got caught in the middle. Child welfare took her away. I hope to get her back [next month]. He is doing three and a half years in the pen for something. He was just sentenced. I never talked to him for two months before. I want a divorce. He was solo then got into gangs. My boyfriend does a lot of gang intimidation now. My brother just got murdered. He was murdered by [gang name]. His two minutes killed him. They tortured him. He was twenty-six.*

Within male gangs, young women are given minor roles, such as being the look-out for the police, dealing drugs, or working in the sex trade.[5] They are typically required to carry weapons and drugs, often intravaginally, because they are less likely to be searched by male police officers.[6] Women are also likely to act as escorts, drivers, and intelligence gatherers. They are involved in debit and credit card scams. Some manipulate rival male gang members into thinking they want a romantic relationship, when in fact these women are gathering intelligence on the rival gang and setting up rival gang members to be assaulted. Young women who do not have prior criminal records are particularly attractive to gangs because they are off the police radar.[7] In some gangs, they are not permitted to attend meetings.

On the other hand, young women who are members of all-female gangs report that they are relatively safe and free from violence and belong to mutually supportive peer groups. Gang-affiliated women (who are part of male-dominated gangs), however, experience little to no support from other women likewise affiliated. Anne Campbell, in her groundbreaking book on female gang members, writes: "Gang girls see themselves as different from their peers. Their association with the gang is a public proclamation of their rejection of the lifestyle which the community expects from them."[8]

There are at least two types of all-female gangs: those that are auxiliaries to male-dominated gangs, and those that are independent. Canada has had few of either type of female gang, but either type is likely to have its own hierarchy and status.[9] Examples include the Winnipeg-based Sisters in Action gang (responsible for the death of a young man in the 1990s in a gang fight), Sisterhood, the Warriorettes (associated with the Manitoba Warriors), and Native Sistahs (reported to be related to the Native Syndicate). The Indian Posse Girls have been identified as the auxiliary to the Indian Posse Gang and have recently exerted control of the Edmonton and Hobbema sex trade. The Sisterhood Gang has also been identified as affiliated with the Indian Posse. The Ace gang has had affiliation with the Deuce Gang, also affiliated with the Manitoba Warriors. The Spadina Girls recruited teenagers from high school in Toronto and was directed by a sixteen-year-old leader. Four members were charged by the Toronto Police in 1998 after a severe beating and a $500 robbery.

Carolyn is representative of the women in all-female gangs. She was in a relationship with the president of a notorious gang and by virtue of this relationship was deemed to be the leader of an all-female auxiliary. Notwithstanding this, she was still under his thumb: she was beaten in (*"I had to do one minute"*) and had to turn over her profits to him. She told me:

> *I was president by association. I was the almighty woman, the boss, what I said goes. It was because of my relationship to him. I had to sign an oath, a blood oath, and do one minute. Drugs, girls, home invasions, partying. I did it because I was told to do it—to save my own ass. I ran my own crew of girls, [name of all-female gang]. It was prostitution, I put them out. It was horrible—he [ex-boyfriend] said, "You have to bring me this much, all by this time."*

Unaffiliated street women or girls are by far the most vulnerable. They are not respected or valued by the male gang members. Even women who are affiliated through a man to a male gang are treated with more respect than street women. These women hang out with gangs but do not have relationships with male gang members. Instead, they are treated as sex objects. They are addicts and sex trade workers, often referred to as "party girls." Many are intravenous drug users and have contracted life-threatening illnesses such as AIDS and hepatitis. Some are wannabes or posers.

Ruth is a good example of an unaffiliated street woman who was brutalized by gangs. She was eighteen years old, an intravenous cocaine and morphine addict, and worked in the sex trade frequently. She told me how she got started: *"My cousin was* *two or three years older than me. I was twelve and she got me started in it. Now I work every week. I keep the money or give it to my mom to help her out. I can make anywhere from $80 to $900 a night. It depends if I get calls. I go out or wait around for people to phone me. I have a couple of marks [sugar daddies]—they help me when I need it."* Her experience of having a family member socialize her into the trade is common, as is the fact that she has a couple of sugar daddies who occasionally have sex with her and sometimes pay her rent and groceries. She also put other girls out. She told me: *"I put girls out to work a couple of years ago. They got a hold of me right away and put me away [in jail]. I told one girl, basically, she'd go and I would do my own thing. We'd go together but she gave me her money for rent."*

The commercial sexual exploitation of unaffiliated street women is common. Ruth's case of being sexually trafficked is representative of the experiences of other women in similar situations. She recounted a horrific experience where she had been kidnapped, brought to another province, and forced to work the streets by an African gang: *"Last month I got drunk and my friend ditched me. I got gang raped and kidnapped. They forced me to go to [another city] and work the streets. One guy held me down and two others raped me. Then I went running out and they let me go. They pulled my hair out, busted open my lip, and punched me all over."*

Although some studies indicate that young women are allowed by male members to participate in violent activities,[10] the majority of studies suggest that this is not the case.[11]

Are they "one of the guys," as Jodi Miller, Professor in the Department of Criminology and Criminal Justice, University of Missouri–St. Louis, argues?[12] Some do take on the characteristics of hyper-masculine male gang members, but others do not. Laura Fishman's work is a case in point. Her account of the 1960s Vice Queens of Chicago (the African-American female auxiliary to the male-dominated Vice Kings), who reported a preference for same-sex intimate relationships as an avenue out of chronic sexual violence and forced prostitution by the Vice Kings,[13] suggests that the social construction of femininity in gangs is a very complex matter. It is likely that girls involved in gangs resist and negotiate their gender roles outside of traditional femininity; the gang provides a social space to negotiate gender differently. Many female gang members in Canada engage in same-sex relationships. Although data are very limited, there is at least one study on this topic.[14]

Sylvie's case is illustrative. She was a leader of her prison-based gang in an all-female facility. This gang was active only inside the institution and was not active outside on the streets. She engaged in same-sex intimate relationships inside the prison, although she had been a member of a male-dominated street gang prior to her incarceration. Her boyfriend had been a higher-up in this gang. She had committed multiple acts of extreme violence.

> In this gang it was different from just stealing cars all the time. It was based on love, loyalty, support, and respect—what I been yearning for all my life. I got jumped in. I remember I couldn't even walk the next day how beaten up I was...that was called love and respect. I was about to start learning to be a part of them! It was the beginning of the end for me how beaten up I was...The decision that made me want to change and not be a part of the gang anymore was an incident that happened in [date]. I was out on parole and some shit happened to me. I was partying with three guys and one thing led to another. They beat me and raped me, knocked me out. I woke up and realized what happened. I couldn't do nothing either. They told me I was free to leave. I was black and blue, bloody, couldn't even close my legs.

New-Canadian women who are members of all-female gangs are especially likely to experience positive peer support and refuge from cultural clashes. The gang functions as a refuge from traditional gender role expectations, which for women are very limited. It is safer to get support in a gang than to be perceived as going against community and familial cultural norms.

Until recently, it was rare for girls and women to be targeted in gang shootings and other extreme violence. There was a street code against killing women. However, a number of women have recently been murdered in BC.[15] As women continue to be involved in drug distribution, it is expected that more will be killed.

STANDING BY YOUR MAN

It is interesting how many gang-affiliated women are willing to put up with unhealthy relationships, as long as there is no physical violence. They seem to believe that they have no other option, particularly if their man is the father of one of their children. The cases of Julie and Lorraine are illustrative.

Julie had made many positive changes since the start of her participation in a group program. She had grown up in a gang family where working the streets was not only common but expected. She was pregnant. During the program she had gotten away from a severely abusive boyfriend, quit drinking, reduced her drug use, and stopped working in the sex trade. Her housing situation had stabilized. She had attended all group sessions. She told me about the violence: *"I split with him. We were fighting too much. He tried to intimidate me, make me scared. I couldn't risk my baby. He would use wrenches and hammers, not nice, especially when carrying a baby. He made me miscarry in September then I got pregnant again. He beat me, hit me with hammers, and threatened me with knives and bats."* However, she had just gotten into a relationship with another man who was a gang member. She said: *"He just got out of jail and is a [name of gang] member.*

When he gets up [in the morning] he is drinking and gets high. He has to leave when he is using. But he is really sweet. He is not violent towards me. I know I have to split with him once my baby is born."

According to Julie, her current boyfriend was a good catch. Although he had been incarcerated for a number of years for a crime of extreme violence and was an active gang member, she was happy that "he is not violent towards me."

In a similar way, Carolyn reflected on her relationships with boyfriends who were gang members. Like Julie, she appeared to be content with her current boyfriend, who was an alcoholic and a higher-up in a gang. Why was she happy in this relationship? The answer was that her previous man, the leader of a notorious gang, beat her to a pulp. She told me: *"My boyfriend is in [name of gang] and I live with him. He drinks every day. When his bros come over, I don't go over and try to get noticed. My ex was president of the [gang]. I left him and came to Saskatchewan. I ran away from him—he beat me."* Carolyn went on to relate an experience wherein this same man brutally assaulted her, kidnapped her, and forced her to work the streets in another city and hand all the money over to him. She said: *"He gave me a minute and broke my collarbone and fractured my wrist; my face was pretty unrecognizable. He took me to [name of a city] from [another city]. He put me out. I snuck out, called the cops; they put me in hiding. I pretended I was drunk and waited for him to pass out. I have been in hiding ever since."*

Lorraine, a white woman aged twenty-four with a three-year-old son, had never socialized with gang members. Yet, she was involved in a long-term relationship with the father of her child. He had been a gang member for many years, but had recently exited. She also had been friends with other gang members for many years. She seemed to accept her affiliation as inevitable, even though it could jeopardize the health of her son. She said:

My boyfriend dropped his rag [quit] after I joined

[the program]. He was [name of gang]. I did not grow up in it. I was not raised in a gang. [My boyfriend] grew up in the middle of it. He was starved, abused, neglected. Although I hang out with gang members, they never pressured me and were respectful. They knew that I never wanted to do gang things. I told my boyfriend that you don't come visit him [his son] when you are drinking or high. You don't bring that to my place...It is hard because they are everywhere. In every bar I go to. I could stay away from them but that would mean I would stay home all the time. When I used to hang with gang members it was through him and before that other friends. You go out with girlfriends and their families are filled with gang members. Then you date one of them. It's all around you.

How is it that Lorraine was never a gang member, never a party girl, despite the fact that many of her friends were gang-involved? She is a rare case wherein her boyfriend, the father of her son, exited his gang while in the relationship with her. She told him things were over "unless he dropped his rag" (left his gang). She was employed in a good job part-time, had completed two years of university, and was planning on returning to school to finish her undergraduate degree. She was strong, resilient, and a good mother.

* * *

The vast majority of gangs in Canada are male-dominated: men occupy the upper rungs of leadership and women tend to be in subservient positions. Young women involved with such gangs face various risks at the hands of the men. Female members of all-women street gangs are relatively safe from male violence, but any women affiliated with male-dominated gangs (mainly as girlfriends and wives) and street women in the sex trade all face elevated levels of violence from gang-involved men. There are two main types of all-female gangs: those that are auxiliaries to male-dominated gangs, and those that are independent. Canada has had very few of either type. There is no evidence to suggest that the number of female gangs in Canada is rising.

The pathways into gang life are gendered. Gang-involved women have typically experienced severe sexual abuse in most areas of their lives, beginning in early childhood. This abuse is almost always inflicted by male family members and other men known to these girls. This seems to set the stage for prolonged sexual exploitation later in life. The levels of woman abuse in gangs are comparable to those in their families of origin for almost all female gang members. In most cases, the gang-related violence against them is just as bad as what these women experienced as children. Child sexual abuse is strongly associated with self-destructive behaviour and can lead to other criminal activities (such as solicitation and substance abuse), which in turn can lead to increased violent offending. A majority of these young women have a history of running from abusive homes, child welfare facilities, and mental health centres. Arguably, young women are "criminalized" for behaviour that is directly related to their having suffered chronic abuse.

✳ **CHAPTER 5** ✳

THE CHILDHOOD EXPERIENCES OF GANG MEMBERS

This chapter investigates the early childhood experiences of Canadian gang members, from birth to age eleven. Early childhood suffering often sets the stage for both prolonged victimization—through physical and sexual violence—and perpetration of extreme violence. This process of "violentization,"[1] or of becoming inured to violence, begins early and includes not only directly experienced maltreatment, but also the witnessing of and listening to violence being inflicted on other family members. Many children are born into gang life—they are socialized by gang-involved siblings, parents, and extended family members.

Another key problem I explore is the impact of brain damage and other cognitive impairments. Typically, these result from fetal alcohol spectrum disorder (FASD) and severe beatings. These problems are exacerbated by social factors such as gender inequality, racism, and poverty, which interact and result in social exclusion and devaluation. Gang members are not "born bad." Instead, they are trained as children by adults to do monstrous things later in life.

Loretta's story is typical, albeit she is an intelligent, vivacious young woman with a self-deprecating sense of humour who is strikingly beautiful and knows how to use her sexuality to get what she wants from men. She tried to flirt with me, and I gently let her know that I was not interested, and that she need not fear I would hurt her. Loretta had keen insights into her younger life and an uncanny ability to link negative experiences in her past to the problems she is experiencing in the moment. It is our fourth interview and she has just finished a beading project. It is remarkable, and I tell her she should pursue a career as an artist.

"What do you think, Mark? Pretty good for a kid who was meant to be killed by her dad when she was in her mom's stomach, eh?" Somehow, Loretta has been able to overcome the severe and long-term sexual, psychological, and physical abuse that has defined her. The horrific abuse she endured started even before she was born. Her father seems to have been a monster. She suffered serious injuries when he tried to beat her mother into miscarrying when she was five months pregnant with Loretta.

Although her father molested Loretta's younger sisters, he did not sexually abuse her. Instead, she was molested by just about every other male in her family. *"I was three years old when it started. Two brothers and three cousins sexually abused me—two years and seven years older. I was with my biological mom. I don't give a shit about my brothers or cousins. Everybody in my family knows."* At the time of the abuse, Loretta tried telling her mom and grandmother what was going on, but they both denied the abuse was happening and told Loretta that she was just a "bad kid." But things had changed for the better just before our interview. Loretta indicated that some people in her immediate family now, finally, realize that she had been telling the truth. *"Some of them believe me and some don't. Both my mom and grandma believe me now."* At this point, she began softly crying.

When she was a child, Loretta's mother and grandmother were unable to protect her from the male family members' ongoing sexual abuse. They refused to get her help. Instead, her mother resorted to physical battering in an effort to make her daughter "behave": *"My mom used to beat the shit outta me. She stabbed me here [pointing to her hand] when I was late getting home. She beat me black and blue, but not on my face where you could see it."* The abuse from her mother and male family members continued until child welfare intervened. Her mother called Child and Family Services because Loretta was "out of control." She did not mention the sexual abuse. Loretta, feeling abandoned by her mother and grandmother, was placed in more than ten foster homes and group homes before she turned twelve years old. She told me, *"My mom and grandma didn't want me anymore. My family was sexually molesting me, disowning me, abandoning me."* Loretta hated the child welfare system and felt that the foster and group homes were colluding with her mother to prevent her from ever returning home.

Loretta had no problem admitting that she was a difficult child, and related it to the abuse she was suffering: *"I was acting out because of my sexual abuse when I was little. I ran for weeks on end. Partied, stayed with friends, then I got sent back [to foster and group homes]."* She was suffering from emotional and behavioural disorders as a result of the abuse. After bouncing around in care, largely because authorities identified her as "conduct disordered," she learned not to trust adults, particularly those in positions of authority. There was one foster mother Loretta liked. Unfortunately, Loretta was moved one month into that placement because the foster mother believed Loretta had brought drugs into the home and had introduced them to her biological daughter. She also thought that Loretta was encouraging her daughter to skip school (they were both in grade six, at the same school). Once again, Loretta felt rejected and abandoned.

By age eleven, Loretta was well on her way to becoming an outcast. She was learning to use violence to protect herself from men, following a rape by two older street males. Loretta described them as "junkies." She stated, "*I didn't know how to fight then—not until I was thirteen. I couldn't stick up for myself.*" From that point on, Loretta decided, no man would ever hurt her again, at least not without a good fight. She used the rage burning inside of her to her advantage. She described as "flicking on the switch," the ever-present state of mind whereby she could erupt like a volcano without warning. For the first time in many years, she felt alive. She committed many assaults, most leaving her victims injured. When I interviewed her she was up on charges and likely to serve time in a correctional facility.

Like other young women in my studies, however, she was engaged not only in monstrous violence against others—she also directed it against herself, attempting suicide many times and cutting her wrists with a razor blade for years. "*I attempted suicide five times by overdosing when my family was trying to give me up for adoption. I felt like a complete failure. I was slicing my wrists when I was younger.*" At the time, Loretta blamed herself for the abuse as well as for being taken away from her mother and placed in the foster families and group homes. The self-injurious violence gave her a sense of peace and tranquility, not unlike the emotions she experienced when assaulting other people. When she attempted suicide, she used prescription drugs she either bought on the street or found in the medicine cabinets of foster parents. Her preferred drug was Oxycontin. After ingesting ten or so tablets, she told me, she would drift off into a dream-like state. She told me that it was as if she were at heaven's gate, waiting for the doors to be opened. She was hospitalized after each attempt.

A BIO-PSYCHOSOCIAL PERSPECTIVE

A bio-psychosocial perspective addresses multiple risk factors. Pathways into gang life are best understood through an integration of biological, psychological, and social factors, including bio-physiological and psychological characteristics, family, school, peer, and social variables. Within each category, social inequalities such as poverty, gender, and race can prevent healthy child and adolescent development.[2] However, health is not determined only by risk factors; resiliency plays an important role. Protective factors such as access to quality health, recreation, education, and other social services and supports can improve the outcomes for children and youth who are vulnerable.

I have identified five main pathways into gang life. This "pathways approach" is useful in identifying the primary mechanisms through which youth find themselves involved in gang activity. These five pathways are: The process of "violentization," rooted in experiences of serious and long-term child maltreatment; the prolonged institutionalization of children into child welfare and youth justice facilities; brain and mental health disorders from childhood trauma and fetal alcohol spectrum disorder—the result being "psychological homelessness;"[3] social exclusion and devaluation; and the development of hyper-masculine and sexualized-feminine gender identities. Given that this chapter focuses on early childhood, I will concentrate here on the first three pathways.

Children have different social, psychological, and familial experiences. They face different risks and their resiliency varies tremendously. Although all children have a right to an environment that is hospitable and nurturing, a significant minority grow up in one that is hostile and threatening. The playing field is far from level. Resilience is the ability to achieve positive outcomes in adverse conditions.[4] It is according to the young individual's resilience that the combination of societal, institutional, and individual factors[5] to which he or she is exposed result in positive or negative outcomes. But different outcomes will occur for young people, even when they live in similarly negative situations: the key to the difference is how well individuals, families, schools, and communities mitigate the risk factors.

FAMILY FACTORS

In the vast majority of cases, the seeds of violence and gang involvement are planted at home. Simply put, children with strong, healthy bonds to their parents have better mental and physical health[6] and are highly unlikely to become involved in gangs.

Violentization is the first pathway into gangs. Extreme physical maltreatment and neglect turn survivors into predators and prey in adolescence. As a child, Michael was abandoned by his mother, who was an intravenous drug abuser. Michael wrote the following letter to her when he was twenty-four: "*I'm writing this letter out of anger, maybe because I have nobody else to be frantic at. Mother, I love you but I ask the question why? Why is it I felt forlorn with you, I used to flounder without your love? They say without love, there's only the soul. Is it because I've tried so hard for your attention? Was I not the brightest kid? I'm left with so [many] questions…I remember once you held me close and promised this will be over soon, but again it was a lie. I still wonder why were you not around just like Dad was never. Is it why I am what I am?*"

Suffering chronic and repeated sexual trauma throughout childhood is another key driver into gang life for both girls and boys. Typical victims experience multiple types of exploitation, including sexual abuse, commercial sexual exploitation, and gang rapes. These children are most often abused by male family members or men who know them. More girls are victims, although many young men who participate in violent gang activities report having been sexually abused.[7] Some women are trafficked by gangs for lengthy periods of time. Lillian, a twenty-two-year-old gang member, penned the following poem about her experiences. It reflects the experiences of most female gang members:

Why Me?
He's in my room again tonight.
Maybe if I pull the covers up tight,
He might think I'm sleeping.
I heard the giggles in the other room.
Please God, not tonight.
I feel a cold hand on my thigh,
My mind goes blank.
Why me?...
Suddenly it's over.
I curl to the corner of my bed...
And silently cry...
It will never be over.

For girls, this betrayal of trust and abuse of power is aggravated in many communities by misogynistic and sexist beliefs, which result in their early sexualization. Julie described childhood and teen years characterized by violence, gang involvement, and work in the sex trade:

> I was in too many group and foster homes to count, since I was a baby. I hated them. My mother drank and did many drugs. Mostly all of my family were into gangs. Brothers, sisters, cousins. [name of gang]. I associated with them because they were my family. I was four years when it started. I used needles for a long time—coke and mo [morphine]. When I was eight years old I was in a foster home and I got raped lots. That's why I started looking after myself when I was thirteen. I shacked up with my ex—I was twelve and he was sixteen. I just managed to do it. I couldn't get on welfare, no allowance. When I was sixteen I started robbing tricks. I went with one

*guy and he said, "You remind me of my daughter."
I took all his money and took off. My brother had
gone away for twelve years for shooting a guy in the
chest. That same guy was trying to get with me.*

When I interviewed her, Julie was six months pregnant and
had quit working the street and using needles. She was told by her
child welfare worker that her baby would be taken away unless
she cleaned up her life. Yet, she still lived with a gang member.

Susan was a sixteen-year-old who had become gang-involved
at the age of twelve, the same year she started using intravenous
drugs and working in the sex trade. The leaders wanted her to
run drugs for them and to benefit financially from her prostitution. There was no shortage of older men to pay her for sex. Her
father had been absent her whole life and her mother, although
loving and well-intentioned, was totally incapable of keeping her
out of gang life. Susan put on paper her thoughts about how early
sexual abuse had set the stage for the unhealthy relationships,
depression, violence, and substance abuse:

*I was 5. My cousin was 20. He forced it on me. I was
sexually abused many other times. My ex-boyfriend
did it too. I wouldn't eat because I was too depressed
or high, wore clothes that showed off a lot of my
body because I thought that's all I was and what
every man will like me lookin' like a hoe [whore].
I was depressed and also angry on the inside,
covered those feelings on the outside, pretending to
be happy or just being quiet, stressed out because of
my feelings. I was violent—lashed out at everyone,
didn't give a shit about anything or anyone around
me, drank all the time too and used intravenous
drugs to flush away my feelings. I wanted to die,*

didn't see anything worth living for, thought I was
worthless and unwanted and unloved.

Like many other teens who have survived traumatic abuse, Susan felt that she was worthless, unloved, and abandoned. Like most of the young women in my studies, she developed a sexualized sense of femininity as a result of the abuse.

In Canada, child maltreatment is a major public health epidemic. It affects many more children than cancer or AIDS.[8] Many maltreated kids have impaired physical, emotional, cognitive, and social functioning. Suffering serious and prolonged child maltreatment is strongly related to experiencing mental health and behavioural problems, such as depression, low self-esteem, self-destructive and criminal behaviour, delayed cognitive development and poor school performance, aggression, and violence.[9] The severity, frequency, and duration of the child abuse are crucial factors in the extent of the emotional and behavioural difficulties the affected youth experience in their future lives.[10] All aspects of children's lives are affected when they grow up in violent homes. Domestic violence can make children less likely to succeed in school, more likely to suffer and to commit violence, and more likely to face a host of health problems.[11] Children who witness or hear chronic and severely abusive behaviour between caregivers can show the same effects as children who experience it directly.[12]

The emotional and behavioural responses to these experiences are very different for boys and for girls. Female victims internalize their distress, which then erupts through substance abuse, eating disorders, self-mutilation, suicide attempts, and depression. They tend to experience ongoing victimization in their interpersonal relationships.[13] Most males, however, externalize their distress. Boys have higher levels of hyperactivity symptoms (impulsiveness, poor concentration, distractibility), conduct symptoms (destroying things, threatening others, fighting, bully-ing, and cruelty), and externalized violence (homicide, physical and sexual assaults, homophobia, racism, bullying, dating vio-lence, and the like).[14]

The experiences of thirteen-year-old Shirley are illustrative. I invited her to put her life story on paper. First, she wrote about how her father had raped her on two different occa-sions, telling her if she told on him he would kill her. She tried to get her mother to kick him out, but the mother was unable to do that:

> *I'm gonna talk a little bit of my life what I went though when I was younger and when I was drinking and doing drugs. Well this is my story. When I was younger my dad raped me! I was about six. He told me if I ever told anyone he would kill me and my brother. Then it happened again when I was about eight and I tried to tell my mom. Every time she kicked him out I always asked her, "Mom, is he coming back?" Every time she said no but I never believed what she said because every time I said that he always came back. Then when I was about ten she kicked him out, then I said, "Mom, is he coming back?" and she said no! Then I said "Mom, I need to talk to you, just me and you!" "What is it?" Then I said, "Dad raped me!!!" About three–four months later he came back. I looked at my mom and said, "You lied to me!"*

The second key pathway into gang life is the experiencing of multiple out-of-home placements in child welfare and correc-tional facilities.[15] Many of these facilities are prime recruiting grounds for gangs, and a significant number of gang members report that they were not gang-involved before being placed in such facilities.[16] When she was ten, Shirley was apprehended and placed in a foster home and, subsequently, in a group home. Shortly thereafter, she was introduced to drugs and alcohol, beat up another young woman, and ran away from the home.

> *That morning a worker came to the school I was going to [name of school] at the time and this woman asked me too much questions. Then she talked to my brotherz and sisters. That same day she took me out of class and said you're coming with me. Then she put me in a foster home. So about one year later I just found out what drugs and alcohol were. I had this friend I was in a group home with this girl. Me and this girl ran away from that group home. That's when I just found out about alcohol and drugs and smoking. I got so drunk that I beat up this girl for looking at me in the wrong way. I don't remember what I did, all I remember is lookin' down at that girl. I thought to myself what did I do. I seen a cop car so I took off right then and there.*

She was later returned to her mother, who again took her father back in. Shirley then went to live with a friend, where her drug and alcohol use escalated. She was picked up by the police at some point, who returned her yet again to her mother. It was then that Shirley understood why her mother had been so unable to protect her from her father: he threatened violence, and had stalked her mother for years.

> *So about 6 months later we went back to my mom. I was mad at my mom because all that time she always took my dad back, so I ran away from her. Went to go live with one of my friends. It was the*

same thing every day, always drinking, smoking weed, smoking. When I was always drinking it's like nothing mattered anymore. But one day I got so drunk that I left that house I was living there and I got picked up by the cops. I was too young to go to the drunk tank [or] the cells so they called my mom and they went to go drop me off there! I don't remember going to bed but I woke up and I asked my mom why did she take [Dad] back all those times. She said to me, "I never took him back. He just [came] and [went] whenever he felt like [it]." My mom told me about how he would break in and wait for her to be home.

Arguably, Canada's child welfare and youth justice systems have replaced residential schools. Currently, one in ten Aboriginal children is in foster care or a group home, compared to one in two hundred non-Aboriginals. Today, the total number of children in care is three times higher than it was at the height of the residential schools period (28,000 Aboriginal children are in child welfare facilities today).[17] The Canadian Incidence Study of Reported Child Abuse and Neglect reported that the main reason Aboriginal kids are brought into care is neglect—severe poverty, substance abuse by parents, and poor housing.[18] In Canada, many Aboriginal children are placed in white settings, where it is difficult for them to develop a cultural identity. Thus, many Aboriginal children in care experience culture loss and are at high risk of gang recruitment and sexual exploitation as ways to get love and survive.

Although numbers are hard to come by, there is a growing body of evidence suggesting that African-Canadian children are also over-represented in the Canadian child welfare system, primarily in central and eastern Canada.[19]

Growing up in care, the second pathway into gang life, often results in attachment disorders,[20] which magnify the impact of childhood maltreatment. Even worse, institutionalization can result in further physical and sexual abuse by the staff and other young people.

Most maltreated kids are not violent, and some violent youth were not maltreated as children. A key moderating variable is the resiliency of the abused children themselves: their individual, familial, and community protective factors that can offset the impact of child maltreatment. Key protective factors at the family level include strong attachment to parent(s) and caregivers, bonding with other adults, effective family management practices (positive reinforcement, consistent structure and discipline, good supervision), residential stability (adequate housing, few moves), and good health of parent(s) and caregivers.[21]

BIOLOGICAL AND GENETIC FACTORS

Biological and genetic factors are key determinants for gang involvement. Children are born with different sets of abilities and potential, and factors such as resiliency, intelligence, cognitive functioning, physical ability, physical attributes, and body type are important factors in determining healthy child and adolescent development. The presence of one or more of these attributes can go a long way toward protecting a young person from involvement in gang life.

The third pathway into gang life—brain and mental health disorders resultant from childhood trauma and fetal alcohol spectrum disorder—fits here. Developmental problems, learning disabilities and intellectual limitations, FASD, brain injuries, predisposition to mental health problems, and certain personality traits are all important risk factors that can lead to poor child and adolescent health.[22] Young people who live in poverty *and* face one or more of these risks are vulnerable to poor health—they are doubly disadvantaged.

Personality traits that influence child behaviour are complex and the product of the co-occurrence of several genes.[23] Temperament (whether children are fussy or calm, upset or happy) and other characteristics such as irritability, low self-control, and irresponsibility are moderately genetic.[24] Children's capacity to learn the social use of language, to interact with others, and to regulate their emotions are influenced by genetic inheritance as well. These factors are directly influenced by a mother's behaviour when pregnant. For example, malnutrition, smoking, alcohol/drug consumption, and victimization by violence during pregnancy all contribute to negative health outcomes on the fetus. Fetal alcohol spectrum disorder, which results in infant brain damage to areas responsible for planning and self-control,[25] is a particular concern in Aboriginal communities. (FASD will be examined later in this chapter.) Risky behaviours during pregnancy are more common in low-income mothers. This is primarily because of a lack of education, and other behavioural risk factors.[26]

The case of Paul is illustrative of those gang members for whom abuse began in the womb. His mother was beaten by his father, she abused cocaine throughout her pregnancy, and was malnourished. Paul was born addicted to cocaine and he had a significant speech impediment. He also was dyslexic and had many other learning delays. In my interview with him, although he did speak about these issues, he found it difficult to do so because of his speech delay. He had just been released from prison, having served a sentence for severe violence:

> Uh yeah I guess I was you know like born one of those babies who are addicted. I dunno, I was you know, I was told that thing 'cause of moms who do drugs. Like when I was in her stomach, see, shit

happens. And I got fucked over, like my teachers,
they said, I was, you know, a dummy. I got that
thing where I see the word "dog" and I say "god."
Whatever fuck it's not me but her [his mother's
problem] so I got grade six. And then there's the
bullets in me, you know the gun did it, did it to me.

It has been estimated that roughly 40 per cent of a child's anti-social behaviours may be related to genetic factors.[27] However, genes interact with important environmental dynamics. For example, so-called "bad genes" inherited by a child (such as cognitive impairment, or low intelligence) most likely will not negatively affect psychosocial functioning if there is positive parenting, quality schooling, and a pro-social peer group.

There is a complex interaction between a child's inborn resiliency and vulnerabilities, and how parents/caregivers deal with the child's needs. In the preschool years, children with difficult temperaments, hyperactivity, impulsivity, oppositional and defiant behaviour, early onset aggression, and social difficulties are at high risk for serious and violent offending trajectories. Without comprehensive early intervention, these children will likely grow into the 5 per cent of all adolescents who commit over half of all serious youth crime.[28] Paul and Loretta are good examples of children who never got the help they needed, and became involved in that small group of serious and violent offenders.

Highly aggressive adolescents like Paul and Loretta usually have a history of conduct problems that began at a very young age. Cognitive deficits and a lack of social skills can lead to poor coping skills and frequent frustration. These children often misinterpret social cues, mistakenly assign hostile intent to others, have poor impulse control, low frustration tolerance, limited insights into the feelings of others, and lack alternative responses to stress. It is estimated that 30 per cent of Canadian boys and 22 per cent of girls aged four to eleven years have symptoms of one or more of these emotional or behavioural disorders; 3 per cent are socially impaired by their problems.[29] Less than 20 per cent of these children get help for their problems.[30] Paul and Loretta certainly did not receive much help, despite their social impairments. They were vulnerable children, whose basic emotional and physical needs were disregarded, and who consequently developed mental health and behavioural problems, which led to gang involvement.

As will be shown in the following sections, healthy child and adolescent development is shaped not only by genetic and biological makeup, but also by personality traits, early interactions with parents/caregivers, socio-economic factors, and early childhood experiences in the family, the school, and the community. However, barriers such as poverty and racism can greatly compromise healthy outcomes when families have limited access to quality health, recreation, education, and other social services.

FETAL ALCOHOL SPECTRUM DISORDER

FASD is a major contributor. In the presence of other risk factors, it can set the stage for a lifetime of engagement in gang activities. In one of the gang evaluation studies conducted by Sharon Dunn and myself, the vast majority of youth reported having a close family member who had a severe drug or alcohol problem. Many of these youth had the visible facial features indicative of FASD.

Fourteen-year-old Chrystal wrote about the impact of addictions on her life. She identified that she was a fetal alcohol spectrum disorder child because of her mother's alcoholism. She felt abandoned and rejected. Her father wanted her aborted and she was left to the care of her sister to raise her. Violence was ever-present in her home life. She wrote:

> *I just turned 14. Still healthy, not into drugs or*
> *alcohol. I am literally scared to death by drugs and*

alcohol. When I was in my mom's stomach she did
really hard drinking. My dad wanted nothing to
do with me, he told my mom to get an abortion.
She just about did but she changed her mind and
was going to give me up for adoption but my sister
[name] cried for my mom to keep me. My sister lived
with my grandparents. My mom told her to keep me
then, that she has to take care of me. She was only
12 or 13. She would have to get up early, change
my diapers, feed me. My grandpa would beat my
grandma every time they drank. I was about 5 when
I moved back with my mom. She loved drinking at
the time, it felt like she never cared for me. My sister
put a big impact on my life, what's right or wrong I
look up to her. I am in this program because all the
drinking has caused me trouble in school.

Fetal alcohol spectrum disorder is the umbrella term used to describe a continuum of disabilities, from most severe to least severe, of prenatal exposure to alcohol. It includes the related conditions of fetal alcohol syndrome,[31] fetal alcohol effects, alcohol-related birth effects, and alcohol-related neurodevelopmental disorder.[32] FASD is the most common cause of mental retardation in North America. The physical, mental, behavioural, and intellectual disabilities (commonly referred to as "primary" disabilities—permanent brain damage resulting in impaired mental function) resultant from maternal alcohol exposure are lifelong and include skeletal abnormalities (for example, facial deformities), physical disabilities (for example, kidney and internal organ problems), cognitive impairment (such as difficulty comprehending the consequences of one's actions), and learning disabilities (such as those related to mathematical concepts).

There are no national statistics on the prevalence of FASD

in Canada, although data exist on rates in other countries. In the USA, fetal alcohol syndrome prevalence is estimated at 1 to 3 per thousand live births and FASD prevalence is reported at 9.1 per thousand live births.[33] Health Canada uses these rates for estimating prevalence in Canada, where it is believed that 1 per cent of the population has FASD (about 300,000 people).[34] There has been a handful of studies estimating prevalence in small Aboriginal communities in British Columbia, Manitoba, Saskatchewan, and the Yukon. These studies suggest that prevalence rates are elevated in these communities,[35] although methodological problems exist.[36] A complicating factor is that it is difficult to disentangle the effects of FASD from the outcomes of colonization, forced assimilation, and the residential schools.[37]

Studies in other countries have also found higher rates of binge drinking in North American Aboriginal communities.[38] These prevalence rates, both in the USA and in Canada, likely show only the tip of the iceberg because diagnosis is quite rare and usually occurs in adolescence or adulthood.[39] Aboriginal people also suffer from many other disabilities (such as learning disabilities, physical disabilities) at a prevalence rate estimated to be double that of the non-Aboriginal population in Canada (32 per cent compared to 16 per cent).[40]

Anecdotal reports in Canada and a small number of investigations in other countries suggest that young people who have FASD may be more likely to be gang-involved and to have experienced sexual exploitation than those who are free of the disorder.[41] Gender seems to play an important role: FASD-affected girls and young women tend to be victimized by childhood sexual abuse and to experience sexual exploitation in gangs, whereas men are more likely to be sexual traffickers and perpetrate other forms of exploitation on girls and women. Boys with FASD are reported to have experienced high rates of childhood sexual abuse as well. A high proportion of Aboriginal youth involved with the Canadian youth justice system have disabilities, including FASD.[42] Many leave their home reserve and get lost in a city,[43] where they are easy prey for exploitation and gang recruitment.

Most children with FASD will never be financially or socially self-sufficient. They are at high risk for neglect, physical abuse, sexual abuse, violence, maternal death, and abandonment. Studies with school children who have FASD indicate elevated rates of disruptive behavioural disorders at home and at school. Boys are highly likely to display early onset aggressive behaviour disorders. Many appear to lack guilt, are cruel to others, and are more likely to lie and to steal. Combined with other social deficits, these traits can result in extremely violent behavior.[44]

Secondary disabilities, which are not present at birth but emerge from primary disabilities (such as brain damage), have also been thoroughly investigated. With appropriate interventions, such secondary disabilities as mental ill-health and school problems can be prevented or reduced because they appear in the social environment in which the child lives.[45] Longitudinal studies on relatively large samples have investigated these lifelong secondary effects. Of particular relevance are the findings related to victimization, violent offending, and association with criminal peers. The vast majority of participants in these studies (three-quarters or more) have suffered long-term physical and sexual abuse as children and continue to be victimized as adults, have disrupted school experiences (suspensions, expulsions, dropping out), have problems with employment and living independently, and have mental health problems (suicide threats and attempts, psychosis, depression, panic attacks). A smaller majority (roughly two-thirds) have histories of youth and adult offending behavior. Their most common crimes are those against persons (theft, burglary, physical and sexual assault, murder, domestic violence, child molestation), followed by property damage, possession/selling of drugs, and vehicular crimes. Approximately two-thirds also have addiction problems. Roughly one-half have attention deficit and conduct problems, including "inappropriate" sexual behavior.[46]

As a result of these serious issues, many of these young people have experienced long-term placement in child welfare, mental health, and justice facilities. There also appears to be an intergenerational aspect to FASD (although there is no evidence to suggest it is hereditary): young women with FASD are highly likely to drink during their own pregnancies and about one-third of their children are born with FASD. The children of young mothers with FASD are thus highly likely themselves to be taken into the care of the child welfare system.[47]

PSYCHOLOGICAL FACTORS

Lillian, a twenty-three-year-old gang member, was a talented writer. She had many indicators of borderline personality disorder and bipolar disorder. She reported that various doctors had prescribed anti-psychotic medication for many years. She took the drugs during periods of incarceration, but when on the streets preferred to self-medicate with morphine and marijuana. She indicated that she felt like a "vegetable" while taking the medication. Her poem "These Eyes" reflects the experiences of many participants in my studies—the process of emotional numbing that follows years of maltreatment:

> **These Eyes**
> *I've seen death, looked him in the eye,*
> *I've done things that would make you ask why?*
> *I've looked down the barrel of a gun,*
> *I've danced with the devil…and won.*
> *I've been beaten and broken…*

For words I have spoken.
I've been raped and abused,
I've been tortured and used.
Yet no amount of pain can break me.
No amount of time will shake me.
They can lock me in a cage,
I'll still put my soul on this page.

Certain psychological factors are key determinants of health. Intellectual and interpersonal abilities, positive self-esteem and mental health, personal responsibility, and pro-social behaviours are key protective factors that can shelter young people from the risks of gang involvement.[48] However, risk factors such as poor mental health status, low self-esteem and body image, learning disabilities, antisocial behaviours and attitudes, internalizing disorders,[49] and externalizing disorders[50] can compromise the healthy development of children, particularly if they live in poverty and do not have protection from some of these risks.

The third pathway into gang life also involves these factors—the mental health disorders and the state of psychological homelessness. Twenty-three-year-old Michael was victimized by chronic and severe physical, sexual, and emotional abuse as he was growing up. He lived in grinding poverty. His poem, "Suicide," illustrates the mental health problems many gang members have after untreated childhood trauma. He wrote this while in a prison in western Canada, halfway through a sentence for an act of severe violence. He told me that his poem was in fact a true reflection of a time when he almost hung himself. He was able to avert the hanging despite having few, if any, supports. He later told me that he wanted to live for his younger brother.

Suicide
Thoughts of suicide once came into play

Sobbing with pain holding the string
Managed to tie,
But just couldn't end my life,
Reminiscence of family and friends,
And how it could be the end,
Contemplating on taking the next step,
Towards an ending life feeling like there's nothing left,
A childhood which wasn't the greatest,
A ruined life I just couldn't take it,
With the noose around my neck,
And the tears dripping like sweat,
Really hoping somebody would help me,
To stop my pain and to stop all the misery,
Was dealt a cruel hand and lived my 22 years sad,
Reasons to live for, I wish I had.

In their preschool years, high-risk children have difficulties in processing information. Their perceptions and cognitions are not wired properly, especially their perceptions of caregivers and other adult authority figures. Children who are aggressive at this early age are far more likely than non-aggressive children to attribute hostile intentions to others and to have external loci of control. These children tend to impute threatening intentions to others, are easily slighted, and evaluate disobedience, defiance, and revenge as positive attributes and as legitimate ways to solve problems.[51]

During adolescence, low-income youth are also more likely to experience emotional and behavioural disorders. Self-destructive and externalized violence are common in the lives of young people who have unequal access to the key determinants of health. The case of Lorraine is illustrative. In the following excerpt from my interview with her, she reflected on how depression had been a constant in her life, as well as in the lives of many family members. She believed that her depression had many causes: early childhood trauma, post-partum depression, seasonal affective disorder, as well as having been passed down from her parents. In her teen years she tried to self-medicate by binge drinking and had two serious suicide attempts.

> *I have had depression ever since I was a child. It got to the point where I tried to kill myself in my teens a couple of times. My doctor increases the dose in winter and decreases in the summer. It helps. I take Zoloft 100 milligrams. I have been on them since age fifteen or sixteen. I am still in the post-partum stage for one and a half years. I have lots of bad memories I am triggered to. My real dad sexually abused me while I lived with him on a farm in [name of city]. It happened in July and August lots. Depression runs in my family. That's why I have become very knowledgeable. My parents both grew up in abusive homes. They have their issues and never got help. Lots of violence and anger. I'm not saying they are bad parents. They'll kick your ass instead of sitting you down and talking. I took a whole bottle of Effexor twice—over thirty pills each time. I was hospitalized for two weeks each time. We were kept in line by fear. You were too scared to cross that line. I binge drank when I was a teenager until age nineteen. When you drink like that you let men do things to you. You are putting yourself in danger. Maybe it was intentional, maybe not. I was promiscuous. I just didn't care. I was not worthy of a normal relationship.*

Ruth, another gang member I interviewed, had attempted suicide many more times than Lorraine. She had bounced around in the child welfare system for most of her childhood and teen years, had been an intravenous drug addict since age twelve, and had been involved in the sex trade since the same age. She talked about the positive aspects of cutting, and of her love for her younger brother: *"I have tried to kill myself about ten times. Overdosing on my mom's anti-depressants, penicillin that I am allergic to, my brother's sleeping pills. For four or five years I cut myself every week. Whenever I felt bad about myself. It made me feel better I guess. I cut on my arms and lower legs. My little brother was the reason I stopped. He is fourteen and he is my everything."*

Gina Brown[52] has demonstrated that the competencies of low-income children with emotional and behavioural disorders can be raised substantially with the provision of no-cost, accessible recreation and daycare services. When health and social services are targeted to and delivered in neighbourhoods with high proportions of low-income families, many more families in need can access required supports. This is important, because traditional approaches to addressing child and adolescent disorders (psychiatric and psychological treatment) reach only 20 per cent of all young people in need. The traditional interventions do not work well with high-risk young people: they are expensive, difficult to access, and have poor outcomes.[53]

School, peer group, and community factors round out the remaining three domains in the bio-psychosocial model. The fourth pathway into gang life, social exclusion and devaluation, is rooted in all three areas.

SCHOOL FACTORS
School success and bonding (high commitment and educational aspirations), attendance, participation in extracurricular activities, and low delinquency rate are key protective factors that lead to positive outcomes for young people. Such youth are highly

unlikely to become gang-involved. Risk factors, though, include academic failure, low literacy, frequent school transitions, low bonding (low commitment and educational aspirations), truancy and dropping out of school, and high delinquency rates. These risks are linked to negative outcomes—in the absence of protective factors in other areas of a young person's life.[54]

Staying in school provides structured daytime activities and supports a healthy socialization process. However, many gang members have negative experiences in school: learning difficulties, behavioural problems, poor grades, frequent suspensions and absenteeism, and high dropout rates. Youth who don't go to school are at increased risk of joining anti-social peer groups and gangs, which can entrench violent behaviour.

Low-income students are disproportionately excluded from participation in academics and extracurricular activities. A growing body of research outside Canada on the long-term impact of "zero tolerance" policies has documented the devastating consequences: large increases in the number and duration of suspensions and expulsions, significant over-representation of visible/ethnic minorities and special needs students in disciplinary measures, large increases in school dropout rates, and criminalization of many behaviours that previously were addressed in school settings without involving the justice system.[55] Suspensions and expulsions, by excluding students from school life, contribute to problem behaviour and youth crime.[56] Low-income students are far more likely than their more affluent counterparts to be suspended or expelled, drop out of school, have low literacy and employability skills, and have emotional and behavioural problems.[57]

Billy's experiences in school are representative of those of many other gang members. At the time of his interview, he was twenty years of age and had been gang-free for nearly three years. He was back in school full-time, working part-time, and had completed a residential drug treatment program. His earlier years had not been so good, however. Although he reported doing well in elementary school, he said he began to experience difficulties in grade eight, which continued into high school. He felt like a loner but wanted to fit in. He felt excluded and devalued as a young Aboriginal man:

> *Three boys in my family, we were all going to be hellraisers. In elementary school I got good grades, I was an A+ student. In high school I got into drugs and alcohol, started drinking more. I started in grade eight, grade nine, and I fell into a bad crowd. Part of it may be just to fit in. When I was growing up I was the loner kid, always by myself. I wanted to be the cool guy, the one everyone respects.*

Like many other gang-involved young men, Billy was athletic and had at least one positive friend at school. However, these strengths were not enough to overcome the influence of family members who were gang-involved and school friends who were turning to gang life:

> *My friend, he was on the wrestling and football teams, he showed me around. There were some positive peers. I was on the wrestling and football team about two years. About grade nine year I started to get into gangs...Some of my family are gang members. I got started in it through my school friends, friends of friends. I started hanging out with them.*

What sparked Billy to get out of the gang life were his two younger brothers. He believed that he was the reason they became gang members. He also reflected on the impact of growing up in poverty. He told me: *"We didn't have much food to eat growing up, I lived in poverty. I had to have some source of income, even though it was illegal."* After spending two years incarcerated, he worked on his employability and developed some skills. He felt good about earning money honestly: *"Two years in the [young offender centre] altogether. First job was at [an employment program], a changing experience for me. I had never worked a day in my life. Respect, learning to wash dishes properly. Eventually I learned how to cook. Money was my motivation."*

PEER GROUP FACTORS

Key protective factors at the peer group level include pro-social siblings and peers and positive peer group membership. Evidence suggests that most healthy peer networks are organized around hobbies, interests, and other activities shared by friends.[58] Positive peer relations are strong protective factors for many children and youth. Positive social support is related to lower rates of emotional and behavioural disorders, crime, and violence. These factors can protect young people from the risks associated with living in poverty.

Risk factors at the peer group level include delinquent siblings and peers, and membership in anti-social peer groups and gangs. Researchers who have studied violence and youth crime in the social context of peer group processes argue that peers play a significant role in enabling and sustaining these anti-social behaviours.[59] Associations with people who are violent role models can result in violent behaviour. These problems can interact with and feed off genetic, biological, family, and school risk factors. Many Canadian gangs have been based on close friendships developed in elementary and high school and in young offender facilities.[60]

The risk factors at the peer level present in the life of fifteen-year-old Ricky are similar to those in the lives of most participants. Ricky joined a crew at the age of ten, engaging in petty crimes. He developed friendships on the streets because he was not getting attention or love at home, where he felt rejected and excluded. His mother was an alcoholic. He liked the idea of being a "little hustler." He wrote: *"When I was a little boy my mom used to drink a lot and when I turned ten I joined a crew called [name]. I used to get into a lot of trouble running from the cops, hitting cars with rocks to get chased, smoking weed, drinking. We used to get chased from other gangs but we weren't a gang, we were a crew. Now that all of us are older that crew ain't around. I used to go steal some candy, pop, chips for everyone. They used to call me a little hustler."*

Things went from bad to worse as his mother's drinking continued. Ricky was embarrassed and felt devalued by the situation at home. He was acutely aware that many of his friends had mothers whom he believed to be better than his own. He joined a crew but got caught *"stealing liquor for my homies."* His mother realized that he needed help so she stopped drinking. With things stabilized at home and the justice system leaning heavily on him, Ricky retreated from his negative peers and spent more time with family. He wrote: *"but now I'm doing 8 months probation. I changed my act from negative to positive. My mom ain't an alcoholic no more but I still got problems with the law since I was 12 years old. Now I'm turning 15, that's been 3 years and I'm still on curfew but I'll be off in a couple months, then I might go find a job so I can have some money in my pocket instead of always stealing. That's been keeping me in and out of jail for a while but I'll be off pretty soon I hope."*

Compared to Ricky, Anthony had been a serious gangster for most of his life. He had been trying to exit for years with little success. At the time of my interview with him, he was twenty-six years old, an intravenous drug user (cocaine and morphine), and HIV positive. He was deeply ashamed of his illness and felt isolated and devalued. He was excluded from family life. He told me about how an absence of positive family supports led him into gang life. He was looking for a place to belong and found it with gang-involved friends. Status came with making money, engaging in stabbings, and reading his name in the local paper:

> *My mom passed away last month, my dad is in jail looking at [doing a lengthy sentence]. I was raised by foster homes and my grandma. I quit [school] three months into grade twelve because I wanted to be a gangster, be cool. I got more hard into it. That's when drugs came in. Started off smoking weed then to harder ones, coke and mo [morphine]. Started off somewhat positive with my friends then we all started taking off from school. Getting high then started off into drugs, violence, selling drugs then in and out of jail, after grade nine. I was doing missions for my gang, scamming and taxing people. Basically we were all drug dealers, doing armed robberies. I made the paper a couple of times. Even when I stayed in [name of city] I made the paper there—for a stabbing. I got a thrill outta that.*

COMMUNITY AND NEIGHBOURHOOD FACTORS

The risk factors at this level include community disorganization (crime, drug selling, gangs, poor housing, high unemployment, transient population), exposure to violence, and racial discrimination. Social infrastructures to promote inclusion and participation in quality health, social, and recreation services are minimal compared to those in more affluent neighbourhoods.[61] There are usually few social networks and ties, with a disproportionate number of single-parent families and individuals experiencing mental or physical health problems. Neighbourhoods character-ized by high-density housing, disorganization, high population turnover, high crime rates, and unemployment tend to have low social capital. Immigrants, ethnic and visible minorities, and Aboriginal people make up a disproportionate share of many social housing communities.

Many of these risk factors were present in the life of Noel, aged twenty-four, who lived in one of the most marginalized neigh-bourhoods in Canada. Housing was poor and few people had jobs. Because of this, many parents engaged in survival crimes to meet the basic needs of their children. Noel's mother worked in the sex trade to bring money into her family—then spent most of what she made on intravenous drugs. He told me: *"My mom always worked. She slammed forever. It was like tricks were always coming and going. She made cash. But we still were poor. Never had much food or clothes. I guess it all went to the coke."* Noel and his brothers had jobs too—they stood watch at the front door of their house as their mother turned tricks upstairs. It was their job to look out for their mom and to collect the money from the johns. Their experience is common amongst gang members who grow up in entrenched poverty. They often feel excluded from community life. Experiences of racism lead to further devaluation.

Protective factors related to healthy adolescent develop-ment include mixed socio-economic backgrounds of families, organized and accessible community and social infrastruc-ture (recreation facilities and activities, adequate housing, high employment), bonding to institutions outside of family and school, and strong cultural identity and racial harmony.[62] Noel did not have access to any of these.

A large body of research on human development shows that health and well-being are linked to financial resources. Children and youth from low-income families are more vulnerable: they generally experience more physical, behavioural, and mental health problems; they suffer more neglect and physical violence; they do less well at school, are more likely to drop out, and experience less labour market success than people from more affluent family backgrounds.[63] The vast majority of gang members grow in severe poverty.

Billy's case is representative of the backgrounds of the majority of gang members in Canada. As a youngster, his job was to steal food from grocery stores to feed his parents and siblings. His parents placed this heavy burden on him when he was very young—he started stealing food when he was eight years old. He told me that none of his other friends had to steal food. He understood that he did not fit in. As he entered adolescence, he realized that he could make much more money dealing drugs. Even then, he gave most of his profits to his mother. She used the money to pay the rent.

Serious delinquency tends to originate in low-income, disadvantaged families in many Western countries.[64] The depth of poverty (or how far a family falls below the low income cut-off) is important. Those families who are very poor, for a long time, suffer profoundly negative effects. Parents who live in high-poverty neighbourhoods experience more stress.[65] Issues such as unemployment and being a young single parent can lead to difficulties in parenting and the supervision of children.

Most of the gang members involved in my studies had next to no supervision from parents. A majority had never met their fathers. Even if biological fathers or other father figures were present, they were unhealthy influences and violent. Most of the mothers could not parent well because of their addictions and involvement in gang or street life. Those young people who were lucky enough to have both parents working in "normal" jobs had only sporadic contact with them. As twenty-five-year-old Junior told me, *"They were gone before we got up and only came back after dinner. They had no idea what we were into and even if they did, they were not around to deal with it. Never went to our schools, even when we got kicked out. Never cooked us meals. Never gave a shit."*

Only 35 per cent of low-income Canadians feel that their neighbourhood is a suitable place in which to bring up children. In comparison, 63 per cent of high earners report that their neighbourhood is suitable for that.[66] The case of nineteen-year-old Jimmy is illustrative. Life was relatively good in his family until they had to move to a social housing project, which was infested by gangs, drugs, and violence. They had to move to this new neighbourhood because both his parents lost their jobs. He wrote: *"I lived on the [name of working class community] all my life with my father, mother, and three brothers. We all had good healthy lives 'til we moved to one of the worst parts of the city at the time. It was called [name of housing project]. They were town houses. My father was the caretaker, he cleaned the place up really good."* Following the move, all three boys dropped out of school because that was what their new friends did. The family experienced a home invasion by gang members who mistakenly believed that Jimmy's father and uncle were rival gang members.

The vast majority of the participants in my studies grew up in neighbourhoods or on reserves where social capital was low, with a critical mass of very poor families. Participants did not feel that they had a meaningful place in their communities, schools, or families. They turned to gangs to fill this void.

Many young gang members come from communities where there is an intergenerational cycle of involvement in foster homes, group homes, and young offender facilities. In some of these communities, it is rare to find a child who has not grown up in care. The impact on a child of having parents and grandparents who have been raised by the child welfare system is significant: many of these young people feel helpless to change the cycle and seem resigned to it as a normal and acceptable part of life. Julie was six months pregnant and was depressed, anxious, and fearful because of what she saw as a culture of baby-snatching. She stated: *"It's about being pregnant, being scared. I am going to be a good mother, but how come all Indian girls are losing their babies? People tell me that I'm going to lose my baby. I have cut down lots on smoking weed."* Her fears were well-founded. She herself had grown up in care all of her childhood and adolescence, as had her parents. Her grandparents were residential school survivors.

* * *

This chapter has focused on the early childhood experiences of Canadian gang members from birth to eleven years of age. For almost all the young people in my research, early childhood suffering sets the stage for both victimization by physical and sexual violence throughout the lifespan, and perpetration of extreme violence against others.

A bio-psychosocial perspective has been proposed to address the multiple risk factors related to gang involvement. Pathways into gang life are best understood through an integration of biological, psychological, and social factors, including biophysiological and psychological characteristics, family, school, peer, and community variables. Within each category, social inequalities such as poverty, gender, and race are significant risk factors that can prevent healthy child and adolescent development. Protective factors such as access to quality health, recreation, education, and other social services and supports can improve the outcomes for youth at high risk of gang involvement.

The vast majority of gang members come from a background of entrenched poverty. This has resulted in economic and social marginalization, along with an inability to meet the most basic needs of life—food, clothing, and shelter. Imploding families are another key problem. Directly experiencing, witnessing, or hearing family violence has had a significant harmful impact on the growth and development of these children. Emotional and behavioural disorders are a common outcome. Unfortunately, none of the young people in my studies got the help they needed to address these problems. Parental addictions, intergenerational incarceration of caregivers, absent or unhealthy fathers, brain damage (as a result of FASD or severe beatings), and socialization into the gang lifestyle are other common challenges they faced in childhood. Far too many young people in my studies were taken into the care of the child welfare system and never went home again.

✳ CHAPTER 6 ✳

TRAUMATIZED TEENS, IMPLODING FAMILIES

This chapter explores the adolescent years of Canadian gang members, from age twelve to seventeen. Twelve is the age of criminal responsibility in Canada, and the youth justice system ends at age seventeen (young adults eighteen and older when they offend are dealt with in the adult system). I continue with the theme that the child welfare and youth justice systems can be sites for gang recruitment for some young people. In some cases, institutionalization of children from gang families actually helps to solidify the gang and supports recruitment of new members. I also turn our focus to the notion that street gangs are perceived by many members and prospective recruits as alternate families. These young people "jump ship" from one family into another, only to realize that their new family is just as violent and unforgiving as their blood family, and some in that situation find themselves left to sink or swim. Finally, some children arrive at birth into families already entrenched in gang life.

In the following poem, "Bonded by Blood," twenty-four-year-old Michael feels he has let his younger brother down by exposing him to gang life and to witnessing a murder. At the time of the interview, Michael had just been released from a penitentiary after a lengthy sentence for serious crimes of violence. He had been incarcerated for most of his life. But this poem offers an insight into how difficult it is to leave gangs that are based on family blood lines. Michael had tried to get his younger brother, Jules, seventeen, who had FASD and was actively involved in a street gang, into a gang exit program. Jules had refused.

Bonded by Blood
Am I my brother's keeper?
Am I my brother's keeper?
I am.
I am my brother's keeper
My loyalty knows no other,
I escalated dishonour between me and my brother
We both started hatred for each other
It's a problem I want to vanish
I can't put up with it
Am I my brother's keeper, you keep asking me this
Man through thick and thin
You and I have been through a lot of shit
Living a life of sin, we both knew this day was coming
Just like you said, we'd live for each other
And die for one of another
Shit
No matter how I put it and look at it
I can't make it fit
The pieces of the puzzle of life that we live
It's personal now and it's with that in my mind that

I think
Blood in our bond
On my life I walk with you till I'm gone
And that's a promise bro
Cut my arm and see the colour that runs through
my veins
To show you blood's thicker than water
Ask me if I'm my brother's keeper again.

About seven years earlier, Jules, their older brother Cal (who had just been released from prison), other extended family members, and Michael had been drinking at a family member's place. At the time, young Jules idolized his older brothers. Cal stabbed an extended family member, killing him. Jules witnessed the whole incident and wound up hiding in a corner, covered in blood, terrified. When the police arrived, Michael was also covered in blood and crying. Michael remained ridden with guilt for exposing his younger brother to this horrifying incident.

Since that time, Michael has tried to protect his brother from gang involvement and the justice system. Michael even served time for Jules, who had been charged with an assault. In a nutshell, Michael is questioning his own ability to look out for his younger brother: "I escalated dishonour between me and by brother." When he writes "blood in our bond," he is not only referring to family ties to the gang, but also to the murder.

Cal, the older brother, was later released from prison and subsequently attacked in the community. The attack was gang-related. He exited his gang following the vicious assault. He reported that he was tired of the constant threat of violence and did not want to be killed.

THINKING PATTERNS SHAPED BY TRAUMA

Young people who end up in gangs start out as children who are socialized into a culture of violence and trained by adults to be gangsters and thugs. They are immersed in a criminal lifestyle and a world of addictions. I have already discussed how maltreated kids have impaired physical, emotional, cognitive, and social functioning, but it is worth repeating that all aspects of children's lives are affected when they grow up in violent homes. Domestic violence can make children less likely to succeed in school, more likely to suffer violence outside the family and to commit it, and more likely to face a host of health problems that can last throughout their lives.[1]

Christine was born into a family which seemed to be imploding. Her mother was an addict and had a series of boyfriends and common-law partners who were violent, gang members, and addicts as well. Christine was groomed, through the process of violentization, for a life of institutionalization, gangs, drugs, and street life. Like many gang members who have suffered extreme abuse, she used violence to stop the abuse. Christine talked about fighting back against her abuser: *"My mom's ex-husband sexually molested my twin sister and I chopped off his fingers. I was eleven years old. He got acquitted and I was never charged. He lost one finger and the other was mangled. I was molested by him too but I was afraid to tell anyone at his trial."* Like many abuse survivors, she did not tell anyone that she and her twin were being violated for several years. Why? He had told her that he would kill her: *"He held my hand on the stove burner to threaten us not to tell."* Christine still thinks of revenge: *"I get this urge to do something fucked up to him when I see him walking."* Life has been cruel to Christine since the abuse. When I asked her how many different child welfare places she had been in, she shrugged and matter-of-factly said: *"I have been in group homes and foster care all of my life, about thirty different places. I have been in jails for seven years."* Despite being only twenty-three years old, she figured that she had been institutionalized for over twelve years. She cracked a smile and said: *"So that's what you get for telling the truth—locked up, forgotten, and the key's thrown away."*

Violentization in the teen years builds upon and further entrenches the violence experienced in childhood. It solidifies. Suffering severe abuse is directly related to the onset of mental health problems and extreme violence. Common mental health problems found in abuse survivors include post-traumatic stress disorder, borderline personality disorder, depression, and bipolar disorder. The youth participating in two projects evaluated by Sharon Dunn and myself are illustrative of this connection between mental health and engagement in severe violence. Of the 229 participants in the gang evaluation studies, 214 (93 per cent) were clinically depressed and 113 (49 per cent) had considered suicide in the previous month. Seventy-six (33 per cent) had attempted suicide in the previous six months, and 191 (83 per cent) had made at least one suicide attempt at some point in their lives.

The case of Sylvie, aged twenty-five at the time of the interview, shows how early childhood sexual abuse can lead to serious mental health problems and perpetration of extreme violence in the teen years. She told me: *"I think this [sexual abuse] is when I started to become bitter, angry, and didn't care about nothing, including life itself. I hated myself. I started running away, drinking, using drugs, skipping school, and doing crime. I even made it on the news when I wasn't old enough to get charged. I was nine years old, that's when my mom moved to the city. Life just got worst for me. I started stealing cars, doing break and enters."* Although the abuse ended when she was nine, she never got any help. In fact, her parents never believed her when she told them that a male family member had been molesting her for years.

Kim is an example of how extreme violence experienced in

the family leads to severe mental health problems. Her stepfather had murdered her mother, then turned the gun on himself. Kim, then eighteen, almost succeeded in killing herself after that. She spiralled into a world of addictions, street life, the sex trade, and gang involvement. She told me, *"I have been depressed since my mom passed three years ago. She got murdered by her husband. He then shot himself. In 2005 after mom died I cut my wrists. In that year I tried to kill myself fifty times."* Kim was wearing a T-shirt at the time of the interview. It was evident that she had cut herself with razors and knives many times. Although the wounds had healed, the scars remained. On each wrist she had a particularly deep wound that had been stitched up, roughly twenty stitches in each. When I asked about this, she matter-of-factly told me that she almost succeeded in killing herself those times. She also had numerous burn marks; some were random small circles, but one set formed a triangle. When asked about these, she indicated that the round marks were self-inflicted from cigarettes, and the triangular burn was gang-related. Apparently a higher-up had branded her as part of an initiation ritual in BC. She also had old track marks from intravenous drug use on both arms.

Mental health problems tend to run in families. It is common for children of parents with a mental illness to have an inherited genetic predisposition to the given illness, which may or may not be problematic. Other factors can also play key roles. Biology is important. Some young people have an imbalance in naturally occurring brain chemicals called "neurotransmitters." This imbalance can lead to emotional and behavioural symptoms, if other factors described here are present. Stressful life events can also be influential. Going through a number of stressful life events or suffering trauma can make some young people more vulnerable to these illnesses. Examples include suffering prolonged and severe maltreatment, witnessing the death of a family member, and witnessing serious violence. And personality traits are also a factor. Young people who have a perfectionist attitude, lack assertiveness, are self-critical, insecure, prone to negative self-talk, or have low self-esteem are also at greater risk.[2]

After enough major childhood losses and a series of disrupted attachments, some young people don't want to feel anything because it hurts too much. Many gang members who engage in violence are in "terminal thinking"—they focus on survival only. Their wounds are so profound that their souls are barely alive. Violence and emotional detachment form an armour to hide behind. Their sense of security, safety, and trust never developed because childhood attachments were repeatedly breached. Their inarticulate sorrow from emotional wounds goes unrecognized and is often devalued, yet it is as real as physical scars. Ken Hardy and Tracey Laszloffy theorize that the net impact of these lacerations to the soul is a state of psychological homelessness. Unresolved and buried grief results in monstrous acts of rage that camouflage deep-rooted sorrow. Kitty's account is illustrative. She spoke about the loss she experienced when taken out of her grandmother's care at a young age and placed in the child welfare system: *"I still don't know why she [her grandmother] made me to go foster care. I came home at lunch one day and she was crying on the couch. I asked her what was the matter and she told me she couldn't take care of me anymore. The foster mom was mean."*

When young people experience cumulative losses, severe trauma, and violence, the result can be extreme violence. Invisible wounds are slow to heal and the healing process is complicated. Unspeakable sorrow and rage are associated with deep injuries to the spirit.[3]

Traumatized young people often repeat negative patterns from their childhoods in self-defeating ways. Many young gang members, recreating the conditions that were so destructive in their childhoods, fall into what have been referred to as "lifetraps."[4] The traumatic early experiences typically involve suffering prolonged and severe physical, sexual, and emotional abuse and neglect. Rage, violence, and detachment are common outcomes.

The effects of childhood abuse are long-lasting and profound. Anger, rage, and violence are directly related to maltreatment. The brains of abused kids develop differently from those of children who have not been maltreated. To understand how traumatized patterns of thinking develop in teens, rewind the clock and examine the thought processes of young people as they experience cycles of abuse. The work of Canadian clinical psychologist Jan Heney on understanding the dynamic after-effects of long-term abuse is very helpful here. Consider the case of Loretta, who was sexually and physically abused repeatedly throughout her childhood and teen years. On a daily basis she was told she was no good and would be placed in care if she did not behave better. She was three years old the first time her older bothers abused her, although her earliest memories of abuse are from about age six. She knew that something was wrong and felt betrayed, but she loved her brothers and did not want to tell any-one. She blamed herself for the abuse and worked hard to please her older brothers. She told herself, "It's my fault and it will stop if I am good." She tried harder and harder. Of course, the abuse never stopped.

As the cycle got entrenched, she began looking for danger everywhere. The abuse usually happened when her parents were not home, so every time they went out she looked for danger, not knowing if she would be hurt or who would harm her. This was the start of emotional dysregulation, which is characterized by exaggerated emotional responses. These distorted thinking patterns are the root of anger, rage, and violence. They cause a young person to feel as if they can be harmed anywhere and at any time—they have to be alert for potential sources of harm everywhere. They are hyper-vigilant, both over-reacting and under-reacting to situations most people would consider "normal." Their emotions are chaotic and unstable. This results in harm being done to others and to themselves.

Loretta blamed herself and continued to make changes in her own behaviour, still thinking that if she behaved better the abuse would stop. She clung to the hope that the abuse was under her control. She started to experience victimization in other parts of her life: she got bullied at school, boys were grabbing at her and making derogatory comments about her body. Male cousins started sexually abusing her as well. As a response to all the abuse, Loretta developed a sexualized feminine identity. Why? Because she understood her only value to be sexual. She equated love with sex. She had learned that, in order to get her needs met, she had to use her sexuality. She had also learned that she could control men through her body.

As she progressed throughout adolescence, Loretta continued to turn her pain inwards, engaging in cutting and burning behavior to release her pain. She felt good when she carved her arms and chest. She felt in control when she attacked her body parts she disliked—her growing breasts and what she perceived to be chubby thighs. She started to make herself throw up after eating. She began to binge drink regularly and to smoke weed daily. This helped her forget. She came to see the very men who hurt her as ones who could protect her. In her mind, pimps and male gang members were on her side. She never perceived that she was being put out on the street to work, no matter how much money she had to turn over to them after working the streets. In her mind, she was in control. In the absence of quality intervention, such as counselling, the cycle continues and problems—emotional and internalized—become entrenched. She came to use manipulation to navigate around men who were potential sources of harm. It is a survival skill.

When child welfare was made aware of the sexual abuse, she

was taken into care. Her mother and grandmother seemed to be unconcerned, being caught up in their own addictions and refusing to believe that family members could have abused Loretta for so long without anyone knowing. They called her a liar. Loretta had at least fifteen different placements in group homes, foster homes, and young offender centres. The rules in the placements were restrictive, keeping her from seeing her younger brother. She would run from the homes when she could, committing petty crimes such as shoplifting food and makeup. She would be homeless often, resorting to trading sex for meals and places to stay. The police would catch up with her after a couple of weeks, and bring her back to the foster home or group home. She would stay for a couple of days, but then her pimp would find out where she was staying and meet her on her way to or from school with drugs and expensive gifts. He got her hooked on crack, and then the gang took over. Leaders demanded payment for the drugs she was consuming. She had two options: work the streets, or traffic drugs along their established drug lines. Loretta chose to traffic.

By the time she reached sixteen she was so deeply traumatized by the abuse and the bouncing around from pillar to post in care that she was telling herself, "I'm worthless. I must be one tough bitch." She never made her probation appointments on time. When she did make a meeting, she just nodded to her probation officer's questions, stared off into blank space, and told herself she did not care about anything. She did not trust any adults, especially those in positions of authority. She believed that her child welfare worker was useless because she refused to put her up in an independent living situation. Her worker reprimanded her when she ran back to her mom's place. Loretta's soul had been so deeply traumatized that she had buried herself under layers of protection. She had given up.

The cycle of sexual abuse for boys begins in a similar fashion. Consider the case of Chase. He was sexually abused by his father

and uncles, beginning at age seven. Like Loretta, the first time it
happened he experienced it as an immense betrayal of trust and
loss of safety. In school, he had learned the difference between
good and bad touching. He knew that what his father had done
to him was wrong, yet he also loved his father. He was incredibly confused. As the cycle of abuse continued and he aged, he
began to act his pain outwards, engaging in property destruction,
fire setting, and bullying. When he hit puberty, he experienced a
crisis in his masculine identity. When his uncles sexually abused
him, he became sexually aroused and sometimes ejaculated. He
put the blame on himself, thinking that he must enjoy the abuse
because he got erections and climaxed. He had no one in his life
who could help him understand that he did not cause the abuse
and had no control over becoming sexually aroused. He blamed
himself and thought he must be gay—what else could explain
what was happening to him?

As he progressed into his teen years, the abuse stopped. He
had fought off his father and uncles, punching them and forcing
them off of him. He began to run from home, for weeks at a time.
There, he found comfort in a gang where many of his cousins
and uncles (not the ones who abused him) were members. He
avoided being beaten in because his two uncles put in a good
word for him, which he supplemented by successfully completing several missions for the gang, including dealing a kilo of coke
and bringing all the money back to his higher-ups, and stabbing
a rival gang member after rushing his house when he was having
a party.

Yet, he was still masking his pain through the violence, addictions, and suicide attempts. He often considered suicide, and
tried to hang himself three times. He refused to deal with the
childhood abuse and did not tell anyone. He coped by becoming
involved in violent crime, armed robberies, and gangs. He figured
that if he was a violent thug, no one would ever know about his

secret. He developed bipolar disorder, experiencing intense, even suicidal, depression for months on end, then suddenly becoming manic for a couple of weeks. During manic episodes he rarely slept, was very violent, constantly craved sex, and spoke so fast that others could not understand him. He self-medicated with cocaine and morphine. He figured that this was a better way to deal with life than the powerful medications that his shrink had him on when he was at the young offender centre (he had been prescribed Seroquel, an anti-psychotic, Lamotrigine, a mood stabilizer, and Clonazepam, to help him sleep). After a couple of weeks of mania, he would crash and sleep for days. Bingeing on cocaine did not help—indeed, it mimicked the highs of the mania, followed by the deep crashes into fatigue and exhaustion.

Like Loretta, Chase developed traumatized thinking patterns as a child. The abuse left a traumatic footprint on his brain. He was never helped. He blamed himself and worked hard to please his father. As did Loretta, he told himself, "It's my fault. If I am good it will stop." He convinced himself that if he changed, his dad would change as well. The longer the cycle continued, the harder Chase tried. He developed emotional and behavioural problems in response. He started to externalize his pain to cover up sadness and despair. As he hit early adolescence, he would step in between his father and mother when they were fighting. He felt he had to protect his mother, even though she did nothing to stop his father from abusing him. He both protected his younger siblings from his father's violence and bullied them. He learned that violence resolved conflicts and got you what you wanted. He took extreme risks, walking over the river on the railway tracks, knowing full well that if a train came he would most surely die. The river was two hundred feet down and very shallow. He also was taking Oxycontin regularly. It was cheap on the street, going for five dollars a pill.

By the time he hit sixteen, Chase was a soldier in his gang.

He liked being a gangster. It gave him lots of good things. He
didn't have to work for minimum wage at a restaurant, he had
fast money and women, and doing home invasions and armed
robberies was a rush. He put girls on the street and didn't care
what happened to them, as long as they brought back the money.
Like Loretta, his soul was so deeply traumatized that it was barely
alive. He had created a violent shell to protect himself from the
outside world. He had learned that you can't trust adults, especially those in positions of authority. They all leave just when
you get to know them and all they do is screw you over anyway.
Unfortunately, Chase's experiences with sexual abuse had not
ended: as a young adult he would be incarcerated in a prison
where he would be anally raped.

How can we know if someone is in a situation like those of
Loretta and Chase? There are a handful of common indicators.
They include disassociation (alterations in consciousness—the
mind seems to split from the body), inappropriate and intense
anger (exaggerated reactions to any actual or perceived conflict),
emotional shutdown (emotional numbing), and hyper-arousal
(exaggerated reactions and apprehension of danger, no matter
how safe the situation). The young person responds to day-to-
day situations as if reliving the violent victimization in his or her
past. Humiliation and rejection, two common feelings when a
child is being abused, are expressed as anger and rage. Teens hide
their vulnerability because they don't want to get hurt anymore.
It would be too painful to expose these deep wounds in their
souls. Young persons, stuck at this developmental stage, actually
feel as though they are experiencing the trauma all over again.
As Young and Klosko so eloquently write, youth don't *remember* past traumatic events—they *relive* them.[5] Specific sights,
smells, and sounds can trigger intense psychological and physical
arousal, flashing the young person's mind back to the traumatic
event as if it were being experienced at the moment.

BONDING PROBLEMS

Young people like Chase, Kitty, Loretta, Christine, Sylvie, and Kim are rejected and abandoned by their families. This dynamic continues in the child welfare system, where they are bounced from pillar to post, having up to twenty different placements in foster homes, group homes, and young offender open and secure facilities. Bonding problems originating during infancy get entrenched while the person is growing up in the "system." Perhaps the only thing they learn is not to trust adults, particularly the social workers, probation officers, and youth workers who staff the revolving door.

Healthy attachment, which children need, is the nurturing relationship between a parent or primary caregiver and child that begins at birth and continues throughout infancy and childhood. It is based on a parent's "sensitive care"[6]—the capacity to identify with the child, to understand what the child is communicating and its needs, and to have compassion for the child. Having an empathetic parent who unfailingly provides unconditional love and support from birth throughout childhood is critical for healthy development.

Children require stability and security to make healthy and successful transitions from childhood to adolescence and then on to adulthood. "Secure attachment" means that children use their parents or primary caregivers as their foundation as they grow up and transition through infancy and childhood. Children develop understanding and the confidence to know that they will be loved and looked after, and that their parents or primary caregiver will unconditionally ensure that they are cared for as they uncover their world. Such children believe that they are safe and sound, self-assured, and capable of exploring their environment as they develop.

Babies who are insecurely attached do not experience unconditional care and love from their primary caregiver or parents, they experience insensitive care. Their parents are uninvolved, unsympathetic, and inattentive to their needs. These children are repeatedly left alone, especially when they are upset. Alone, their cries for human contact are ignored or disregarded. They grow up understanding that their environment is harsh and cold. They learn that adults are not dependable and are anxious and frightened themselves. As they mature, they perceive that they have no hope and cannot change their circumstances. They are likely to be pessimistic, have a sense of helplessness, and an external locus of control.

There are three types of insecure attachment: resistant, avoidant, and disorganized. In the first case, resistant attachment, the pattern of behaviour between infants and parents or caregivers is ambivalent. Infants get frightened and upset when separated from their parent, but will become irritated despite wanting to be consoled. In the second case, avoidant attachment, babies avoid their caregivers when distressed. These infants do not demonstrate a preference for their own caregivers, and usually are more affectionate with strangers. This affection is misplaced. Finally, disorganized attachment is evident when there is disoriented or incongruous attachment behavior in babies. They give blank, bewildered looks when held by their parents or cry without reason when in their caregivers' arms.[7]

Adolescents who suffer from insecure attachment are more likely to have mental health problems, to abuse drugs and alcohol, to be antisocial and violent, or to experience sexual exploitation. Familial attachment problems are exacerbated by institutional abuse—the lack of permanency planning for children in the care of the child welfare system. Of the 229 participants in the two evaluation studies conducted by Sharon Dunn and myself, 191 (83 per cent) had grown up in the care of the child welfare system.

It is important to understand that although insecure attachment in early childhood can set the stage for further risk factors, consequences can be overcome by later positive attachments. Unfortunately, few young people in my studies bonded to healthy adults in adolescence.

Most maltreated kids are not violent, and some violent youth have not experienced maltreatment as children. The key moderating variable is the abused children's resilience: the individual, familial, and community protective factors that can offset the impact of child maltreatment. Lorraine is a good example of how healing from prolonged sexual abuse is possible with family and therapeutic supports. She was also resilient from birth: she was intelligent, securely attached to her mother, and self-reliant. Lorraine said, *"I overdosed two times on anti-depressants when I was fifteen. I was hospitalized both times. When my depression got bad I slashed my arms and legs."* But, although she attempted suicide twice and battled lifelong depression, she had been able to get the support of a good psychiatrist following the sexual abuse by her biological father. She still maintained contact with that psychiatrist, going for booster sessions when necessary. Her mother and stepfather were instrumental in getting her help. Although her parents were by no means perfect, they stood by her when needed. She also made the choice to become involved with a gang member, the father of her baby. She is one of the few female partners who have maintained such a relationship without getting sucked into the gang lifestyle. She attributes this to having been crystal clear with him when they started dating: she expected him to drop his gang involvement, "get his ass into school or a job," and get help for his drinking. She was firm, and he accomplished all of these things.

VIOLENCE AND MURDER, AND ABORIGINAL GIRLS AND WOMEN

The victimization of Aboriginal females deserves special attention. Aboriginal girls and women in Canada suffer much higher rates of physical violence, sexual violence, and homicide than any other group in the country.[8] Arguably, the rate of extreme violence experienced by these women is among the highest in the world. In the vast majority of all incidents, men are the perpetrators. An Ontario study found that eight out of ten Aboriginal women in Ontario had personally experienced family violence.[9] First Nations women aged twenty-five to forty-four are five times more likely than other Canadian women of the same age to die of violence[10] and are roughly three times more likely to be victims of spousal violence. In a Statistics Canada study, 54 per cent of Aboriginal women reported experiencing severe and potentially life threatening violence, compared to 37 per cent of non-Aboriginal women.[11] Rates of female abuse are even higher in the lives of incarcerated Aboriginal women: 90 per cent of all federally sentenced women report having been abused physically, or sexually, or both.[12] The Native Women's Association of Canada has documented 582 cases of missing or murdered Aboriginal women and girls.[13]

It is likely that rates of violence and murder for Aboriginal women who are involved in gangs are even higher than that of those who are not. In particular, anecdotal evidence suggests that Aboriginal women seem to be much more likely to be commercially sexually exploited than any other group of women in Canada. Chapter Seven will examine this issue. I believe that racism is at play here. If it were white women who were regularly going missing and occasionally found murdered, cases would be solved quickly and solid prevention and intervention strategies would be put in place. For some reason, Aboriginal girls and women seem to be disposable in Canada.

SUPER-GANG FAMILIES

Some families are imploding, consuming themselves from the inside out. They socialize children into gang culture. They raise their sons to become pimps and traffickers and daughters to become sex trade workers. Children are socialized into drug and alcohol use at a very young age. Those children who remain with their families throughout childhood and adolescence suffer greatly. Yet, those who turn to the streets or are swallowed into the foster care and group home system rarely seem to do any better. These families have exceptionally high rates of violence against mothers, including murder. The men, including fathers, are absent—either they are uninvolved in parenting, are drunk or high on drugs, or are doing time in correctional facilities. Arguably, the young men in these families are more likely to graduate from adolescence into prisons than they are to graduate from high school.

I developed the concept of "super-gang families" after having conducted hundreds of interviews with gang members across the country, and after examining the data from the evaluation of gang intervention projects conducted by Sharon Dunn and myself. I was astounded at the sheer volume of cases where young participants recounted how many family members were gang-involved. Although a minority of participants reported having a couple of family members who were gang-involved (typically uncles, or cousins), the vast majority had many, many immediate and extended family members who were involved in gangs. Most of these cases had between ten and fifteen relatives in gangs. I thus developed the idea of being "born into the gang." This pathway is very different from the other routes into gangs. For example, the vast majority of children who are born into gangs do not get beaten in, nor do they have to "show their papers" (demonstrate evidence of having committed serious crimes). Yet, most still have to undertake missions as directed by their higher-ups.

I make the distinction between children who are born into the same gang as that of their family members and those children who are born into situations where family members belong to rival gangs. Life is very complicated for the latter group of children, particularly when it comes to using violence against rival gangs where cousins and uncles are involved. I discuss this concept further in the next section of this chapter.

The good news in Canada is that there are simply not that many gang members in the country. Gang activity is problematic in pockets, but it is by no means everywhere, or in every region. Because there are only a couple of dozen super-gang families in Canada, we can solve the problem one family at a time. These are the families that seem to produce a high number of gang members, many of whom are leaders or occupy upper ranks of gangs.[14]

Many of the organized crime groups in Canada are likewise blood related. Brothers seem to be the most common type of familial relationship in gangs. There are many examples of what I call "brothers in arms": when brothers are involved in gangs, most often they have founded their gang and occupy high ranking positions. Some have been killed, others are in prison, and some are still active on the streets.[15]

In one super-gang family, Justin, aged five, was sitting on his father's lap. His dad was a leader of a local street gang. A rival gang member burst through the front door of their house and shot Justin's father in the head. Justin himself went on to become an active member in the same street gang as his father. All of his brothers were likewise members. Following the murder of his father, Justin was apprehended into the child welfare system, where he spent most of his childhood bouncing around from one foster home to the next. At age twelve, he was sentenced to secure custody for numerous assaults on other foster kids. At the time of the interview, he had been out of jail for roughly one year and was expecting his second child. He was working full-time as a shift supervisor at a fast food restaurant. He was going to church every Sunday and attributed his recent success to his religion.

About two months after the interview, he fell back into gang life and was incarcerated yet again. His girlfriend had just given birth to a baby boy.

Billy, aged twenty years, told me that friends got him into his gang. Family members were also part of the same gang, although Billy denied that he entered the gang with their help. His case was unusual in that he got beaten in, despite having family members who were already involved. After he joined, his two brothers followed. *"My dad left, he went away somewhere. My life, I kinda knew about gangs because some of my family are gang members. I was aware of it but didn't think it would affect me. I didn't know much about them. My role, how I got started in it, was through my friends, friends of friends. I started hanging out with my school friends. Then I got my first minute. That was my initiation…I seen my little bros going into gangs. I kinda felt bad, it made me feel, like I led them to that life, to go into gangs."*

Billy's exit process from his gang is illustrative of that of many other participants who were involved in gangs with relatives: he decided that enough was enough, and his uncle got approval from the higher-ups to not give him minutes. *"I was able to walk away. I had some help. My uncle, he talked to the higher-ups. He was very connected. And he asked them to just let me go."*

Billy was forthright about how difficult his life was. Although there were benefits being a "family man," he longed for the money, power, and respect that came from gang life. Yet, he knew deep down that he had made the right decision.

> *Right now it's a struggle, my life, because I have a daughter and everything. I'm not used to getting up every morning and usually when I was in the gang life I would get up at twelve, sell drugs, and come back home. I am a family man. I have to. What I miss about the life is power and respect, especially*

when we did not have the money. My family and friends, people at [a gang program], they are a stepping stone. I feel I am more caring and kind, not so much ruthless. I'm not mad at the world. I'm just trying to help people now. I would say to the young guys it's not worth it. All it brings you is pain. You may see all the jazz about it, the cars, women, drugs, and booze, but it's not worth it.

Jordan, aged twenty-one, had an unusual process for entering his gang. His cousin was involved with gang members, and exposed Jordan to them while she was babysitting him. The girl's most recent boyfriend was a soldier who trafficked drugs and put young women out on the street. She apparently never was involved in the sex trade, although she was an intravenous drug user. Jordan also recounted the many problems in his immediate family:

I'm from Ontario and I grew up in [name of city]. Half my bros, we are all split up. One passed away in a fire. My dad is deceased and I got my mom who is still alive. We all got split up, foster homes. One still lives in the city…I grew up without a father, a father figure. My mom was always drunk, drinking and what not. I went to at least ten different elementary schools. In high school I ended dropping out, going back, dropping out. The streets, getting high, partying, smoking too much weed. 2002–2003 when I was in elementary, I started getting high, drinking. I was just in elementary. Half my life—I am twenty-one now. I tried working and going to school at the same time. Too hard for me—I wanted to work, make money. I work now. Pretty much just hung out with anyone and everyone. Started getting into music, the arts. High school was good, all about the music. It all depends, the ones I went to school with were positive, the ones I dropped out with were negative, the drugs, weed, ecstasy. Probably since I was young I started hanging out with gangsters. Babysat by my cousin, she had boyfriends who were gangsters. They would say to me [later], "hey I remember you when you were young."

At the time of the interview, Jordan had been out of his gang for almost two years. He was an alcoholic and had partially completed a gang intervention program. Recently, he had been convicted of beating up his girlfriend. He had a roofing job.

BORN INTO MULTI-GANG FAMILIES

In some cases, participants had multiple family members in different, rival gangs—cousins, uncles, stepbrothers. Most of these participants said that they had ten or more family members who were gang-involved, and a minority reported that they had over twenty family members in various gangs.

Paul's case is reflective of just how dangerous the life is, especially when you are looking over your shoulder for family members who might kill you. Like George, he had been shot numerous times and had been left to die in a pool of his own blood. Twenty-three years old, this former gang leader was born addicted to cocaine and was an intravenous drug abuser at the time of the interview. He had been convicted of manslaughter. He likely had Fetal Alcohol Spectrum Disorder and did have a significant speech impediment. He came from a "super gang family" where members were in rival gangs.

My cousins are yeah umm in fuckin' [two different gangs]. I tell my cousins to leave me alone. I have

*bullets in me—two by my heart, one you know in
my arm and I don't know where the other is. They
said it could, you know, paralyze me. I grew up in
them [gangs]. Everyone I grew up with is in gangs
and in jail. They offer me...positions [in the gang].
I got offered to run the [name of city] for them
[name of gang]. I said no, no. They said why? I said
because I don't wanna. I have lost all my friends,
fuck, all of them—the people I grew up with. I went
out a few times to see my family on the reserve.
Both times I got into shit, trouble. Fist fights, guns.
They're all into different gangs.*

ABANDONING NATURAL FAMILIES FOR GANGS

Some of the young gang members in my studies came from families where there was no prior gang involvement, yet plenty of other serious problems: violence, parental addictions, parental incarceration, homelessness, and an overall chaotic environment. These participants sought refuge in street gangs. They made a conscious decision to abandon their families and sought out gangs as alternate families. The family of origin did not exist as a viable place for most participants, whether they were born into gang families or not. For those who were not born into gang families, they abandoned their biological families for a sense of belonging, status, and acceptance in gangs. They defined these gangs as their "new" families.

Most of the participants spoke of their gangs as refuges from their abusive and chaotic childhoods. For these youth, their gangs had replaced their natural families. With no familial reference point from which to gain acceptance and a sense of belonging, the importance of gangs escalated for these youth. When talking about their gangs, most of these participants used distorted images of happy nuclear families, even though their words about "family" did not fit the violent street behaviour of their fellow gang members. They told me that these gangs provided them with feelings of acceptance, status, and identity. The gangs were described by these youth as the families they never had.

The following brief accounts demonstrate how that worked. Carl said: "*What the fuck do you want? It's my family. I got nothin' else. It's like I'm divorced from those fuckers who said they were my parents. Now I've got no parents and lots of brothers. It's great. No asshole parents to beat you all the time. So, yeah. Gang is family.*" John told me: "*What home? I've got nothin'. The old gang [name] were my home. I'm looking for a new one now. I think the new gang [name] will be it...Yeah. I've got no other family. I mean I do but they're not my family. Too much violence and shit. Too heavy for me. It's a lot better this way. No one to tell you what the fuck to do.*" Finally, Peter said: "*Well, I see my mom occasionally. No one else. They all fucked me too bad. I mean, a guy can only get hurt so much and then he moves on.*"

Carl, John, and Peter grew up in families where violence was the norm. Like many other participants, these three youth seemed to indicate that their gangs were their home, their family. Their use of distorted images of happy families when describing the brutal violence of their gangs is striking. That is, they articulated their own victimization by child abuse, but appeared to be able to neutralize their own engagement in collective gang violence. None of these youth verbalized an awareness of this apparent inconsistency. Instead, they talked about having an identity, a sense of belonging, and a feeling of acceptance in their gangs.

Kelly, twenty years old, was an Aboriginal woman who had been convicted of manslaughter. She said her experiences with the child welfare system were just as bad as her home life. After having been sexually abused and beaten at home, she turned to the streets to live. Instead of jumping ship, she was tossed off the ship by her parents without a lifeline. Her parents were not gang members, nor were any of her close family members. She was apprehended from the streets by the police and taken into the care of the child welfare system. She described how, as a twelve-year-old caught up in an ineffective child welfare system, she quickly became violent and started prostituting when placed amidst older females. She reported that she did not start prostituting until she had been taken into care by child welfare services. When she began running from child welfare homes, she turned to the sex trade to financially support herself.

> My [biological] mom was abusive to all of us, so my grandmother took me from my mother and she used to beat me every day and then I just got tired of it...I didn't like it 'cause it was far away from home, and then I ended up o.d.'ing [overdosing] when I was there...I was placed in about four group homes and thirty different receiving homes...I hated it, I was always being shipped around...I always wanted a family setting, and I used to beg my social worker that I wanted to be in a foster home, but they would tell me there was nothing available, so I was always stuck in group homes and stuff...I was put in with fifteen- to eighteen-year-olds...I think putting me in with the older [kids] was bad, 'cause when they run away, they all were working the streets, they have these pimps...I got involved and it didn't help matters much...When I was still in the shelter 'cause I had run away [from the child welfare home]...I would hang around there, and this guy [a pimp] said if you are going out, I will pick you up. If you wanted to leave [the sex trade], there was a leaving fee. I didn't know all about that stuff. All I knew was all these girls made lots of money, that's what they said.

Her initial encounter with the young offender system is illustrative of how many girls enter the justice system: for prostitution, for running away from child welfare facilities, and for being violent while in care. Here, she talks about how being victimized by the violence of older girls resulted in her using violence for self-protection, which landed her in a young offender facility.

> *I started being assaulted, and that's how my youth charges started was from there...I was twelve. I never knew how to fight and they [older girls in the child welfare home] would always hit me. They would always fight me, and I would start fighting back...I took it [an object] and kept hitting her [another youth] and hitting her. And the next day they moved me to secure. But I wasn't hitting her just to be violent, I was hitting her because I thought if I got her then maybe the other girls would leave me alone. First I got thirty days, then I got sixty days, and then I got ninety days.*

Charlie, aged twenty-four, was a long-time gang member who jumped ship as well, after experiencing severe abuse and neglect at home. When he ran away, he joined a gang. He considered his gang brothers to be his biological brothers, who were "tight like family." He took pride in the fact that he had an important purpose in prison life: to ensure that "skinners" and "hounds" feared going to prison because of people like him. He kept them in line. He wrote the following:

> *How the hell did I end up here?...[My gang career is] the underlying reason why I'm here. When I try to remember my reasons for joining, I find*

myself thinking of reasons I don't want to drop [gang colours]. Brothers. Brothers that depend on other brothers. Brothers never grow apart. Brothers that stood by me. Brothers I don't want to let down 'cause brothers are tight like family. How would I justify my alibi between my brother and I? Skinners are sexual offenders that come to prison for touching, diddling, and raping girls and women. Someone's got to keep these hounds in check. How would this city be if skinners weren't scared to go to prison? Yeah the pros outweigh the cons, the time reminding me of why I persist in my thuggish ways, but not all the time. Alot of days I find myself deep in a mental tug of war, contemplating my motives, so why must I sacrifice to coincide?

PARENTAL ADDICTIONS

Almost all the young gang members I interviewed had serious addiction problems, and likewise almost all came from families where caregivers were addicted. Stephan, twenty-three, spoke about the impact of his parents' drug dealing and addictions on his family. He felt humiliated by his parents' prioritization of their drugs over him and his siblings. Unfortunately, he turned to a gang, alcohol, and drugs to deal with the pain he experienced at home. At the time of the interview, he was an alcohol abuser and cocaine addict.

> *My mom and dad had me—I was born. They were not fit to keep me or whatever. From there my grandma took me. I went to my grandma and spoke Sodo, Ojibway, until I was five or six. Then I went back to live with my parents. I went to public school then I was home schooled by my grandma...I*

was in and out of foster homes. She would give me back to my parents. They would go to treatment, get out and do their thing, get high, welfare would take me away. Grandma would bail us out. That's where that is. They would slip again. My brothers and sisters we all went together. School was a little difficult. My parents sold drugs so lots of money. I still never experienced being wealthy or secure like that. It was weird and stupid yet we still struggled with food…But we never had food.

The root causes behind these young people's drug and alcohol abuse cut across almost all five pathways. Most began drinking and drugging at a very young age. They were socialized into this culture by parents and older siblings. They used substances to cope with the trauma associated with violentization. Many were exposed to peers with addictions issues, in child welfare and youth justice facilities. Those who had Fetal Alcohol Spectrum Disorder or suffered from other emotional and behavioural disorders self-medicated with illicit drugs and alcohol. Many coped with exclusion and devaluation through drugs and alcohol.

Like Kelly, Ruth also had suffered prolonged abuse. Her mother, an alcoholic, was unable to protect or to care for her, so she was bounced around in the child welfare and youth justice systems. She attributed these experiences to being "crazy." Like Kelly, she had been thrown off the ship without a life raft:

My mom was a drunk. While she was a drunk she left me with people she trusted. I got sexually and physically abused. My brother and sister were always with my mom but I was bad. I acted out and was miserable. I used to beat myself up a lot, blame myself. All my life I was in group homes and foster homes, since I was a baby. Every group home in [two cities]. Since age twelve I have been in juvie and jail. My uncle raped me when I was three or four years old. At age eight my older brother raped me. My family did not believe me. That's what fucked me up. Ever since then I've been crazy. Then when I was thirteen I was molested by random people. I was always running away and foster parents could not handle me. We got moved lots and physically abused by foster parents.

Although Ruth had stopped her hard drug abuse, she continued to binge drink many days every week throughout a gang program in which she was a participant. She related this to the tragic loss of her sister and her relationship with her mother. She told me:

My sister passed away two years ago. I am kind of grieving now. She died of hypothermia—she passed out. We found her four months later. She was out partying and froze to death. My mom does not know how to cope. She blames me for my sister's death. I freak right out in my mom's house. I hit her with candle holders, plates, I am angry. I black out when I drink. She said she was going to stab me up and I told her I was going to stab her in the face.

Michael, twenty-three, was an insightful and passionate writer. While incarcerated for a serious crime of violence, he wrote this piece. It is a reflection on how drugs and alcohol masked the pain of his childhood and resulted in emotional numbing. He wondered if his spirit was alive. In the first excerpt, he talks about his early introduction to marijuana and how fear was always present in his life:

> *Listen, I always said that I would never use drugs. Looking back, everything I said I wouldn't do, I ended up doing. I had nowhere to turn, I felt that no one could help me, as my situation was so much different than others. I thought I was doomed to continue in an insane drive toward self-destruction that already sapped me of any determination to fight. For many years of my life, I felt that the world had dealt me a cruel hand, which left me with many inadequate feelings. Fear ate a hole in me that I was never able to fill with drugs and alcohol. My first introduction to drugs was at the age of eight, a young male, born to be a man. I started with pot. I loved it and got used to it. If I didn't use it I didn't feel cool. Growing up only the negative evolved around me. Drugs, alcohol, abuse, and fear, it goes on and on.*

Michael then goes on to relate how his mother apparently loved him only on the day when her welfare cheque came in. His mother was an addict and very abusive. Violentization was a defining feature of his childhood and he was abandoned into the child welfare system at a young age. By the time he committed the crime for which he was incarcerated, he was psychologically homeless. But, he still had enough insight to understand that his addictions were only masking his suffering:

> *It's not like my household had gifts to give, faith, happiness, responsibility, or love. Only time we had love was the beginning of a payday. And when that*

*was gone, back to guilt, pain, and my mother asking
for forgiveness all over again. I had no tolerance for
none of it, because I knew what to expect when it
was over. Through drugs I tried to avoid reality,
pain, and misery, but when the drugs wore off, I
realized I still had the same problems I started with.*

As a result of childhood trauma, Michael had mental health
problems: depression and post-traumatic stress disorder. He self-
medicated to relieve his symptoms. Suicide was an ever-present
option. He was devalued and excluded from his family and community. He also developed a rigid, hyper-masculine identity.
Given all the losses and suffering in his short life, masculinity was
down to the basics for him: violence, gangs, guns, and women.
This culminated when he committed several violent assaults.
But, there was a glimmer of hope: he was looking forward to
returning to school after his release from prison:

*Thoughts of suicide became an issue and depression
set in at a young age. I was sick and tired of all
the pain and trouble I put myself through. I was
frightened and ran from the demons and fear. No
matter how far I ran I always carried fear with me.
When I lied, cheated, or stole, I've always degraded
myself in my own eyes. Growing up I tried so much,
I cried so much, and still I do things that aren't so
great. I have so much close friends, family. Deep
down, I keep fooling myself about changing. It's
only lies upon lies. After today there's tomorrow but
tomorrow is today. A cycle of dishonesty to myself.
My life feels like a closed door, my childhood is my
burden, this disease I've carried for some time, the
patience I never had, my attitude was different each*

day. My personality changed, I was always hiding behind a mask. When you spoke to me, I was high or just not paying attention. My life, I need it to be changed and I'm trying.

* * *

The young people in my studies "acted bad" during their teen years for very good reasons. They were traumatized. They had suffered neglect, abuse, and physical violence as children, and now they continued to experience the same thing as teenagers. Almost all were excluded from school, either because they had been suspended for long periods of time, were permanently expelled, or had dropped out. Many had literacy challenges. Many experienced racism on a daily basis, which contributed to their psychological despair and hopelessness.

Mental health problems surfaced in many of these young people during adolescence. They experienced illnesses, such as post-traumatic stress disorder, borderline personality disorder, depression, and bipolar disorder. Although there is a genetic aspect to these problems, traumatic suffering also is a key cause.

Many participants in my studies were recruited in foster homes, group homes, and young offender centres. In some cases, the institutionalization of children from gang families actually helps to solidify the gang and supports the recruitment of new members. Street gangs are perceived by many members and prospective recruits as alternative families. These young people "jump ship" from one family into another, only to realize that their new family (i.e., their gang) is just as violent and unforgiving as their blood family. Some are thrown overboard by their parents and left to sink or swim on their own. Finally, some children are born into gang life because their families are already entrenched in the gang lifestyle. Life is particularly complicated for young people who have family members involved in rival gangs.

Bonding problems that originate during infancy and childhood are entrenched while the young person is growing up in the social welfare system. These young people learn not to trust adults, particularly the social workers, probation officers, and youth workers who maintain the revolving door.

✳ CHAPTER 7 ✳

SEXUAL EXPLOITATION, GENDER, AND GANGS

Susan was checking me out. I could tell that she was trying to decide whether I was like all the other men in her life who had disrespected, abused, and exploited her. I can hardly imagine a case of a young woman more profoundly impacted by sexual abuse and exploitation. She encountered it everywhere: cousins, boyfriends, Johns, sugar daddies, and gang members. It must have been hard for her to make sense of it all. On the one hand, she had learned to use her sexuality to control men and make money off of them. On the other hand, she hated being a prostitute, and made very little money doing it: the gang let her keep only about 20 per cent of what she made. The sexual abuse she had experienced at home had morphed into sexual exploitation by her gang. She had no choice as a child, nor did she have any as a young woman.

At sixteen, Susan looked and sounded like a hardened street woman many years older. She weighed no more than ninety pounds and had dark circles under her eyes. When she talked, she looked at the floor. She rarely made eye contact with me, even on this, our third interview. She had begun injecting cocaine and morphine, as well as working in the sex trade, shortly after our first conversation in 2007. She had been only twelve then. She had been in a series of abusive relationships with male gang members, two of whom had been incarcerated for beating her up. She sustained serious injuries in both attacks. By now, she also had a number of serious health concerns and was not taking her prescribed medication. She said, *"What's the point? I'm gonna die anyway."* I got the sense that she was fed up with gang life, but was resigned to the fact that there was no way out. Her most recent boyfriend, the father of her one-year-old daughter, would soon be released from jail. He was in his mid-twenties and very violent.

Susan was wearing a T-shirt and blue jeans. She had fresh track marks on both arms from injecting drugs. She also had many scars on her inner wrists from cutting herself with knives and razors. She told me that she had worked the streets the night before, and had given some of the money she earned to her cousin, who was babysitting her daughter. She had to give most of her earnings to her higher-up in the gang. Normally, that money would have gone to her boyfriend, but he was in jail.

In this chapter, I examine the lives of young gang members up to the age of thirty. By the time gang members have entered young adulthood, they are emotionally numb and resigned to, probably, getting out of their gang only if they die. Their souls are barely alive.

Chronic and repeated sexual trauma throughout childhood is a key driver into gang life for the young people in my studies. These youth are most often abused by male family members or men who know them. More girls are victims, although many male youth who participate in violent gang activities report having been sexually abused.[1] I also investigate sexual exploitation and the sexual trafficking of young women in this chapter.

Trafficking is different from other exploitation in that it involves a commercial element, in which the trafficker makes a profit from the young person's sexual acts. Pathways into pimping and trafficking are also examined here, as well as the rise of the female pimp. Some women resort to pimping out other young women as a strategy for getting out of prostituting themselves. I also examine what I call "traumatized" gender identities, the process whereby young gang members develop rigid gender roles and behaviours. Finally, I look at the experiences of gay, lesbian, bisexual, and transgendered young people who are involved with heterosexual gangs.

I pay special attention to the unique situation of trafficked Aboriginal young women in this chapter. Although there is little information on domestic trafficking in Canada, what research does exist indicates that Aboriginal young women make up the vast majority of victims.[2] Gang-related sexual exploitation is different. Although Aboriginal young women make up a substantial number of victims, other groups of women (Africans and Asians, for example) are also at elevated risk of being exploited.

SEXUAL EXPLOITATION AND GANGS

In general, sexual exploitation occurs when a child or youth is sexually abused by adults; engages in sexual activity to support a friend, partner, or family member; or trades sexual activities with adults for money, drugs, food, shelter, gifts, transportation, or other items. Sexual exploitation is not employment or a chosen occupation.

Many youth who have suffered childhood sexual abuse engage in survival sex (providing sex for a place to sleep, a meal, or for a ride) after they have run away from home or child welfare facilities. Prostitution includes commercial sexual activities where sex is exchanged with adults for food, housing, money, or drugs.

Like Susan, Nora was actively involved in the sex trade and an

intravenous drug abuser. She had been sexually abused on numerous occasions while growing up and she was introduced to the
gang and to street life as a young teen. Nora wrote regularly in
her journal. She wrote about the need to respect her body and
felt ashamed and worthless. She used drugs to "feel an artificial
happy."

> *Why is my body important to me? My body is
> important to me because it's the only one that I
> have, and my body is the reason why I'm breathing,
> eating, drinking water, and, just basically living. So
> it is very important. How do I respect myself? I take
> pride in how I look. I take pride in my cleanliness.
> I buy myself nice clothing. (I have a lot of work to
> do). I have to start respecting my health and body
> a lot more than I do. How do I disrespect myself? I
> disrespect myself in a lot of ways, that I am ashamed
> to say. I prostitute my body to old disgusting men for
> money, in most cases to buy drugs, not intentionally
> to self destruct, but to feed my addictions. I drown
> myself in drugs day after day. I stick needles in my
> arms to feed them with drugs just to feel an artificial
> happy, that just never comes. I have a lot of work to
> do on myself. Hmmm. Where to begin?*

There is a dearth of research in Canada on the relationship
between gangs and sexual exploitation of girls and women. In
particular, very little is known about the men who are doing the
exploiting.[3] As we learned in Chapter Four, there are at least
three categories of young women who are involved in gangs:
female members of all-women street gangs, women who are
affiliated with male-dominated gangs, and street women in the
sex trade. Many gang-involved females, no matter what their

category, are sexually exploited, and the degree of exploitation depends on the nature of their relationship to the gang. Gang crimes related to exploitation include gang rape and other forms of sexual assault, witness intimidation, extortion, and forcible confinement. Most females who are gang-involved have personal relationships with male gang members: they are sisters, nieces, daughters, granddaughters, or girlfriends. Those who don't have these prior relationships get recruited through violent intimidation. Most girls are gang raped as part of their initiation.

Anecdotal evidence on gang-related sexual exploitation from many northern communities in western Canada suggests that there is significant under-reporting on this issue. For example, it is common for family members in such communities to identify female relatives who have gone missing. Such reports are unofficial for a variety of reasons, including shame, humiliation, lack of education, fear of outside involvement, fear and mistrust of the police, and family ties to gangs. Larger, systemic issues are at play here as well, such as colonization, racism, and the intergenerational impact of residential schools. In western Canada, it is primarily Aboriginal young women who are sexually exploited by gangs; in central and eastern Canada, it is mainly African-Canadian young women.

Loretta related how she had survived a childhood characterized by severe physical, sexual, and emotional abuse, neglect, gang involvement, and addictions. She had become psychologically homeless. She felt ugly and unloved. The suffering was intolerable: she wanted to die. Loretta was suicidal at the time she completed this narrative.

> *I learned physical, verbal, sexual, and mental abuse.*
> *I grew up with my parents being very abusive and*
> *dealing with my mom on drugs. I see myself in my*
> *mom, especially her anger, the way she smokes weed.*

I have her personality, her looks. I am trying my best to lose my mom's habits. My mom hit and beat me, she always yelled at me and called me down. I was sexually abused by my family. My mom always put negative thoughts in my head, always made me think I was ugly and not wanted. My mom always played with my emotions, always making me cry and getting me mad. My mom was very abusive, she had a problem with her drugs, always drinking and having gang members at the house wearing white and black bandanas. A few times, actually more than that, my mom would disappear for days and my brother would have to take care of us. There were times when we had no food and I don't know how my brother did it but he always had something to eat for me and my other brother. I take my mom's habit of being generous and her habit of smoking weed. I took her habit of getting mad and doing the silent treatment. I took my mom's habit of being a cuddly. She always cuddled with me, always after she got mad at me and when she was happy...I was so messed up I'm not sure on how I behaved. I always got drunk, always got high, I acted out by fighting. [I thought] I'm not beautiful, I'm ugly, I'm not wanted, nobody loves me. WHY? I wanna Die!

Almost all young women in my studies reported that family members had got them involved in the sex trade around the age of ten or twelve years. There seemed to be a relationship between mothers turning tricks in their homes and the introduction of prostitution to their daughters. Ruth told me: *"My mom's trick said [to my mom] I'll give you $200 if you let me sleep with your daughter."*

SEXUAL TRAFFICKING

Commercial sexual exploitation (or trafficking) involves the use of violence and threats of violence, coercion, deception, fraud, abduction, abuse of power, and giving payment to achieve consent for the purpose of sexual exploitation. The trafficker recruits, transports, transfers, harbours, or receives girls and women.[4] The trafficker makes money from the sex acts victims perform. Trafficking is not prostitution or sex work—it is a form of slavery. It is common to confuse other forms of sexual exploitation with trafficking. For example, an adult who consents to engage in prostitution is not being trafficked. The case of Ruth is illustrative: *"Last month I got drunk and my friend ditched me. I got gang raped and kidnapped, they forced me to go to [another city] and work the streets. One guy held me down and two others raped me. Then I went running out and they let me go. They pulled my hair out, busted open my lip and punched me all over."* Clearly, she was not voluntarily involved in prostitution. She had been taken against her will by gang members, brutalized, and forced to work the streets. This is trafficking.

Trafficked girls are hard to find—gangs usually confine them within homes or other closed environments. Prior to being trafficked, many have lived lives characterized by severe poverty, lack of opportunities, violence, and poor health. As a result, many migrate from remote communities to cities, where their lack of job skills and city "smarts" makes them vulnerable. Some become homeless and can't even meet such basic needs as food, clothing, and shelter. Many girls become isolated and lose contact with their communities; they experience culture loss. Some go to bars for friendship—where traffickers hang out. They find love in "boyfriends" and street families. Traffickers approach the girls who appear most vulnerable to offer jobs, opportunities, education, and a glamorized city life. Data from my studies and those of others indicate that this process of ensnarement is widely spread in western Canada.[5]

Nora was injecting cocaine and morphine daily, binge drinking daily, and trading sex for money, drugs, and shelter on a daily basis. She overdosed regularly, which usually resulted in hospitalization. She had a gang-involved boyfriend, partied with gang members, and was moderately depressed. She had suffered brutal physical and sexual attacks regularly from traffickers and tricks. She had been commercially sexually exploited four months prior to my interview with her:

> *I got trafficked to [name of city in another province] by six black men, they took me out on the stroll. I made money, gave it to them, they gave me drugs. I ended up getting lost. I did not get much money for them. My friend did not work. They got mad at her and threatened to kill her. I was trying to smooth out shit and they threatened to kill me. They told me "you are blood money. You can't go." It was the [name of gang]. They threw us out of a moving car and gang raped us. My friend's dad called the cops. We stayed with an auntie. My friend said, "I'm safe, I have a knife." I said, "Please, [name], you are not safe. They will kill you."*

Females trapped into sexual slavery in gangs often have long histories of sexual exploitation by adult men, most often family members. Susan and Nora are examples. Many youth who have suffered childhood sexual abuse engage in survival sex (providing sex for a place to sleep, a meal, or a ride) after they have run away from home or child welfare facilities. Many of the young women in my studies had extensive histories of engaging in street crimes, working in the sex trade, and living on the streets. Most started very young. Some felt they were not being exploited and that they had willingly chosen to exchange sex for resources, but it was clear to me that this was not the case. Barb wrote: *"It started with drugs. I started slammin' [doing intravenous drugs] and I liked it and I needed my supply. I had some family who were looking out for me—spotting. They were using me. I was sixteen. My family members never made me. They just chiselled me for dough."*

Sabrina said: *"I was fourteen and a guy asked me and said he would give me drugs."* Susan said: *"I was twelve. I just started in the 'hood on my own. I work the street every day."* Finally, Christine said: *"A friend got me into it. She told me that we were going to a place and what to do. She was seventeen and she had influence. I was thirteen. I got picked up on the stroll and a john picked me up. He put something in my drink to fuck me up. There were a couple of incidents of sexual assault."*

In many communities, family members socialize girls into the sex trade. It is a common way for families to make money and the practice is perceived as legitimate employment. Often, young women would speak of an older family member who got them involved in prostitution. For example, Trina wrote: *"I started in [name of city], I was nine years old. My cousin showed me. She was eleven years old. No one has ever made me. I keep all the money. Once a trick beat me up when I was seventeen years old. My face was swollen and I got cut inside [in her vagina]."*

Christine spoke of how she was born into a gang family and what would happen to her if she refused to work the street: *"I ran around in a car because I had a licence. A lot of my family are higher-ups. A lot of girls I know worked the streets. I used to work the streets, dealing drugs. I was pressured by family. If I said no I would have gotten a licking. I would have gotten disowned. Family is all I have. I felt used, it's pointless."* She also revealed how violent street life was: *"My boyfriend stabbed me in the arm last month. My best friend who killed herself stabbed me in my arm. I got stitches the first time. I taped it with duct tape the second time so the cops would not ask me questions."*

The case of Nicki is illustrative of those young women who experience both sexual exploitation and trafficking. She recounted how she got started in prostitution and how she got commercially sexually exploited (sexually trafficked). "*I was eleven when my friend showed me, she was sixteen, she was supposed to be my best friend but not no more. Last year I got taken to [name of city in another province] by a black gang, they forced me to work the streets and gang raped me. I was kidnapped. They said they would kill me if I did not work for them...My ankle was wrecked and I was covered in bruises and had to get stitches. They'll get what's coming to them. I am HIV positive.*"

Sexual trafficking of Canadian girls and women is most common within the borders of Canada. Trafficking networks are found both in major cities (such as Vancouver, Winnipeg, Regina, Edmonton, Montreal, and Halifax) and in smaller towns. Traffickers tend to move women and girls to locations where the economy is booming. The men who work on the oil rigs and in mining industries in Alberta, for example, in places such as Fort McMurray, have lots of money to pay for sex with young women.

TEACHING BOYS TO PIMP AND TRAFFIC

Females who are harmed tend to be extended family members or intimates of the perpetrators.[6] Little is known about the gang members who traffic women. Several in-depth interviews with gang leaders reveal men whose backgrounds include an intergenerational dynamic of mothers, aunts, and grandmothers who were forced into work in the sex trade or trafficked. Many of these young men bitterly report that their mothers were absent during their childhood—some having gone missing for extended periods of time, or having been murdered. Some expressed hatred for their mothers. These gang leaders seem to have learned very young how to sexually exploit and traffic the girls in their own families.[7] Data from gang evaluation projects conducted by Sharon Dunn and myself support current estimates on the widespread nature of these forms of violence.[8]

George's case is illustrative. He is a twenty-four-year-old gang member with a long history of extreme violence against female intimates and gang girls. He is the father of two girls and an IV crack addict.

> *My mother worked the streets all her life and she was murdered...I used to treat girls really badly—I tortured them. I would be all nice to them—I have a good smile—I know I was born with that gift. I would be all sweet then get them all hooked on pills, morphine, crack. I would fill their needles for them. Then I would lock them in a room for three or four days and not let them out. They would scream and moan and yell—they were hooked on my drugs— and I tortured them by locking them in that room for days with no drugs. Then they would work for me on the streets. I guess I treat them like that because of my mother.*

I asked Noel, twenty-four years old and out of his gang for two years, how he got involved in pimping and challenged him to accept responsibility for his actions. He said: *"I didn't really make them—they got their cut and I got mine. It's their choice."* I then said, *"I disagree. I don't think girls choose to be hooked on crack and sell their bodies."* He replied: *"Well, yeah, if I was to be really straight up, I sure wouldn't do it. I mean when I was a kid that's what I remember. Me and my brothers used to stand watch, make sure that the marks respected her, didn't fuck her over. And we'd slang [deal drugs]...it's just normal. It happened all the time. My mom chose to do it. She shouldn't have done that stuff around us."*

THE RISE OF THE FEMALE PIMP AND RECRUITER

Kitty, twenty-one, was the only female in an all-male street gang from the age of fifteen until she was nineteen. She had to show the male gang members that she was tough, and deserving of their respect. She also needed a strategy to avoid being forced to work in the sex trade to bring money into the gang. She resorted to pimping out a stable of six to ten fifteen- to seventeen-year-old girls over a three year period. She was widely feared on the streets for her propensity to engage in severe violence. She continued this lucrative operation until she was charged and incarcerated for four years. She explained putting out girls on the street with a reference to her father. *"My dad was a dealer and a pimp—that's why there were always lots of girls and drugs around. That's how they took me [child protection]."* It is interesting that Kitty chose to pimp out girls after being taken into the care of the child welfare system because her father was doing the same thing. Kitty hated being in care. Loretta, who also had a history of forcing girls to work the streets, told me: *"I used to put girls out on the street when I was fifteen. One girl I filled her with needles and she overdosed. I saw a kid I sold to overdose. One girl I sold to turned into skin and bones."* She reportedly had stopped doing this, and dealing hard drugs to young people, because she realized the harm it was doing. She was twenty-one years old when she told me she had stopped.

Carolyn's experience pimping was a bit different from Loretta's. She had no option than to force girls into prostitution. She was the girlfriend of a violent gang leader who routinely beat her, especially if she did not follow his direction. Carolyn told me: *"Drugs, girls, home invasions, partying. I did it because I was told to do it—to save my own ass. I ran my own crew of girls, the [name of gang]. It was prostitution, I put them out."*

Finally, Kim discussed with me how drug dealing, prostitution, addictions, and the struggle to meet basic needs were commonplace in her young life. She admitted to putting out family members on the street, but denied that she forced them into prostitution. She said that she needed the money to pay for her drugs (she was shooting morphine and crack) and that she tried to make the work as safe as possible for her family, keeping track of who went with which tricks. *"I was selling drugs, finding new clients, driving to get drugs. I put people out on the street, my cousin, my auntie, my friend. I went on the street with them and asked if they wanted me or her. They usually choose her—I'm not as pretty. I would write down licence plates and call the cops if they did not come back. I was fifteen when I started. I needed money to get high."*

Female pimps and gang recruiters tend to be former sex trade workers who rely on their own experiences to entice runaways, prostitutes, and vulnerable girls to become part of their gang's stable. Often, this is the logical outcome of coming from a family where there is intergenerational pimping and sexual exploitation. I have many reports in my studies of impoverished mothers pimping out their daughters.

There is considerable evidence that female recruiters operate under the control of male gang members—that they are owned by male pimps. Male-dominated gangs often use gang-involved young women to recruit other girls. Female recruiters operate by seeming to be instantaneous best friends to vulnerable girls, gaining their trust through gifts, drugs, money, and jewellery. Recruitment into the sex trade does not seem to be bad, when it is facilitated by one's best friend. Once the recruiters have introduced their underlings to the sex trade, the male pimp usually takes over.

ALCOHOL AND DRUG ABUSE

Almost all the participants I interviewed had serious addiction problems. Almost all came from families where caregivers were addicted.

The case of Nora is representative. She had three sugar daddies and was living with her boyfriend, a gang member. She wrote about her body, and her heart.

> *I love my body and my heart. But not to the best of my ability. I've put it through destruction, pain, and deadly situations with no care at all. It is my job to take care of my body and my heart, and in my case I haven't. If I continue to put my body and heart in self-destruct any longer, I WILL DIE. I don't want to die. I have a lot of work to do on myself and in order to learn to value my body and its worth, and I need to learn what my body and heart is actually worth. I'm stuck in a rut. I am a beautiful person. And that I need to tell myself every day, along with no longer abusing myself with fucking DRUGS!*

She addressed her body:

> *Dear body of mine, I am extremely sorry for the disrespect and filth of disgusting old men that I've brought upon you. I do love you. I need to learn to love you more, and I need to learn your true value. I have a lot of work to do, and that has to come from within. I'll do my best to respect my one and only beautiful body.*

It is obvious that she was ashamed of being with and feels devalued by the "disgusting old men," but it is not clear whether those were her sugar daddies or the men who bought her services on the street.

Then, she wrote directly to her heart:

> *I apologize for all the damage that I've caused you.*

For taking you for granted, and causing you pain, when on numerous occasions even now, you've told me enough's enough! I would like to take the time to get to know you, and begin to understand your worth, and why you are so important to me. You are my only heart, and I would like to start off fresh, and begin to value the great heart that I have. I'm sorry for the pain that I have endured you, and myself.

She ended by writing about the impact of her daily intravenous drug use. When she wrote that her death would come soon if she were to continue the drug abuse and sex trade work, she was being quite realistic. She had overdosed many times during the previous two years and had survived being trafficked by another gang. When asked why she was an addict, she replied that she had begun abusing drugs when she was ten. She had been sexually abused at a very young age, and there was an intergenerational pattern of addictions in her family. She told me that she also got high to deal better with trading sex on the street.

Consider also the cases of Nicki, Kim, and Carolyn. All were abusing cocaine and morphine intravenously at the start of a program and were on methadone when they completed it. By the end of the program they were, however, also smoking marijuana frequently—which was at least less harmful than cocaine and morphine. Nicki, who was HIV positive, stated: *"I got off needles in January because I was sick of being sick, sick of working the street to pay for it. I am not taking care of my illness [HIV]—it will kill me. I went from using needles every second day in January for mo [morphine] and coke to only doing weed now. I have been on methadone since then."* Kim told me that she had quit hard drugs and was going into treatment. Alcohol abuse was clearly still problematic for her. *"I registered to go to [name of treatment centre] in February. Drug treatment. I quit meth [methamphetamine], heroin, E [ecstacy], peyote, crack. Going on methadone got me off the other drugs. I used to drink for days. Crack open a beer when I wake up."* Likewise, Carolyn, who also was HIV positive, was on the methadone program to ease withdrawal from morphine. Earlier, she told me that severe sexual abuse and the loss of a close friend who had once saved her were root causes of her addictions. *"One and a half years ago I tied a shower curtain around a pole in the basement. My friend who just died found me. I went to the hospital and was put in the psych. ward. I also overdosed eleven times in my life. It was morphine that I slammed most of the time."*

TRAUMATIZED GENDER IDENTITIES

Violentization, brain and mental health disorders, and prolonged institutionalization had resulted in traumatized gender identities for almost all of the participants in my research. Because of psychological numbing, the soul was barely alive in many gang members. To cope, many young women developed sexualized femininities and many young men developed hyper-masculinities. Their gender identities were malleable, constructed and reconstructed daily. Dominant and subordinate gender types are the outcome of both passive gender role socialization and active negotiation and resistance.

For many gang-involved young people, violence is a resource one uses to construct masculinity, and sexuality is a resource one uses to construct femininity. Agents of socialization in society[9] contribute to implanting complex cultural messages about the appropriateness of gendered behaviour during childhood and adolescence. In general, masculinity is associated with power, independence, aggression, dominance, and heterosexuality. Femininity is related to dependence, nurturance, passivity, serving others, and maintenance of social relationships.[10]

High-risk young women learn that they can use their bodies

and sexuality to get needs met, especially in the face of controlling and dangerous men. They learn to compete with other young women over male attention and to defer to male authority and privilege. Through the process of sexual objectification, they learn to starve, purge, and injure their bodies. Committing violence is contrary to the gender role expectations for girls.

Many gang-involved young men learn from an early age to hide feelings of fear and pain. They are taught to use violence to mask sadness, insecurity, rejection, and humiliation. They learn that not being powerful means not being masculine. Perceived failure to meet societal standards for being a "real man"[11] results in insecurity and anxiety. Violence compensates, and is usually directed at individuals who are physically weaker or more vulnerable. The pain of grief, guilt, stigmatization, and shame defines gender identity for many. For male gang members, the experience of prolonged sexual abuse by men relates directly to their own construction of violent gang identities. Many young men who were abused around the time they reached puberty told me about having deep-seated fears about their sexual identities. They said that they felt responsible for the abuse because they became sexually aroused while it was going on. Many believed that they must be gay because they "had sex" with men. Their violence compensated for these threats to their heterosexuality.[12] Even for those male gang members who have not suffered violent trauma, the elimination of traditional means of achieving masculinity (such as supporting families through hunting, trapping, or a job) is compensated for by a hyper-masculine exertion of power and control over women and children.[13]

GAYS IN GANGS

There is a sound body of literature on the high-risk issues faced by many gay, lesbian, bisexual, and transgender youth. These youth are at elevated risk for developing mental health problems, attempting suicide, living on the street after being kicked out of home by parents who do not accept their sexual orientation or gender identity, engaging in criminal activity, being victimized by violence, and being taken into residential care.[14] There are considerable data on collective gay bashing by heterosexual male adolescents,[15] and there have been a number of high profile murders of gays in the USA, apparently committed by young men who themselves have unresolved issues around sexual orientation.[16]

Yet, the participation of gay, lesbian, bisexual, and transgender youth in gangs has been ignored in the literature, most likely because these youth are primarily viewed as victims of bashing, and as highly unlikely to participate in violent gangs where their own personal safety would always be at risk.[17] For this reason, I wanted to learn more about if and how sexual and gender minorities[18] are involved in gangs, and how such gang members made sense of their violent behaviour within their heterosexual-dominated gangs. I wanted to better understand their world from their viewpoint.[19] Of the 290 participants in my six qualitative gang studies, 25 identified as sexual minorities.[20] Sixteen identified as male, eight as female, and one as transsexual.[21] Of the sixteen young men, thirteen reported that they were gay and three said that they were bisexual. All of the eight young women identified as bisexual. Four had children, although none had custody of her child. The youth who identified as transsexual was preparing for gender reassignment surgery. None came from families that had gang-involved members.

All of the twenty-five young people were severely homophobic,[22] and had participated in extreme acts of violence against victims their gangs believed to be gay (including murder, aggravated assault, assault causing bodily harm, sexual assault, armed robbery, home invasion, and hostage-taking).

The various gender strategies employed by some participants are illustrative of these points. The accounts of Phil, Breanna,

Kristy, Kathy, Amy, and Bob highlight the different strategies employed by the young people in this study.

Phil was a fourteen-year-old first-generation Italian who was on probation for assault. He had recently been released from a young offender facility. He was a member of a street gang organized around pimping and gun running. Other gang members were much older than he, ranging in age from eighteen to twenty-four. They were all male and heterosexual. Phil had grown up in poverty. In the absence of material possessions, masculinity was down to the basics for him—strength and guns. *"We fuckin' roll faggots for a laugh. Sometimes they have money—sometimes a jacket. Goddam queers. They're not men. Bitches. No, they're worse than bitches. They haven't got any balls, you know? What the fuck do they have balls for—to ram each other up the ass? What a laugh when we find one. Fuckin' right. So I'm no faggot. And at least I've got my strength. Nobody can take that away from a guy—even if he's got nothing else. He's still strong and can pound the crap outta anyone. A guy can never lose that. Strength and guns. If you can't beat 'em, shoot 'em."*

When Phil said, "at least I've got my strength. Nobody can take that away from a guy," he may have meant that he had nothing left to lose—he identified as gay later in the interview. Though indicating that his masculinity was in jeopardy, he seemed to be trying to neutralize the issue by presenting himself as powerful and invincible. Guns, fists, and gay bashing appeared to compensate for his dark inner secret. Phil was likely coping with his own self-loathing by beating up anything resembling himself.

Breanna was a nineteen-year-old Lebanese male-to-female transsexual who was attracted to women. Her family came to Canada before her birth. She was on social assistance and taking hormones in preparation for gender reassignment surgery, and was on medication to control depression, aggression, and paranoia at the time of the study. Breanna said that she had witnessed serious violence between her parents as a child, and that her father had inflicted the most injurious. She said that both her parents had often been violent with her and had subjected her to humiliating psychological abuse over her gender identity. She denied ever having been sexually abused.

Breanna described rigid gender roles at home, stating that *"females should stay home, cook, and wear dresses...males should provide for the family, work, and be macho."* She said that her family was extremely homophobic. Breanna reported that all her life she had been ostracized by peers because of her ethnicity and gender identity. She was a loner, yet occasionally participated with a local gang in collective beatings of male prostitutes. Breanna said that she had fooled other members into believing she was a tough, macho male. She told me that she always wore baggy clothes to conceal the development of her breasts.

Breanna had perpetrated severe beatings on strangers, physically and sexually assaulted family members, made numerous bomb threats, stalked individuals, and had been convicted of arson. She had been committed to hospitalization under provincial mental health legislation on many occasions because of the risk she posed to herself and to others. According to Breanna, members in her gang thought she was "psycho," and apparently let her in on only the occasional activity, because they feared her. Breanna was extremely homophobic, often bashing victims she perceived to be gay, with other gang members. Breanna indicated that she felt equal to, even superior to the other gang members because of her power; other members thought she was crazy, knew she was capable of extreme violence, and had no idea that she was transsexual. Her violence likely compensated for the mistreatment she lived with on a daily basis outside of gang life. Thus Breanna found, as Jodi Miller puts it, "protection from gendered vulnerability" in the gang.

Breanna wanted to undergo gender reassignment because

"women could get away with more criminal activity, as society does not think they are dangerous." She expressed regret at not having been born female, thinking that she could have gotten away with more violence if this had been the case. She said that if she had female sex parts, she could gay bash more often. She said *"it is okay to hurt someone as much as they hurt you,"* referring to the many times she had been victimized by peers because of gender identity issues. She said she was "under threat," and that it was *"good to intimidate people so they are afraid of me."* She strongly denied any wrongdoing, claiming that *"faggots were all child molesters"* and that it was *"my time to pay back all those gays who picked on me all my life."*

Like Breanna, the other sexual minorities in my research were traumatized as a result of abuse at home, and were searching for a sense of belonging and family. Having experienced rejection and abandonment by their families of origin, they lived on the street or in the care of child welfare. They all turned to street families and gangs for a sense of belonging and support. However, most indicated that if other heterosexual gang members discovered their sexual orientation or gender identity, they would be severely beaten or killed.

The gang violence used by the bisexual females was very different from the harmful actions of the gay and bisexual males. Kristy is a good example of a young woman who is "doing gender" differently. She was a twenty-three-year-old Caucasian in a white supremacist gang. Her one-year-old baby had been apprehended by child protection officials because of her alcohol abuse and street-entrenched lifestyle. She was abusing substances and was in unstable housing. She had turned to the streets to get away from severe violence at home from both her biological parents. They also rejected her bisexuality. *"Dad used to beat the fuck out of me. I think it was built into my genes…He said he owned me—he could marry me off. His ability to beat the crap out of me had an effect on me."* Once on the street, however, her idyllic image of a peaceful, loving "street family" was shattered. She needed to be violent to survive. *"I've used it to protect myself— best way I know how. I'm not gonna call the police—they'd laugh in my face."*

Although she acknowledged her responsibility in the violence, she rationalized it. *"But there's rules downtown. It's all about power. As long as I keep my power, I'm happy...It's about control over everyone. They can't ever touch me...you have a reputation to keep...If I feel threatened or my reputation is threatened [I'll fight]. I take care of big things like that."* Kristy reported that she had been in too many serious street fights involving weapons to count. She had been convicted of a number of offenses, including possession of narcotics, aggravated assault, possession of a weapon, and assault causing bodily harm. Somehow, she had avoided serving lengthy periods of time in custody. She maintained that she had spent no more than a total of six months in youth facilities from age fourteen to seventeen years. She had never been incarcerated in an adult facility.

She had lived on the street for most of her teenage years, and lived by a street code. *"You rat on somebody, you're out of town. It's a respect thing. If you charge someone, the police [get involved]... There's a whole bunch of street rules."* When she was seventeen, she was dealing drugs to survive. At one point, two black males flashed a lot of money at her, asking for drugs. She asked them to meet her in a park nearby. Kristy assembled a group of her street friends and *"boot-fucked him [one of the victims]—took everything, his jacket, his money."* She used a gun in the attack. Although a number of her friends were convicted of aggravated assault and assault with a weapon, Kristy avoided charges by leaving town with her boyfriend.

Kristy used excuses to explain why her behaviour was violent, and why she was not in the wrong. She said: *"I'm a faggot. It's me killing them or they're [heterosexual gang members] gonna kill me.*

I've been picked on all my life because people think I'm a dyke." She also distanced herself from heterosexual violence—in effect, she excused her own actions because she was bisexual. *"I watched my Dad kick the shit outta my Mom, and he beat me. He's straight. I'm not."* Her gang clearly offered her protection from and retaliation for the street violence she routinely faced. Her gang provided her the space to resist the traditional gender roles of her parents and to negotiate a situationally specific identity that provided her with self-definition and empowerment.

Did Kristy do gender like the "straight" young women in my studies? It is likely that her gender strategies were different, partly because of her bisexuality. Yet, Kristy's strategies were also different from those of the other bisexual young women in my research. Consider the case of Kathy, who was seventeen when she pleaded guilty to manslaughter. She had originally been charged with second-degree murder, along with a string of other serious, violent offences. She had suffered traumatic sexual and physical violence throughout her young life, and had engaged in self-mutilation and suicidal behaviour since late childhood. She related her bisexuality to the fact that almost all the men in her life had beaten and raped her. She was deeply ashamed of her sexuality. She had been prostituting and drug dealing as a means of survival since age twelve, when she ran away from her tenth child welfare facility. She had her first baby at age thirteen, her second at age fifteen. Family members adopted them both. She said that she had been diagnosed with Fetal Alcohol Spectrum Disorder at a young age.

Although she denied being a gang member, police and prison records suggested otherwise. She maintained that she merely "hung out with a bunch of bikers." Her pathway into gang life was similar to that of the four other bisexual young women in my research. Vulnerable on the streets with no family, addicted and turning tricks to feed her cocaine habit, she was easily lured

into an outlaw motorcycle gang that provided her with protection from johns, other dealers, and the police (because of her
age and state wardship, police could have apprehended her).
She described herself as a "biker chick," essentially a sex slave
to her thirty-year-old co-accused gang member. She was one
of three young females in the gang (all were Caucasian). Kathy
reported that the gang hated "fucking Indians," and that there
were roughly fifteen males in the gang, all in their late twenties
or early thirties. She described what happened in the homicide:

> They [the police] said I was really violent, they said
> I had enough force to snap his neck back. The police
> said I was stomping on his chest, broke all his ribs.
> They made me sound very mean. I don't think I
> could because it would take a lot of force, I was 150
> pounds when I came in, it would take a lot of force,
> especially drunk, you don't have that much force.
> And they said I had to have metal shoes to snap his
> neck back, that's what the doctor said when he was
> testifying, and at the time I had Nikes. They didn't
> find nothing of mine, no footprints, no fingerprints,
> no gloves, no hair, no saliva, nothing...I don't know
> whether to believe them or not, I was scared and
> that. I didn't know, and they [gang members who
> got off] were saying that I was saying to them "don't
> rat, don't rat." And yet I remember them saying "no
> one say nothing." They twisted it and mixed it up.
> They know me for a person not to say nothing. So
> they all got picked up and they pinpointed me.

She denied her involvement and justified her behaviour by
deflecting blame onto her co-accused. Instead of blaming the
victim, she said that her co-accused caused it and provoked her.

She also denied causing any injury to the victim, because she was wearing Nikes. She also said that she could not have inflicted any serious injury because she was "drunk," "just protecting myself," and weighed only 150 pounds. Medical records and police reports indicated otherwise.

When Kathy was questioned about her sexual experiences with other females, she noted that these relations began in early adolescence, long before she was incarcerated in female-only correctional institutions. Her sexual relations with other women were different from those of Kristy or Amy. Kathy's and Amy's intimate relations with other female inmates in prison may have been situationally specific gender strategies, but it is interesting that they both reported having had sexual experiences with other females before incarceration. Both were in male dominated gangs. Whereas Kathy was one of three females, Amy was the only young woman in her gang.

Amy was twenty, in prison for a manslaughter she committed at the age of eighteen. She had been beaten and sexually abused throughout her childhood by both male and female caregivers. She identified as bisexual, and carried much shame and guilt about this. She made it clear that if her family found out about her sexual practices, she would be shunned. She had been part of a street gang heavily involved in pimping, running guns, and drug dealing. She described how she got involved in the streets:

> I was supplying myself and my sister, on the street, 'cause she was on the street to use, but she just, I don't know how she came into my life that way, I didn't want to bring her around that type of life, but I had to 'cause she had nowhere else to go, I had no place for her, I sold drugs here and stuff like that…I was in care of child and family group homes and stuff, and they never gave me a foster family, I was

always stuck in these places, and I started getting anger being in the block treatment and stuff. I think I tried suicide thirty times and slashed a lot. My mom was abusive to all of us, so my grandmom took me from my mother and she used to beat me every day and then I just got tired of it, and my dad phoned the cops on her and [child welfare], and my sister was already in care...I've had four [group home placements] and about thirty different receiving homes...I have seen her [biological mom] be abusive to herself and her boyfriend and stuff... She used to slash in front of us. I remember being scared and watching her, and begging her to stop.

Amy went on to describe her involvement in the drive-by shooting of a drug dealer with her co-accused gang members:

There were four people when we were arrested, we were all offered a deal to testify and to get off the charge of first degree murder. Me and my other co-accused didn't take the deal. Four of them did [the other gang members]...I was driving the vehicle, but like to begin with I wasn't the person [who shot], didn't know where he [leader of the gang] was going at that time. I was a drug dealer and a prostitute. I owed them [the gang] money. I was actually leaving to go home. I was halfway home and they pulled up at the other end and called me and then I asked them if they could drive me down there so I could pay off my dealer.

Amy reported that she was the only female member of her gang, and her experiences were very different from Kathy's and

Kristy's. It is likely that she accomplished her gender by using different strategies than theirs. Being the lone female in an all-black gang was a source of pride for her. She spoke passionately about how her cultural identity developed in the gang, almost as if this masked the sexual dominance she endured on a daily basis. Her account is characterized by denial. Her self-injurious behaviour (cutting with a razor, burning with matches) was also more frequent and severe than that of the other participants. She showed me her cutting journal, which she used to detail emotions and at times to prevent incidents of self-harm. Blood was spattered over many of the pages. An excerpt: *"So now I feel somewhat in better control. I hate myself for doing this. When I was younger, it was all good and happy. Now, I'm sad, and I hurt myself to like myself better. I'm a fucking mess. I hate my life, I hate myself, I hate what I have become. Even though I feel in control after I cut, it doesn't last for long. I'm a train going 500 miles a minute off the tracks."*

Bob, an Afro-Canadian, sixteen, belonged to a black street gang primarily involved in the cocaine trade. He reported being terrified that other gang members would discover he was gay. He talked at length about the terrible experience of gang initiation, when he was forced to have sex publicly with gang "hoochies" (young women associated with the gang who were traded as sexual objects among members, sold cocaine on the streets, and acted as lookouts for other criminal activities). Bob had spent the majority of his teenage years as a ward of the state, bouncing from one group home to another. He was never placed in a culturally sensitive setting, nor did he ever have an opportunity to get counselling support about his sexual orientation. Bob said that his mother was unable to protect him from beatings by her boyfriends. He broke down when telling me about his sexual anxieties: "[Sobbing] *I guess I am trying to prove myself to my friends. I mean, would you like to be called a faggot and a pussy all the time? I gotta show them that I can fuck, and fuck a lot. I'm no queer...What's the point to life if you're a faggot? You would be nothing."*

Bob spoke about the tremendous pressure he was under to demonstrate to his friends that he was not gay or female, along with his fears about his sexuality. Although Bob told me a number of times that he was not gay, he was very emotional, and towards the end of the interview disclosed that he was in fact gay. Within the heterosexual gang context, he said that, for his own safety, he had to prove that he was "no faggot." Bob said that one way to protect himself in the gang was to have a girlfriend, and publicly to degrade her sexually. Bob admitted to using violence against female peers as a means of covering up his own sexual orientation. Although distraught, he repeated that he was terrified about what would happen if fellow gang members found out he was gay.

These young gang members were socialized in a culture that demands heterosexism,[23] and protected their own self-image and personal safety by publicly denying any affiliation with gay culture. Many had tremendous feelings of guilt, shame, and self-hatred from rejection by family and from their experience of bullying and other forms of intolerance. They gained temporary relief by publicly beating anyone who resembled themselves. Although by no means uniformly, many of these young men appeared to play out their marginalization in a hyper-masculine, hyper-sexual fashion. Interestingly, the girls, all bisexual, seemed to adopt many of the traditional heterosexual male behaviours: violence, toughness, independence, and hyper-sexuality. They resisted and negotiated gender roles outside of traditional femininity—the gang was a space to "do gender differently."[24]

Their construction and expression of gang identities were distinct from their relations with others outside of the gang context. Their actions can be seen as a means of resisting gender oppression, both within and outside of gangs. Gender role construction was an ongoing process for these youth, to be negotiated and developed with the limited resources at hand. Some said that they chose a pathway out of traditional gender roles to separate themselves from the violence of their caregivers. Other participants reported that they always had known they were gay. Finally, some disclosed that they became aware of their gender identities in early adolescence.

Gangs provided participants with an identity, feelings of acceptance, and a sense of belonging. Many of them referred to their gangs as the "families they never had." It would therefore appear that the participants' desperate search for belonging and acceptance not only led them to use extreme violence, it also likely amplified the hatred they had for themselves. The participants seem to have had an extreme form of internalized homophobia.

✳ CHAPTER 8 ✳

THE GANG AS WORK

The concept of gang membership as employment has received some attention, yet it needs further exploration. In the absence of meaningful jobs paying an adequate wage, gang crimes come to be seen as viable sources of income. After all, as one young man told me, "It's better than flipping burgers." Most gang members have little education and limited traditional employment skills. In their view, unskilled, minimum-wage work is demeaning and should be avoided at all costs. A tiny percentage of gang members come from relatively affluent families, although their parents are absent, often working long hours outside the home. Many of these gang members are racial minorities, and their work within the gang is seen as a matter of cultural pride and status. But many more gang members experience racism and are blocked from opportunities to get good jobs in the legitimate employment market.

GRINDING POVERTY

The case of Jimmy, Julian, and Andrew, all brothers, is illustrative of how poverty, and its accompanying social exclusion and devaluation can lead to gang involvement. Jimmy, aged nineteen, told me they had hard-working and caring parents. Their life was going well until his father lost his job, forcing them to move into a social housing project that was gang-infested. The family hated the neighbourhood and felt humiliated about not having enough money. When the boys were in early adolescence, their father and uncle were stabbed to death by gang members, right before their eyes. Two of the brothers also sustained life-threatening injuries.

Jimmy gave me his written account of the event. In the first excerpt, Jimmy talked about his father, who was employed as a handyman. He explains how their house was rushed by three men one night while his father was at work.

> We were doing terrific till one night my dad was working late on one of the [row houses] and there was a hard knock on the door at my house. We were all asleep at the time. My mom got up to answer the door and she thought it was my dad when suddenly she seen three males with their hoods up and she went to close the door and the three suspects kicked it open and started beating on my mom. I was sleeping on the couch at the time. I woke up and started trying to fight off one of the guys and he knocked me on the ground. My dog was tied up at the back door and got loose and chased one of the guys out of the house and caught up to him and bit him really badly. And one guy went upstairs and started fighting my brother while he was sleeping and my brother fought him off. And my dad heard the noise from two [row houses] down and come running home. By that time two of the men ran out of the house and there was still one upstairs so my dad ran up there and beat the fuckin' shit outta this

*dude for what he did to my family. As my dad was
beating on this dude one of my brothers jumped in
and they just messed the dude right up, broke his
leg and he was charged for home invasion. He was
in a wheelchair for about a month 'cause of what
we had done to him. He did I think about three
years in jail. So after that the guy my dad worked
for called my dad and they got into an argument, so
dad told him to shove the job up his ass, so he evicted
us from the townhouse. We could not find a house
to move in so we moved to a worse neighbourhood
to another townhouse called "the projects." This
neighbourhood was full of gangs.*

Next, Jimmy described how his father and uncle were stabbed
to death at a house party. Apparently, two parties were going on:
one was a gang party, attended by the guy whom Jimmy's family
had beaten in self-defence a year before; and a second party
attended by Jimmy's uncle and brothers. His dad was called to
the party by a friend, who indicated that Jimmy's brothers were
in trouble. Subsequently, Jimmy's father and uncle were murdered and his two brothers sustained life-threatening injuries:

*One night [date] there was two house parties going
on and the guy my dad and brother had beat up was
a part of this gang and was at a party across the street
from another party where my brothers and uncle were
at. Some dude came over and tried to start shit but
they chased him off. Where this party was was where
my brothers were at. I just live about eleven houses
down. I was sleeping at the time and my dad and mom
were up and all of a sudden my dad got a phone call
from a friend Alex who lived at the house. My brothers*

> *and uncle [name] were drinking and Alex said to my*
> *father get over here! Your boys are in trouble. So my*
> *dad went over there, didn't stand a chance. Him and*
> *my uncle were rushed, beaten, and stabbed to death*
> *and my two brothers were both stabbed. Julian almost*
> *died, stabbed two inches away from his kidney and*
> *Andrew just about lost his hand by catching a knife*
> *instead of getting stabbed in the face.*

Following the loss of his father and uncle, Jimmy's life spiralled downwards. Jimmy joined a gang only after the killing. In response to the violence inflicted on his family, Jimmy constructed an identity as a violent gangster himself. He retreated into a world of hard drug abuse and street crimes. He was psychologically numb and developed a violent exterior shell to keep from getting hurt. His emotional wounds were deeply hidden. Jimmy did not want to expose his vulnerabilities.

> *And after that, my life was a total disaster. I started*
> *doing really hard drugs, getting into trouble. I*
> *joined a gang, started stealing, started selling drugs.*
> *I bought a gun and went to jail but after I got outta*
> *jail I kept my nose clean. We stayed in them fuckin'*
> *shitty townhouses that ruined my life for another*
> *year, then we moved out. Finally found a house on*
> *the [name of neighbourhood] and me and my mom*
> *live here till this day.*

Jimmy exited his gang, quit hard drugs and stopped his criminal activities after having taken part in a gang intervention program for two years. He became a peer counsellor at this program. He attributes his success to moving out of the social housing project where he lived and into a healthier neighbourhood.

"IT'S BETTER THAN FLIPPING BURGERS"

Gerry, sixteen years of age and incarcerated in a young offender centre, told me he was never going to achieve the economic standards of a middle-class lifestyle and therefore was choosing a future of crime for material gain.

> *I wasn't born with a silver spoon in my mouth. There's fuck all I can do about that. So now it really pisses me when I see some rich motherfucker my age driving around in a fast car with lots of gold. 'Cause I know that'll never be me. I'll never have any of that shit from a real job—like a lawyer or a doctor. If I get a job it'll be picking up garbage or flipping burgers. Well, excuse me. I think I'll steal cars and deal.*

Gang members like Gerry often lack legitimate employment opportunities because of factors like a lack of education or poor school performance, entrenched poverty, and high unemployment in their communities. Unlike those young people who do find legitimate employment, the vast majority of gang members have dropped out or have been expelled from school. (Gerry was in school, but only because it was mandatory in young offender centres. He did not go to school on the outside.) A significant minority are in grade seven or eight when their schooling is terminated. Gerry had always struggled in school. He had dyslexia and other learning disabilities related to reading, and knew he would never succeed there. Although he felt ashamed and worthless, he knew that the education system was stacked against him and would not prepare him for college or university. Even when gang members do get through high school, the vast majority do not have the money to pursue post-secondary education.

The lack of legitimate employment opportunities for the

young where they can make a living wage leads to an alternative underground or gang-based economy. In the 1930s, sociologist Robert K. Merton began thinking about this concept, and his work was further developed by Richard Cloward and Lloyd Ohlin. Cloward and Ohlin coined the term "illegitimate opportunity structures."[1] Gangs, like legitimate businesses, provide an opportunity structure for earning a wage. They just happen to do this in criminal ways. Aboriginals, ethnic minorities, and racial minorities are most likely to experience blocked opportunities in school and the labour market. Because of racism, their access to legitimate business opportunities is also blocked. In fact, they are pushed out of the legitimate economy. When low-skilled manufacturing, service industry, or manual labour jobs dry up, it is difficult for longer-term gang members to find legitimate jobs. Gang members who have been involved for a relatively long period of time usually stay in the gang for social and economic reasons. Typically, they have been out of the legitimate labour market for too long to be able to return to it. The longer they are in a gang, the harder it is to upgrade employment skills to get a legitimate job. Those young people who are involved for relatively brief periods of time have a much easier time getting legitimate jobs once they exit their gangs.

Many gang members are legally employed in the legitimate labour market at the same time that they are employed in the illegal economy. These young people are identified as "floaters."[2] Some have exited their gangs but continue to be self-employed, dealing drugs or running girls on the street. Why? It has been theorized that gang participation may be responsive to changes in the legitimate job market. When legitimate jobs are scarce and there is a constant threat of unemployment, members view their opportunities in the underground criminal economy to be better.[3]

Most members in such organized gangs as the United Nations and the Independent Soldiers are employed by the gang, in a clearly defined pyramid structure. However, for members of loosely organized, low level street gangs, things are very different. Such gangs emerge specifically to make money, often cooperating with mid-level and organized crime groups and quickly disbanding after the job is done. In these latter gangs, many members consider themselves to be self-employed. The money they make from drug trafficking and prostitution provides autonomy, dignity, self-esteem, and a chance to avoid "flipping burgers." Some gang members mature out of their gangs relatively quickly, eventually finding employment in the legitimate labour market. Finally, some members stay forever in the underground drug and sex trade economy to feed their addictions. New recruits view sales from illegal drugs and from putting women out on the streets as their career.[4]

THE PYRAMID MARKETING MODEL OF GANG WORK

Both Billy and Anthony were part of street gangs that were based on what I call the "pyramid marketing model of gang work." These gangs are organized on a model similar to the schemes practiced by companies like Amway, Avon, and Mary Kay. Of the work he did, Billy told me, *"It was business, nothing personal."* Anthony had clearly defined roles and reported to his boss, the higher-up. He told me, *"I was doing missions for my gang, scamming and taxing people. Basically all drug dealers, doing armed robberies. I did what I was told and brought my money back to my higher-up."*

Many gang members talk about the large amount of cash prostitution and drug trafficking can bring in on a daily basis. Yet, despite all the money that apparently is being made, why is it that so many gang members live in grinding poverty? Many lack stable housing, are constantly hungry, have no bank accounts, and do not own cars. If money is being made, where is it going? As in a private company, it goes to the leaders. Lower-ranking members simply do not have the same revenue and purchasing power as their bosses. This is the pyramid marketing scheme of gang business.

Pyramid marketing companies are companies that use multi-level marketing to sell a variety of products—primarily in the health, beauty, and home care markets—directly to the public. Multi-level or "network" marketing pays commissions to salespeople for the products they sell, on products sold by others they recruit, and often pays bonuses when their teams reach a certain level of sales. There are different levels of sellers. Such companies bring in hundreds of millions of dollars every year in profits. While Amway, Mary Kay, and Avon are the best known legitimate multi-level marketing companies, there are hundreds of other firms in the industry. Product commissions can be as little as 1 per cent or much higher on high-margin products.[5] The more senior people get a cut of the sales of everyone whom their recruits bring in. Distributors rarely sell products to outside customers. Instead, they only sell products to their new distributors, who must in turn find their own recruits in order to make money.

The average net income of lower level gang members is probably not much different from minimum wage levels in legitimate jobs. Gang members at the bottom bring in lots of money through drug trafficking and prostitution, but don't get to keep much of it. Those at the top of the gang make lots of money. Obviously, this arrangement also parallels the salary structure of many private companies. Take, for example, any of Canada's major banks. Tellers may make minimum wage, financial planners make somewhat more, managers make even more, and executives make millions. The wage disparity is significant. The structure in illegal franchises is similar to that in legal franchises.[6]

Let's take a specific example of a common gang crime and

apply the pyramid marketing model to it. Two leaders of a low level gang invest $2,000 to buy the chemical compounds required for cooking methamphetamine. They have rented a house for $1,000 monthly. The house serves as the lab. It produces $30,000 worth of methamphetamine over a one month period. In order to traffic the methamphetamine on the streets, the gang "hires" four new recruits, who are paid $100 per day each, plus commissions on sales. One collects the cash, another delivers the product to the buyer, and two recruits keep a lookout for the police. The four recruits also spend two days cooking the methamphetamine. If the crew works for ten days over one month, they are thus paid $4,000 in total. This means that the leaders of the gang, after making an initial investment of $3,000, and paying four members $4,000, make a profit of $23,000. Then, they reinvest twice the amount of their initial investment for an even greater profit. Like pyramid marketing companies, the new recruits are responsible for finding buyers who will pay for the drug. The more buyers they find, the more methamphetamine they sell, and the more they get paid. As the business evolves, other local drug dealers who are not members of the gang negotiate with the leaders to be allowed to continue to sell their chemicals in the community, provided they pay a weekly tax. The tax can be calculated as a proportion of their sales (such as 10 per cent) or can be a flat weekly fee (such as $500). The gang increases its profits and starts to generate revenue from work it is not directly involved in—the taxing of drug dealers who are not gang-involved.

THE DANGEROUS NATURE OF GANG JOBS

It is obvious that gang work is much more risky than that in other professions. Perhaps one of the main differences is that gang members do not get danger pay, despite the fact that they are much more likely to get killed or maimed than employees in other industries. In the urban gang economy there is a high risk of serious injury, death, and arrest. Clearly, this type of work would never make it through today's health and safety committees. Job accident rates are far too high. Why is it that gang members put up with making comparatively little money given the risk of death? There are many reasons, including protection, respect, a sense of belonging and family, easy access to drugs, and psychological thrills.

* * *

Many members see their gangs as acceptable sources of employment. They have turned to the underground economy because their access to the legitimate labour market has been blocked—in effect, they have been pushed out of the job market. Given school exclusion, racism, and high unemployment, gang work would seem to be a rational choice. In more sophisticated gangs, work is often modelled on a pyramid marketing scheme, with a rigidly structured hierarchy. Loosely organized street gangs are different. In these latter groups, members are free to make as much money as they can, although they still have to turn over a portion to gang leaders. Gang members are often believed to rake in huge profits from drug dealing, prostitution, and other crimes. This is a myth. Those occupying the upper echelons of crime groups do make lots of money, but those underneath them make very little. At the very bottom, new recruits likely make no more than minimum wage.

Gang work is dangerous. It is hard to imagine another line of work that carries such high risk. Death is not uncommon and serious injuries are frequent. Those members who have spent long careers in the gang are the least likely to find legitimate employment if they do manage to exit. Typically, they are out of the job market for so long that their employability is low.

✳ CHAPTER 9 ✳

STRATEGIES FOR PREVENTING GANGS

When I interviewed him, Randy, a participant in a gang intervention program, had just been released from prison. While Randy was behind bars, he felt it was necessary to demonstrate to the other inmates that he was still a gang member—even though he had exited his gang prior to his imprisonment. He pretended to be gang-involved because it gave him some protection from other offenders and prevented him from being beaten into one of the many gangs that were active in the jail. Once released, however, he felt safer on the streets and did not represent himself as a gang member. Nevertheless, he was still very caught up in the street lifestyle—using alcohol and drugs, partying, and hanging out with gang-involved friends. Randy had been involved in his gang since early adolescence, and all his friends still participated in gangs and street crimes. They all were heavy drug and alcohol abusers. His biological family was no better. Many were gang-involved, and his father, brothers, uncles, and grandfather had all done many years in prison for crimes of serious violence. Many family members struggled with addictions. If Randy were to leave the criminal lifestyle and partying behind, he believed he would be isolated and lost. He told me that he would not have any friends, or family. His situation is illustrative of how difficult it can be to leave gangs behind.

Canada cannot continue to build more jail cells and to put more cops on the street indefinitely. These traditional responses are very expensive and are proven to have little, if any, effect on the growth of either new or existing gangs. Nor can we punish our way out of this, either. Increasing sentences have no effect on recidivism. The total spending on corrections (provincial, territorial, and federal) for the 2010–2011 fiscal year was $4.4 billion ($2.5 billion for Correctional Services Canada).[1] The total spending on police resources in Canada was approximately $12 billion in 2009.[2] We need to make tough decisions, such as diverting money from corrections and policing and investing in prevention initiatives. We can't incarcerate our way out of the gang problem. Randy—and other gang members like him—told me that incarceration had no effect on his gang involvement. In fact, it likely entrenched it and prolonged his exit.

The best way to prevent young people from joining gangs is to address violentization: Help those children who experience severe violence day in and day out while they are trying to grow up. In Canada, child maltreatment is an undeclared public health epidemic. Many more children suffer from the adverse effects of child abuse than are affected by cancer and AIDS combined.[3] Many abused kids have impaired physical, emotional, cognitive, and social functioning. [4] Good evidence suggests that successful interventions target high-risk neighbourhoods using a public health approach. In-home visitation by public health nurses to disadvantaged first-time mothers is a proven strategy for preventing child abuse.[5] Yet, we do not dedicate nearly enough resources to this enormous problem. Children, like the ones in my studies, suffer.

New models of child welfare and justice are also required. Instead of ripping kids out of dysfunctional families and pushing them into the revolving doors of child welfare and youth justice facilities, we need to adequately support high-risk families by investing resources into programs known to work. Programs known to work include parent training, fetal alcohol spectrum disorder prevention and intervention programs, promoting healthy relationships (for example, by supporting women so they are able to leave violent partners, by providing effective therapy for abusers, and so on), addressing poverty and unstable housing, and providing parents with drug and alcohol treatment. A good example of one such effective program is the women's group offered by a federally funded gang intervention project.

Loretta, aged twenty-one, wrote about how this program was helping her make changes. The program, which involved classes on parenting, addictions, self-esteem, child abuse and neglect, life skills, and violence against women, was an extremely cost-effective intervention compared to taking Loretta's child into care or imprisoning Loretta.

> I came here to better myself, and to help my well-being. Coming to this program and learning life skills helps me better myself, teaching me that what I do is wrong and how stupid it is for me to do such a dumb thing. I'm learning new ways to cope with situations that will get me into trouble. This program stabilizes me and shows me a better way to do things. It helps me with my decisions. The positive [girls] that are trying to change their lives gives me a better crowd to hang with and pushes me toward positive situations. People who want to change help me also, give me encouragement. I come here because I want change in my life. I'm only 21

*years old and a single mother to a 3-year-old. My
son is the whole reason why I'm here. This gang exit
project is the perfect environment because I don't
sell myself for sex. I'm not into hard-core drugs, but
I am a troubled female dealing with my past. I'm
not in a gang but I am affiliated, a lot of my family
and friends are in gangs, which pull me in too. I'm
in this program to better my life and better myself.*

A radical change in thinking is required if we are to implement
effective prevention, intervention, and exit initiatives. If we fail to
act now, we can expect gang membership to grow and violence to
increase in Canada, if for no other reason than that the birth rates
of Aboriginal and new Canadian families are very high. And we
can expect more women to be exploited and murdered.

THE DANGERS OF DECIDING TO LEAVE

For many, the gang exit process can be just as difficult as was joining the gang in the first place. Some young gang members do find
it relatively easy to exit the gang, but virtually impossible to leave
the lifestyle. Elements of the lifestyle particularly hard to give up
include intravenous drug abuse, trading sex for money and basic
necessities, and having close friends and even family members
who are gang-involved. Sabrina, aged fifteen, and Carolyn, aged
thirty, talked about these challenges. Sabrina wrote:

*I constantly keep going back to the street life, family,
and illegal activity. I'm so frustrated and miserable
with myself because I don't know why I keep going
to this way of living. I'm sick and tired of having to
live the same thing every single day of living to die!
Living to die slowly, having to feel better because
of the feeling of hurting someone else! I want*

*happiness. I want a happy life even though I know
I will always have struggles going on but know for
myself that there will be something to live for and
not always have to think I'm useless, and that living
in [name of city] doesn't have to feel like living in a
cruel world.*

She equates her current lifestyle with dying. She is at a loss for
a way to get out of the sex trade, crime, and drug abuse. Although
she idolized her gang-involved boyfriend (he was much older
than she), she recognized that the gang life was a dead end.

Carolyn, although much older than Sabrina, told us about
how she had been street and gang-involved for most of her life.
*"I have been part of gang or street life for seventeen years. We had a
part in all kinds of gang activity. From stealing to selling and buying
drugs to pimping and prostitution. For me, that was just the way life
was. I had to make money to survive in the world. I had to do drugs,
to make the money to survive in the world."* Although she was not
a gang member at the time of the interview, she was living with a
boyfriend who was. He also was an alcoholic. Somehow, Carolyn
was able to compartmentalize these concerns and continue on
the road to healing and moving on with her life in positive ways.

Charlie, aged twenty-four and a long-time gang member,
wrote about how complicated it was to leave the lifestyle, particularly when he had a reputation to fulfill. He was finding it very
hard to not be gang-involved in the penitentiary, particularly
when in the midst of other gang members:

*I came to a long-sought conclusion that I wanted
to exit gang life and my current political status
in gangs which is high. Regardless, this proved
to be difficult due to my lifestyle and reputation
which has always preceded me. I eventually got*

released June 21st and before I could establish my independence there was a few obligations I had to tie up. Like I said, my reputation, which I spent years building, preceded me and I got mixed up with gang life once again, which led to my arrest and my current incarceration. Gangs, as you know, are difficult to exit. After years of being involved my life is woven deep in the fabric of gang life. Regardless of my downfall I want to get back up and try again. I succeeded in convincing my sister to exit. I need help and support. I'm in a difficult unit which is filled with gang members so in order to exit I need to get out of this unit.

Methods of leaving a gang can involve one or more of the following:

- doing minutes (suffering a beating) at the hands of gang members
- gang rape by multiple gang members
- getting pregnant, having kids, or getting married (Many gangs purport to have honourable and romantic ideals, which include permitting members to leave to start families.)
- joining a gang-exit program (This can be dangerous because higher-ups usually do not want members to leave.)
- death (Being killed or committing suicide is a common way of ending gang membership.)

Being Beaten Out

Anthony had been out of his gang for twenty-two weeks after two years of trying to exit. His exit process had been sparked by a desire to retreat from criminal peers and fully engage in family life. *"Twelve years of my life a gang member—half of my life. I am out now. I dropped my rag [left my gang] because of family life. I have three kids. I started basically seeing the better side of life, having friends who actually cared."*

He was a soldier in his gang and got "stabbed out." He told me that he was not at all sure that he could stay out of gangs. Like many other participants in my studies, he had friends and many family members who were still actively in. He felt that he was leaving his gang-involved friends high and dry—even though he acknowledged that they were not true friends he could count on. *"It wasn't easy getting out. Not just takin' a lickin', but I still got problems. I don't answer to anyone but myself. The hardest part was abandoning them. When I needed them, they were there. But when I really needed them they were nowhere to be found."* What Anthony meant by this last statement was that periodically he was hospitalized because he had HIV. He found it hard to stay on his medication because of his hard drug abuse, his transient lifestyle, and the cost of the medication. When he was hospitalized, his "friends" did not visit.

Despite what he had come to realize about them, it was hard to abandon his gang-involved friends. Will he remain gang-free? Time will tell. He certainly seemed to have benefitted from the support of the gang-exit program: *"Having people like you guys [staff at a program] around, for showing the positive side, what I never seen. There's more to life than that. Someone listening to you and you being heard. 'Cause I know I don't have to answer to anyone, I am in charge now."*

Jordan, twenty-one, was emotional when he spoke of the murder of his higher-up. He clearly liked the gang life and had had difficulty exiting his gang. He got "stomped out."

> *In 2007 it all started out with the big fight, the gang. I went to get back up. I ended up getting down with [my gang]. Always partying and being down for them, having fun, making a name for myself.*

I felt good, I reminisce about those days. It was fun, I got respect at times. I was not into it hard-core. I felt good. Just hanging out with all of them. My higher-up got rushed, got stabbed in the neck. He got killed, rushed by [a rival gang]. I just got stomped out, just stopped repping it, hanging out with that group. I took it pretty hard, my higher-up who got killed. I did not want to be down. Just thinking about that day, the next day after he got rushed. I was just on the next block. Just thinking about [him], in his white suit. Next morning when they found him, he had died. Crying, it was nothing but a hurtful time. Looking around for his bro, the house just got rushed, looked like. I started doing my own thing. If I was to rep anything, I repped myself. I came up with my own crew, rappers, not hard-core gangsters. I don't need to be hiding behind a gang. I feel happy, not heavily into gang life. At times I fall back into it, gets crazy at times, it is just life. Coming to [a program] helped me out.[6]

Gang-Raped Out

The exit process for ex-girlfriends and ex-wives of male gang members is particularly brutal. Recall that in Chapter Four we discussed the different risk levels for the three categories of gang-affiliated women. Women can be part of all-female gangs, part of male-dominated gangs, or working the street and affiliated through the sex trade and partying. Sylvie's status was very low when she exited her gang. Because she was not attached to a "man," she was beaten and gang raped. *"They beat me and raped me, knocked me out. I woke up and realized what happened. I couldn't do nothing either. They told me I was free to leave. I was black and blue, bloody, couldn't even hardly close my legs."* If Sylvie had had a boyfriend or husband in the gang at the time of exit and they were getting married or having a child, she would have been permitted to leave peacefully.

Exiting through Geographic Relocation and Witness Protection Programs

In one Canadian gang intervention project, seven participants were or had been in witness protection as a result of testifying against fellow gang members in homicide trials. All seven had exited their gangs prior to entering the witness protection program. The outcomes for these seven cases are mixed; four are doing well (or were, at the time of my research), and three are experiencing serious challenges. Witness protection relocates witnesses to another geographic location and creates new identities for them. In Canada, there are no published data on the outcomes for ex-gang members in witness protection. The four cases where witness protection is working well have a number of common characteristics: financial support, stable housing, employment and school support, daycare for children, addictions programs, legal support, and counselling. It seems that, in order to do well, ex-gang members in witness protection need a continuum of supports immediately available. The three individuals who are experiencing major challenges do not have one or more of these supports, and they have all moved back to their communities of origin, thereby exposing themselves to serious risk.

Many young people who successfully exit their gangs move out of neighbourhoods where gangs are active or they relocate to different cities. This is not witness protection, rather a choice to move on their own accord. Again, what seems to determine whether or not outcomes will be successful is the availability of supports that can immediately respond.

Being Killed

George's case is typical of how some gang members exit: they survive a vicious attack and are left for dead. In his case, he was shot by a young man in the same gang who thought George had stolen money from him.

> *Last year I got shot, rolled up in a plastic sheet and thrown in a bathtub and left to die. I was all caught up. I paid out what I had to pay out [money made from crack dealing] and I took my share. I loaded up my rig and took it [crack, intravenously] and was chillin' and I looked up and he [a member of the same gang] had a gun pointed at my head. The next thing I knew it felt like I had been punched really hard. I felt my gut and I was bleeding and I fell down. I was stoned so I didn't feel any pain and I got up and they wrapped me in plastic and threw me in the tub—to die I guess.*

George was found in the tub, dying, by another member of his gang. This young person called 911 and an ambulance arrived on the scene shortly thereafter. Doctors told him that they had no idea how he managed to survive, given the large amount of blood he lost before making it to the hospital. George refused to give a statement to the police. He believed he would be killed if he did. In his mind, you never rat on a member of your own gang.

Jamie, the president of his gang, was twenty-three years of age and had been attempting to exit the gang for six months. Two weeks prior to its intervention, he called the program at 3:00 a.m. after having been stabbed with a knife and broken bottle at a party. A staff member called the police and arranged to have an officer pick Jamie up from the gang house. Jamie was taken to a hospital, where he received twenty stitches to his face. In the counselling session I attended, the staff member asked him how many more attacks it would take for him to exit his gang:

*I'm trying to get out but it's hard. I'm the president.
I have my bros to take care of. I've got business. Who
will replace me if I go? Do you know what it's like
to be looking over your back forty times at night?
Yeah, you got power but you always have to know
who's around you and what's going on. You can get
stabbed or shot up. I was drunk a couple of weeks
ago and walking home in this alley and someone
just stomped me. I was too drunk and passed out.
When I woke up my face was all swelled up and my
ribs really hurt. You're always a target. It's not like
in the movies. You can't relax.*

The staff member asked him, "So maybe you will have to get killed to get out?" He responded, "Maybe. I hope not. I will get out before then."

Paul's case is another that shows just how dangerous the exit process can be. Like George, he had been shot numerous times and was assumed to be dead. But Paul had survived being shot eight times by a rival gang leader (who was a family member), and entered a gang exit program, only to be kidnapped by his higher-up who beat him, forcibly injected him with cocaine, and only set him free after Paul disclosed information about the exit program: the person who kidnapped Paul wanted to harm staff. Paul survived another assault by family members who were in a rival gang. They were displeased that he had left his gang.

*It's my choice to drop [gang colours]. It's my life and
I want to change my life. I want to work here [at the
gang program]. That's my, you know, my thing, my
plan. I'm not willing to try to give up—I wanna do
more, fuck you know...the hardest thing for me to*

quit was leaving gang life. I said in detox. That the drugs were the second hardest thing to, you know, quit. The gang was the hardest. Us who left, we all left the gang for the worst way. Like [name of friend] got shot. This one guy he said it fuck was 'cause of his mom. That's not the way for us. We left because we got shot...I feel uneven, in the middle. It is hard to fly straight now, like drunk driving all over the fuckin' road. Like that TV commercial where they put one bottle in front of you. I am trying to look for a job but it's hard—I have forty-some convictions."

When Paul told me that "I feel uneven, in the middle," he was referring to being caught between wanting to leave the gang and being pulled back in by family and friends. This is a common dynamic among those who try to exit. He compared staying out of the gang to impaired driving. He did not have a road map for life outside gangs because he had spent just about all his life in them.

Finally, Stephan, aged thirty, was a gang leader and by his own accord he had either directly committed or had ordered many vicious attacks on rivals. He attributed his exit to having being almost killed by a rival. *"I was lucky to get stabbed just below my heart. It was done by one of my sworn enemies on the street. He saved my life. That's what got me to leave—almost getting stabbed to death."*

Suiciding Out

Tragically, some Aboriginal gang members see suicide as the only way out of gang life. Although I can speak about only the roughly five hundred young gang members in my research, it appears that suicide is not so much of an issue for other groups of gang members (young African men, for example). Why then is it viewed as an option by young Aboriginals? Charlie gives us a few clues in this poem about leaving his gang. He had seriously contemplated killing himself, even having the noose already tied around his neck and being in the process of tying it to a ceiling joist when a friend intervened. He attempted suicide on many other occasions. Suicide seemed to be the only way out. He had survived unspeakable abuse, had done hard time for serious crimes of violence, and believed that he was the cause of his younger brother's problems. He believed that suicide would bring him to a better place where his suffering would end.

> **Gotta Go**
> *Death always crosses my mind,*
> *But suicide attempts are difficult when I try,*
> *Grasp the noose*
> *As my body shivers and intenses on what I'm about*
> *to do,*
> *After death comes rebirth*
> *I wonder if death hurts*
> *I'm built inside with depression and so much cries*
> *I keep telling myself life's hard when a close friend*
> *dies*
> *Emotional feelings run deep in my soul*
> *Alone with so many thoughts I can't control*
> *I love to love death because my life aches*
> *As minutes go by the more I want to end my pain*
> *I hate this life I live*
> *My suffering has got to end*
> *Give me a bullet and gun and I'll finish it quick*

WHAT WORKS?

Which programs, strategies, and supports truly help reduce the growth of gangs and gang membership? In Canada, about 1 per cent of all children and families—the ones with the most complex mental health needs—take up roughly one-third of all the available resources in traditional services.[7] The long-term outcomes for these traditional, high-cost services (primarily residential and out-of-community) are poor in many cases.[8] These young people usually display early-onset aggression before they are six. If left untreated, most turn into serious, violent offenders and some become gang members. Research indicates that positive outcomes also depend heavily on the motivation of the individual young person.[9]

The programs that have the best outcomes are those that combine primary, secondary, and tertiary prevention in a multi-disciplinary and multi-systemic community approach. It is less costly and more effective to prevent youth from joining gangs than it is to help a member to exit a gang,[10] and the best way to prevent youth from joining gangs is to intervene early in the lives of high-risk children and families.

Primary prevention addresses the entire child and youth population at risk and the biological, personal, social, and environmental risk factors linked to criminal behavior. The emphasis is on awareness and education. It is thought that if resiliency is enhanced and youth develop a capacity to recognize risky situations, then they may be better equipped to resist engaging in gang-related activity. Unfortunately, most projects in Canada are stuck at this primary prevention level and do not work. For example, many youth squads in police departments engage in the "spray and pray" approach: they target all students with one program. Unless it is enhanced with other interventions, this strategy will be ineffective.

One of the easiest primary prevention strategies to implement is to make recreation and arts programming accessible to low-income, high-risk young people and families. Accessible, high-quality recreational opportunities increase a community's capacity to provide youth with a dense network of social ties and meaningful opportunities for engagement.[11] Rates of criminal arrest are reduced *by as much as 71 per cent* when young people have the chance to participate regularly in structured recreational activities along with other therapeutic programming. In addition, anti-social behaviour is reduced and success in post-secondary education is increased.[12] These activities can also provide safe, developmental opportunities for latch-key children, who have reduced opportunities for physical activities and socialization because of the lack of parental supervision. Youth crime peaks in the after-school hours, and structured after-school programming benefits young people in situations where supervision would be otherwise absent.[13] For example, Britain's *Youth Inclusion Programme* targets the fifty most at-risk youth ages thirteen to sixteen years who live in high-crime neighbourhoods in various cities in England and Wales. It aims to engage each group of fifty in activities ranging from sports and recreational opportunities to skills training (literacy, anger management, dealing with gangs and drugs). A 2003 evaluation found that the program reduced school expulsions by 27 per cent, reduced youth arrests by 65 per cent, and overall crime in the neighbourhoods by 16 to 27 per cent.[14]

The most cost-effective way to increase quality infrastructure and programming in low income communities is to adopt the "school as hub" model, wherein schools work with local service providers to help create a network between the school, the community, and opportunities for recreation, arts, and health services. In some cases school boards have signed funding agreements with ministries of education regarding the community use of schools, allowing for low cost or no cost recreation programming during after-school, evening, and weekend periods. By turning schools into centres for human development from birth onward, we can mitigate the many risks faced by low-income people. Empty classrooms and gyms in neighbourhood schools can be transformed into daycare centres, sites for parent training and family literacy and baby wellness programs, and food and clothing banks. Some school boards are already doing precisely this—using freed-up classroom space to offer expanded early childhood development programming.[15]

There is a large body of research pointing to the importance of increasing school bonding as an effective way to reduce drop-out and expulsion rates among high-risk students. Staying in school and bonding with the adults there develops the aspirations of high-risk students, leading them to a successful transition into adulthood.

Investments in the voluntary recreation sector achieve substantial savings to the municipally funded health, social, and police budgets while at the same time improving the quality of people's lives. There is indisputable scientific evidence that high-quality recreation and arts programs can achieve significantly more benefits than they cost.[16] Ontario data suggest that participation in recreation by low-income families pays for itself in the reduced use of professionals and probationary services and in the mental health benefits for mothers. Savings have been found for the tax system when people exit welfare and gain employment.[17] Children and youth who participate in at least one thirteen-week skill development program per year can substantially increase their cognitive, physical, and emotional competencies. Ottawa studies by Dr. Dan Offord showed similar results in the 1990s.[18]

Successful programs reduce the funding-silo effect that complicates provision of public health, recreation, daycare, education, and social assistance. There are promising approaches toward razing these silos in a handful of Ontario municipalities. Hamilton, Peel, York region, and London have created historic partnerships between sectors within their municipalities, increasing the participation of low-income families. Typically, these services become housed in the same building, providing consumers with "one-stop-shopping."[19]

Secondary prevention services target individuals and groups identified as being at greater risk of becoming gang members. Community assessments frame the strategies. The focus is on reducing risk factors rather than on describing variables that cannot be changed.[20] Both social problems (such as poverty, social disorganization, unstable housing, discrimination, and poor living environments) and individual risk factors (such as addictions, family violence and child maltreatment, poor parenting abilities, fetal alcohol spectrum disorder, school drop-out, and unemployment) are targeted. Protective factors such as the development of strong family bonds and positive peer groups and the completion of school programs are promoted. The National Crime Prevention Centre (Public Safety Canada) has adopted a risk-protective framework to increase protective factors and assets by building positive relationships and patterns of interactions with youth, creating positive social environments surrounding youth, and promoting social and economic policies that support positive youth development. A handful of Canadian programs are doing this type of work.

Tertiary prevention targets gang members and recruits directly to rehabilitate or suppress their gang activity, address the needs of victims, and provide exit strategies and support for youth who wish to leave and stay out of gangs. There are a few therapeutic programs in Canada at this level. Unfortunately, the majority of them are police- and corrections-based.

New models of youth justice are also required. Often, Aboriginal young people are criminalized, in effect, because they have suffered child maltreatment. The child welfare system acts as a pipeline into the youth justice system, and incarceration often leads to recruitment into gangs; alternatively, it can enhance gang cohesion and membership for those who are already gang-involved. The Canadian Aboriginal Justice Strategy is broken. There has been no reduction in rates of crime, victimization, and incarceration among Aboriginal people since the strategy was introduced in the 1990s. The Youth Criminal Justice Act has a special set of criteria and measures for Aboriginal youth, but provinces and territories are not abiding by the act in many instances. Unless we can dramatically reduce the number of young Aboriginals who are incarcerated, gang violence will only increase.

SPERGEL'S COMPREHENSIVE GANG MODEL

Irving Spergel's *Comprehensive Gang Model* is a community-wide response to gangs that has been adopted by the Office of Juvenile Justice and Delinquency Prevention across the USA. This model consists of five core strategies, which flow from an integrated and team-oriented problem-solving approach using secondary and tertiary prevention. The model's underlying assumption is that a lack of social opportunities and the degree of social disorganization in a community account for the youth gang problem. Contributing factors such as poverty, institutional racism, poor social policies, and a lack of or misdirected social controls are important. Each aspect of the model is described below. The five core strategies are: community mobilization; social intervention; provision of academic, economic, and social opportunities; gang suppression; and facilitation of organizational change and development.

Community mobilization: This involves mobilizing community leaders and residents to plan, strengthen, or create either new opportunities or linkages to existing organizations for gang-involved or at-risk youth. Community organization around prevention of gangs in neighbourhoods with an emerging gang problem is one of the few approaches to gang interventions that does have a positive outcome.[21]

Social intervention: Gang members are more likely to respond to programs taken directly to them, as opposed to those they have to seek out for themselves.[22] Teams of workers from different disciplines target specific youth, gangs, and social contexts to engage the gang in more pro-social activities or to influence members to exit. Detached workers take part in social activities (such as recreation) and provide social services such as tutoring, employment counselling, advocacy work with the police and court, individual counselling, and family services.[23] A good example of an intervention that involved recreation, counselling, and legal support is the case of Ricky, aged fifteen years. He wrote about the various supports he received in a gang intervention program:

> I've been going to school every day so I don't get breached and go to jail for a couple of months. But now that I'm 15 I'm going to try find a job so I can help out my mom. I never really had a dad, he left my mom when I was like 8 months old but now he's around but things changed in my life. When I was 12, I got kicked outta [public school name] but before then I used to go to a program called [name of gang program]. They used to take us to go bowling and talk about lots of things. Now I'm here at [the cultural school].[24] They have been helping me out for a long time with my probation, so that's pretty cool of them and the staff is fun. We always go on trips. I'm getting my education here and they give us five dollars if we help around here five times so that's good and they drive me to go report so I don't get breached and go to jail. They help out people who are in gangs.

Thirteen-year-old Shirley also wrote about the impact of the same project's services on her life. She wrote about addictions and how much she liked the cultural supports, school, and counselling: *"I started going to school, that's when I started to see some counsellors and even an elder. That elder took me to sweats and round dances. I asked him one day, I said I want to powwow dance, so he helped me out. I stopped with the drugs and drinking and went to [the school]. That's when I started this group [name of therapeutic group]. It helped me talk about my story, my past and share with other people."*

Provision of academic, economic, and social opportunities: Many gang intervention strategies have failed to implement an ecological framework to address educational and employment opportunities in the community.[25] Such programs would encourage members to stop or to decrease participation in gang activities. Other social opportunities that can be provided include programs to address poverty, malnutrition, and mental illness. Educational and vocational programming for high-risk youth are proven to result in lower crime rates.[26] School and employment bonding initiatives provide structured time and hope for the future for potential gang members. High-risk youth who graduate from secondary school are much more likely to be employed, compared to school drop-outs. Unemployment is one of the key predictors of youth crime.

Julie, six months pregnant, developed an employment plan to address these issues over the course of her program. She told me, *"I want to move and get a job. Work with kids. Daycare. I'll stop having boyfriends who are gang members. It's different now. It feels good to make legit money that I worked hard for."* Loretta also developed an employment plan. She stated, *"I wanted to be able to fix myself and all the bad I do. I want to be able to control my thinking, like the negative thoughts and how I control myself through thinking. To gain full-time employment, and keep that job, so I can pay off all my debt. Practically pay off all my debts and start fresh with my new credit."*

Initiatives that support returning to or staying in school are very important. Bonding to school develops a sense of hope for the future, which is sadly lacking in the lives of many young gang members. Completing school also opens up employment options. A number of participants in the evaluations conducted by Sharon Dunn and myself developed plans in this area. Lorraine had plans to complete her post-secondary education. *"I am registered to go back to [university] in the fall for psychiatric nursing."* Julie stated, *"I'm going to graduate and I'm going to be a mom. Finish off school to get a better job. And move outta this city. Finish off my credits. I need to get my grade 12 then I will look after my baby until he gets old enough to get into daycare then I will get into university and take my Early Childhood Education training hopefully to get a better place, a better area, or maybe even a better city."*

One Canadian project has a cultural school embedded in its continuum of services. The following three accounts speak to the positive role this school played in the lives of gang-involved youth. Thirteen-year-old Terri wrote: *"[Cultural school] helped me because I got kicked out of another school I used to attend and I was behind in a lot of work because I never really went. The teacher never really helped or told you what you need to work on or they never really pay attention to the kids in the back rows. So being a teenager and getting kicked out of school and behind a lot of work and bad attendance, I'm sure another regular school would not want that so I decided to come to this school. The teachers are nice and friendly and very supporting and flexible so you can come whenever and bring work home to catch up."*

Fourteen-year-old Chrystal wrote: *"I am in this program because all the drinking has caused me trouble in school. I really like this school. It helps me work better and when you're here they help you through everything. And my mom stopped drinking 4 months ago and I seen my dad a year ago but [he's] still not a part of my life. I am happy my life's better. My grandparents still drink but I barely see them. My sister is like a mom. I miss my dad, I don't love him but miss him. I always wanted a dad but 2 moms are awesome."*

Finally, nineteen-year-old Jimmy described how being expelled from a public school led to his involvement in a cultural school. This in turn introduced him to music and counselling. He is now a junior youth worker at the project:

> *So I started back at school at [name of public school] and I got kicked out of there so I came to [cultural school] and they help a lot. I got to be a junior youth worker there and started in a group called [name of therapeutic group]. I am the sound man for them. They also helped me change big time. I give a BIG thanks to that school for sure. I quit the bad drugs, quit stealing, but I still have a really, really bad temper and some nights I get so upset and feel like dying but it's not worth it. Life has more to it than drugs and gangs so I started writing music and recording. That and my family. Without my music and family I don't know where the hell I would be.*

Gang suppression: This includes activities that hold gang-involved youth accountable, including formal and informal social control procedures in the justice system. Over the past number of years, many municipal police departments have developed gang units (including Toronto, Edmonton, Regina, Ottawa, Montreal, Winnipeg, and Abbotsford). The RCMP and various provincial forces have also initiated gang strategies, often in collaboration with municipal squads (such as the Combined Forces Special Enforcement Unit in BC). Deportation of gang members has also been a popular response. The Immigration Act allows for the deportation of any landed immigrant convicted of a crime involving criminal organizations or gangs. For example, Montreal deported roughly two hundred immigrants with known gang ties between 1992 and 1997. Finally, it has become popular to kick gangsters back to their home communities from other provinces where they are found to be doing business. BC's "Con Air" program is one example. Some police forces have also chased gangsters away from their cities into other parts of the province. The Abbotsford Police Department has had considerable success doing this, although the cities on the receiving end of this have not been so enthusiastic (Prince George, BC, for example, has recently experienced an influx of gangsters from the BC Lower Mainland).

Facilitating organizational change and development: This strategy helps community agencies better address gang problems through a team-based problem-solving approach, not unlike the community-oriented policing framework.[27]

Overall, Canadian organizations have much work to do to make headway on the Spergel model. For it to work, community-wide, cross-sectoral strategies need to address the individual, economic, and social factors related to gang activity. Broad collaboration and problem-solving partnerships are required. All of Spergel's strategies flow from this. In Canada, almost all communities are miles away from this model.

The silos—the isolated and entrenched approaches—that separate sectors (such as public health, education, corrections, child welfare, and recreation), including Indian and Northern Affairs Canada, must come down. But, at present, most communities are stuck at either the consultation or the co-operation level of partnerships. *Consultation* means "show and tell." Organizations and groups inform other organizations and groups about what they are doing. *Co-operative relationships* are a move in the right direction, but only in a limited way. Organizations and sectors that are stuck in this phase plan things together, meet regularly, and get along with each other. There is a lot of good will, but not much sharing of resources. Often, groups provide in-kind supports (such as one organization's sharing a staff person with another group). A small number of communities, usually the smaller ones, *coordinate* what they do. There is joint planning and decision making, formal protocols, and in-kind supports. For example, a community that has many youth-serving organizations providing elements of an after-hours emergency service may decide to pool those resources (staff and budget) and provide one after-hours service, with a common phone number and one intake assessment service. All youth in the community have access to the same emergency support. The savings realized through efficiencies are reinvested in youth programs, in such ways as the elimination of user fees for advanced skill development sports programs.

OTHER SUCCESSFUL GANG INTERVENTION PROGRAMS

The *Little Village Project* has shown the most positive outcomes of any comprehensive gang intervention program. Little Village is an inner-city area of Chicago that has experienced long-term gang violence problems. Roughly two hundred young gang members took part. Data consisted of 127 individual interviews over three time periods, monthly activity reports to the Chicago Police Department, gang member surveys and self-reports, project worker summary reports, field observations, focus group findings, and police arrest and incident data. These data were compared to data collected during a three-year pre-project period, and with two control groups obtained through arrests of non-targeted young people at program entry.[28]

Multivariate statistical analyses indicated that gang members who participated in more individual counselling sessions were more likely to reduce involvement in gang activities. There was a significant decrease in the number of self-reported offences and arrests over the two-year period, and the strongest predictors of this were the following factors: participants' perception that their probation officers were addressing the gang problem; gang members spending more time with female partners; being aged nineteen years or older; having a stronger connection between future goals and expectations; fewer family and household crises at follow-up periods; and the participant's perception that the gang was smaller at follow-up time periods. The program youth experienced a significant reduction in violent crime arrests compared to the two groups of control youth. The hard-core gang youth demonstrated the most significant decreases in arrests, although there was no major decrease in overall gang crime in the Village.[29] This latter problem could be a result of any number of factors, one of them being that many gang members in Little Village did not participate in the project.

Many other programs have demonstrated success. Boston's *Operation Ceasefire*,[30] which engaged a broad array of local, state, and federal officials, as well as community and neighborhood leaders, proved to be an effective and efficient response to youth firearm violence and gangs. Established in 1996, it was a coordinated city-wide strategy, using a problem-oriented policing approach with zero tolerance on gun violence. Suppression tactics included using all possible justice system options to address violence committed by chronic offenders. Police and probation officers also made nightly visits to the homes of youth on probation to ensure they were complying with their probation conditions. Street outreach workers worked together with law enforcement, helping resolve conflicts and linking youth who wanted help with the appropriate services. The program was associated with a statistically significant decrease (63 per cent) in the number of youth homicides per month. Operation Ceasefire was one element of a collaborative, comprehensive strategy, and has been replicated in Minneapolis, St. Louis, Los Angeles, and other cities.

Another program that has been highly effective with serious, violent, and chronic juvenile offenders is *Multi-systemic Therapy* (MST).[31] This is a cost-effective program that provides serious offenders with intensive therapy, supervision, and monitoring. The MST worker accomplishes supervision strategies in a more supportive manner than is usually found in traditional monitoring by probation and police. It focuses on the multiple determinants of criminal and anti-social behaviour, and provides services in the youth's own neighbourhood. Offending is viewed as having many causes; therefore, interventions address the multitude of factors influencing anti-social behaviour. The family is the primary area of work, and building on the youth's and the family's strengths is a main focus. There is an average of sixty hours of contact with the families over a four-month period. Interventions follow the trademarked intervention strategy developed at the Family Services Research Centre at the Medical University of South Carolina,[32] which has been tested in many sites.[33]

Wraparound is another example of a quality approach for high-risk youth. It is a complex, multi-faceted intervention strategy designed to keep youthful offenders at home and out of institutions whenever possible. A comprehensive continuum of individualized services and support networks are "wrapped around" young people, rather than forcing the young people to fit into categorical, inflexible therapeutic programs.[34] Individual case management is a cornerstone, but Wraparound is not like conventional case management programs: in those, a case manager or probation officer navigates the young person through traditional, established social and youth justice services.[35]

Baltimore's *Choice Program* and San Francisco's *Detention Diversion Advocacy Program* have demonstrated positive outcomes through intensive supervision and individualized treatment plans for both young offenders and those at risk, but their outcomes are not nearly as good as those of Wraparound projects, which target serious cases and violent youth. Wraparounds conducted in Canada and the US have been effective in reducing the frequency of residential or institutional placement of children and youth, reducing recidivism and arrests.[36] In particular, Wraparound Milwaukee and the Connections Program in Clark County, Washington, have had excellent outcomes. In Canada, the Surrey Wrap Project has demonstrated promising results. Wraparound is usually part of an *Integrated System of Care* model, where every complex-need child and family receives an individualized service plan tailored to their unique needs.[37] Unfortunately, most of Canada has been slow to develop this type of model.

California's *Repeat Offender Prevention Program* (ROPP, also referred to as "The 8% Solution") is a multi-site early intervention program targeting young offenders who are at high risk of becoming serious repeat offenders and gang members. Originally developed by the Orange County, California, Probation Department in the early 1990s, the program integrates intensive supervision with Wraparound-like services in eight counties. Evaluations showed that youth enrolled in the ROPP significantly improved their academic performance and were twice as likely to complete probation orders than comparison group youth.[38] Replication of the Repeat Offender Prevention Program has had mixed results, largely because of failure to implement the program fully, inability to deal with community risk factors such as poverty, and problems with interagency collaboration, high staff turnover, and inadequate documentation (the Los Angeles ROPP, for example, did not document any difference between control and experimental groups).[39]

The *Philadelphia Youth Violence Reduction Partnership* has demonstrated effectiveness with offenders who are at high risk of being killed or of killing others. Youth-serving organizations and criminal justice agencies collaborate to balance intensive supervision with comprehensive therapeutic support. The Youth Violence Reduction Partnership provides youth with increased supervision and supports their access to relevant resources (employment, mentoring, school bonding, counselling, health care, and drug treatment). Street workers and police help probation officers supervise participants, resulting in almost daily contacts with seriously violent youth and in smaller caseload sizes. Street workers mentor youth and broker-in other services. A key goal is to stabilize the participants' families through such efforts as finding jobs for the parents and locating housing. Analysis of youth homicide rates in Philadelphia suggests that the Youth Violence Reduction Partnership is effective.[40]

The *Warrior Spirit Walking Project,* delivered by the Prince Albert Outreach Program, Inc. agency, is a Canadian leader in evidence-based prevention and intervention for gang-involved Aboriginal youth. Peggy Rubin, its highly respected executive director, is a passionate advocate for youth and is committed to engaging them as partners in every aspect of programming. The National Crime Prevention Centre provided rich funding for this project between 2007 and 2012. The project also serves youth at high risk of gang involvement. It is nested within the broader Prince Albert Outreach Program, Inc. agency and serves youth aged ten to twenty-four years with daily intensive services. It is based on the Circle of Courage model. Key programs include the youth activity centre, the Won Ska Cultural School, intensive counselling, street outreach to youth in the sex trade, and court outreach. Evaluation data demonstrate statistically significant reductions in overall levels of risk for treatment group participants over time. In addition, statistically significant positive changes were found in levels of gang involvement, substance abuse, violent and non-violent offending, and employment. The treatment sample of 147 youth was matched to a control group of 48. Most participants were followed over a three-year period.[41]

The *Regina Anti-Gang Services Project (RAGS)*, housed within the North Central Community Association, is a unique initiative for gang-involved Aboriginal youth and young adults aged sixteen to thirty years who live in the North Central neighbourhood of Regina. It is the only comprehensive gang exit project in Canada. Jacqui Wasacase is the director. A constant whirlwind of energy, she is fiercely protective of her clients and is a skilled counsellor. Compassionate to a fault, she is well-loved by program participants. The National Crime Prevention Centre also provided rich funding for this project between 2007 and 2012. The program engages clients in intensive daily services aimed at reducing their involvement in gang life and facilitating their exit from gangs. The four core programs are life skills programming for young men, the Circle Keeper program for young women, intensive gang exit counselling, and outreach to schools and institutions. Core services are based upon the Wraparound and MST models. As with the Warrior Spirit Walking Project, RAGS evaluation data demonstrate statistically significant reductions in overall levels of risk for participants. In addition, statistically significant positive changes have been found in levels of gang involvement, substance abuse, and offending. The treatment sample of seventy-four young adults (eighteen of whom had been convicted of murder, attempted murder, or manslaughter) was matched to a control group of twenty-nine high risk gang members. Most participants were followed over a three-year period.[42]

THE IMPORTANCE OF GENDER-RESPONSIVE PROGRAMMING

*I come here because this program means something
2 me. It gives me some kind of direction, it helps*

me have some stability in life. I would rather come to program and talk about drugs and alcohol and sex than sit at home and actually do it. I like the direction it is taking me. Myself and others can see the change. I learned a lot, how to be strong to say no to drugs and alcohol. I never knew how 2 talk about what happened in my past or my feelings until I came here. They taught me I am somebody not a nobody.

These words by Nicki illustrate the key elements of high-quality programs for young women. These programs are founded upon specific principles rooted in the developmental, psychological, social, educational, and cultural characteristics of young women, which are not the same as those of young men. Nicki valued the friendships she had made with other women in the group. She liked the conversations and the way childhood trauma was linked to her current behaviours and thought patterns. She understood that she had value as a person, not just as a gang member and a sex trade worker. She liked finding out that other women were facing serious health issues, not just herself.

Services for young women need to include a number of key ingredients. They are founded on a theoretical understanding of young women's gendered trajectories into street life, the child welfare system, and the justice system. This perspective rests upon the belief that most young women are *criminalized* for having been abused, for having mental health problems, and for committing *crimes that arise out of powerlessness*.[43] Programs should take place in a safe, supportive, and nurturing female-centred environment that encourages trust, bonding, and healthy relationships between staff and young women. A strengths-based approach is utilized, which builds protective "pillows" against the specific risks young women face and develops resiliency.

This approach uses female staff who are reflective of the client population in gender identity, ethno-racial origin, and sexual orientation. Young women report that they feel safer with female staff, are more likely to bond and to engage in therapy with women practitioners, and tend to view them as mentors.[44] The principles of a relational approach to young women's bio-psychosocial development should be adopted. Male staff, no matter how competent, should not work with young women until the women have had time to heal from the various forms of traumatic abuse they have suffered at the hands of men. Failure to adhere to this basic principle will result in the young women being retraumatized by male staff and continuing to relate to men in unhealthy ways.

Counselling should address a number of key areas, including healing from physical, sexual, and emotional abuse; overcoming the limiting gender-role socialization that results in the sexualization of femininity, the emotional caretaking of men, the deference to male authority and privilege, and the equation of love with sex; dealing with childhood disrupted attachments and traumatic losses; family relationships; substance abuse; self-mutilation; eating disorders; mental health problems that are rooted in childhood trauma;[45] and assertiveness skills. The nature of healthy relationships is also a major area of focus. The case of Nora is illustrative. In a young women's group, she discussed her boyfriend's violent behavior and wanted feedback from the other participants and staff as to whether or not it was a problem. The group responded, in a non-judgmental fashion, saying that she did not have to put up with this kind of behaviour, and that she had the right to a violence-free relationship. After that discussion, she wrote: *"I have learned about different types of relationships both healthy and unhealthy, self-worth. I just need to put more practice into it. I am in the process of learning more."*

Finally, high-quality gender-responsive programs for young

women should employ a harm-reduction approach to reducing risks and increasing health (in such areas as drug and alcohol abuse, prostitution, cutting and other forms of self-mutilation, and abuse in dating relationships). For example, it is unrealistic for many addicts to try to stop their drug use and drinking completely. Instead, getting off hard drugs and reducing binge drinking are realistic goals. In one gang program, many young women had stopped their intravenous use and had gotten off hard drugs by the end of the program, although they still smoked marijuana regularly. Carolyn informed me that prescription methadone had helped her get off hard drugs and that participating in the gang intervention program had helped her slow down on her drinking: *"I have been off hard drugs for a while. I still smoke weed every day. I quit drinking the day I joined [name of the program]. I drank every day for eight months straight—just coolers. Since I started here, I have been able to slow down on my drinking. It has given me something to look forward to."*

The case of Christine, aged twenty-four, also illustrates how a harm reduction approach can be woven into a women's program. She wrote: *"Before I heard about this program, I sat at home and drank all day with my partner. Day in, day out we would find different ways to feed our addictions. I knew for myself, I need a change! I would talk to my friends and tell them 'I am bored, I am tired of drinking and getting high every day, I want to do something!' My friend had told me about this program and it seemed like it came to me just in time. I liked the fact that it is there, when I don't want to be at home."* The program supported Christine as she improved her health and decreased the risks related to her heavy drug and alcohol abuse. For example, though she had a serious illness she would not take her medication when she was high, and her boyfriend would get violent after drinking. Through the program, Christine was able to reduce her drinking and use of illicit drugs. She was able to tell her partner that his addictions made it hard for her to become healthier. She even found she had the courage to talk with him about his violence, and to give him an ultimatum: Stop the abuse or get kicked out.

Christine also like the bonding and support she felt with the other young women in the group: *"I liked the other girls here, because they are in the same situation that I am, willing to change ourselves and others. I like the workers here because they are non-judgmental, open-minded, and willing to help or just be there. I like the program because it gets me thinking about where I been, where I am, and where I wanna be. It shows me the different things I need to change in my life and achieve my goals. I am here because this is the support I need in my life!"*

The case of Lorraine, aged twenty-four, is an excellent example of how mental health issues are addressed in quality women's programs. Lorraine had battled depression for most of her life and felt devalued and isolated as a result. This was rooted in early sexual abuse by her father and a family history of depression. The program was a safe place where she addressed these issues without being judged. She wrote:

> *I come to this program because I feel good when I'm here. I have lots of support here. The thing I like most is that I can come here and get guidance from [staff person] and the other girls in the program. For once in my life I feel like I belong somewhere. I come to group and nobody judges me, nobody tries to fuck with me, nobody tries to hurt me. I feel comfortable and safe when I am here. When I'm not here, I think about the next time I will be here. I get excited about what we're gonna learn, who I'm gonna see. Most of all I get excited about working on myself and becoming a happier, healthier person.*

Lorraine was able to connect the dots between her early childhood trauma and her current behaviours. She learned that she was tiptoeing around her boyfriend's drinking, without addressing it directly. She felt that there were no other good men around, so she had to put up with his gang-involved friends and addiction. As a result of her membership in the group, she was able to address these issues directly and establish some ground rules (for example, she told him that he was not welcome at her place when he had been drinking). She wrote:

> *I have learned a lot about myself and my behaviour. I've learned about why I do the things I do. I've learned to recognize things about myself that I've never recognized before. I'm still learning, and I'm excited about what I am learning. I've learned how to do things that I never thought I could do. This program gives me confidence. I am slowly learning how to feel good about myself. I would like to achieve self-confidence, self-understanding, self-esteem. I just want to be able to look in the mirror and like the person looking back at me. I don't want to say or think bad things about myself, but that is all I know how to do at this point.*

FETAL ALCOHOL SPECTRUM DISORDER PREVENTION AND INTERVENTION

Given the high proportion of Aboriginal gang members who have fetal alcohol spectrum disorder, it is important to develop approaches that both prevent women from drinking when pregnant and also intervene effectively with children who have FASD. The root causes of pre-natal alcohol abuse are complex and include victimization by violence from male partners and childhood trauma. Although FASD is a permanent, lifetime brain injury, it presents a broad range of characteristics that vary from person to person. For example, 75 to 80 per cent of people with FASD have IQs within the average range.[46] The severity of FASD-related problems is directly linked to the level of prenatal alcohol consumption: mothers who drink frequently and have many drinks at one time have babies with more severe impairments than do mothers who drink less frequently and have fewer drinks at one time. Several protective factors, too, can lead to better outcomes for individuals with FASD, including early diagnosis and intervention, living in a stable home, protection from violence, and school bonding. Early diagnosis can identify a child's problems and support the treatment needed to maximize his or her abilities. It can also help in the identification and support of high-risk women, to prevent FASD in other babies. Caution is required when FASD is diagnosed, however. Diagnosis can result in negative labelling of the child, and that may be used to predetermine negative pathways and limit the child's potential.[47] It is important to develop resiliency and strengths in these young people.

In 1999, the federal government created the National FASD Initiative through the expansion of the Canada Prenatal Nutrition Program. Since then, yearly funding has been allocated to address FASD issues in the Aboriginal population.[48]

WHAT DOESN'T WORK?

Kitty, now in an employment-training and academic-upgrading program, reflected on what would have prevented her from joining a gang. We have a lot to learn from young people, like Kitty, who have exited their gangs. Kitty told me she would have maintained family connections instead of running away. She would have stayed in school if there had been supports to address her needs. She would have taken parenting classes so her son would not have been adopted. She would have avoided jail. She would have engaged in her culture at a younger age. Poverty was also a precipitating factor for gang involvement.

What would I do different? I witnessed my bro'
stabbed to death at a party a couple of years ago. I
woulda went to school and took care of myself and
my son. I would've stayed connected to my family
and grandma. I would have stayed home. And stayed
outta jail...Maybe if my teachers paid attention more
to me. And realized that I needed help. And maybe if
I would've listened to my grandma instead of pushing
her and the rest of my family away. And if my mom
and dad weren't using drugs and alcohol it would've
made a difference. If I learned more about parenting
I probably would've done better. No one taught me
anything. I didn't even smudge or go to a sweat till I
went to [secure facility]. Maybe if I didn't grow up in
a low income household maybe I wouldn't want the
money so much. I hung around a lot of older guys.
And girls that we used to get each other in trouble. I
lived in a good neighbourhood but the 'hood and [area
of city] attracted me, that's where my friends were. It's
different now. It feels good to make legit money that I
worked hard for. I still have some of the same friends
but I'm closer to my grandma after I opened up to her
and she knew what I was involved in. I was drawn to
the [neighbourhood] 'cause that's where the money
was and the bros [gang members] were.

Historically in Canada, gang suppression strategies have taken precedence over evidence-based treatment and prevention. Unfortunately, scarce resources have been spent on "get tough" approaches, where young gang members are incarcerated at huge financial cost. These ineffective approaches should be stopped.

Gang suppression programs have had, at best, mixed results. Based on the prosecution and conviction of gang members, especially gang leaders, these programs are effective in decreasing gang-related crime in the short term, but fail to address the underlying psychosocial and economic issues that cause gangs to emerge, issues such as child maltreatment, poor mental health, substance abuse, and lack of education and employment opportunities. Suppression initiatives should be used only to complement a range of other interventions.

Incarcerating gang members is the most common approach in Canada, and that does nothing to reduce future criminal behaviour.[49] Studies in both the USA and Canada demonstrate that locking up gang members can *increase* the chances of re-offending and staying in the gang.[50] Likewise, grouping early onset, high-risk youth together can increase the negative bonding among gang members and can lead to even more entrenched anti-social and criminal behaviour. In Canada, a comparison study of 1,955 gang members and inmates who were not gang-involved found that the incarcerated gang members, compared to other inmates who were not gang-involved, were more likely to re-offend, to have employability problems after release, to associate with criminal peers, and to be involved in assaults on prison staff and inmates and in incidents of alcohol seizure.[51]

Grouping young women with young men in the same facility or program can do more harm than good. The boys tend to prey on the girls, and programs designed for young males do not address the needs of young women.[52] When gang members are incarcerated, individualized approaches (such as cognitive-behavioural individual and family therapy) in the facilities work best, but gains are maintained only if adequate resources are provided to support long-term transition into the community after release.

Curriculum-based prevention programs that target youth at

risk for gang involvement (such as the American Gang Resistance Education and Training program and the RCMP Drug Awareness Resistance Education program) produce modest, short-term change. However, follow-up studies have found program participants to be as likely as non-participants to become gang members eventually.[53] Such programs can be enhanced, though, by intensive mentoring and supervising of high-risk students, along with engaging their families.

The conventional detached worker programs, in which social workers, youth and recreation workers, or cultural leaders do outreach into gangs, are particularly ineffective. They can, in fact, do more harm than good by increasing gang cohesion.[54] Modern detached-worker programs have included curriculum components addressing consequences of gang involvement, peer pressure, and substance abuse, but remain ineffective unless they are integrated into a comprehensive and coordinated community-wide approach.

Further, "community development" approaches that assume that there is a single, cohesive "community" do not work, either. There are many competing interests in most reserves and urban neighbourhoods, resulting in divisions according to religious and spiritual lines, access to income and wealth, gender, clans and ethnicities, familial blood lines, and gang allegiances. Effective community development programs must therefore engage these subgroups and address the concerns and priorities of each. Like other successful models, community development approaches must be integrated into a comprehensive and coordinated strategy that includes the *whole* community.

Child welfare models that are based primarily on bringing children and youth into care don't work. Grouping teens with varying degrees of anti-social conduct and attitudes can amount to delinquency training. Negative-attention-seeking behaviour is highly resistant to change: reprimands serve as rewards because they are reinforced by the reaction of peers. Many longitudinal studies demonstrate that association with deviant peers is the strongest variable associated with escalation in problem behaviours in the teen years.[55] Children living in group care face much higher risks of being victimized by bullying, sexual abuse, and physical restraints by staff, and, ultimately, of criminalization. A lack of permanency planning contributes to many children being moved from placement to placement, developing attachment problems and deep-rooted feelings of rejection and shame.

LESSONS FROM CANADIAN PROJECTS

There are a number of lessons to be learned from Canadian projects that prevent high-risk youth from joining gangs and that support the exit of members.

The first lesson relates to the importance of building long-term relationships in multi-year programs: Long-term interventions are best. Short-term projects (i.e., those that are one or two years in duration) cannot address the complex needs of gang-affiliated high-risk youth. Many gang members have grown up in the care of child welfare and justice facilities, often experiencing a high number of placements. Because almost all have suffered severe maltreatment by adults known to them, it is very hard for these young people to trust adults, particularly those in positions of authority. It can hardly be surprising, then, if it takes time for participants to engage in programs.

A second lesson concerns the importance of situating projects within a broader continuum of services. Gang projects that are nested within a larger youth-serving organization or within a community-based spectrum of services have a greater chance of success. Given the complexity of their needs, these young people require interventions that address basic needs (e.g., food, clothing, shelter, and medical needs), schooling, employability, use of leisure time (such as recreation and arts activities), and specialized health problems (such as mental health and FASD).

Next, case management should be a key ingredient of programming. Recreational, artistic, and mentoring programs alone cannot address the complexity of needs in this population. Intensive counselling is required. Staff members should be trained and carefully supervised. Clinical supervision should be regular (for example, bi-weekly) and should include both individual and group supervision. The primary function of the case manager is to coordinate the case plan, ensure that the needs of the clients are addressed, provide regular counselling interventions, and maintain the case files.

Another important lesson relates to the particular needs of girls and young women. Therapeutic programs for girls and young women should be separate and distinct from those geared to boys and young men. Implementing a separate and secure young women's space at a confidential location is important. Female clients do not feel comfortable, nor is it safe, to mix them with male participants in the same program space. Since most gang-affiliated young women have limited employment skills and resort to providing sex, dealing drugs, or both to pay for child care, rent, food, and drugs, paying stipends will motivate women to attend programming consistently. It also decreases their involvement in criminal activities, because they are no longer forced to work the streets or deal drugs for income. Providing access to short-term transitional housing services is also important for women who are escaping from violence or from the control of gang members. Providing access to medical services is critical, because many of these women have serious health problems.

Next, all aspects of programming should be permeated with traditional teachings and cultural practices. The assumption here is that gang identity will decrease when there is increased attachment to a young person's culture. For example, Aboriginal youth should be offered the opportunity to participate in talking circles, sweats, ceremonies, drumming and singing, dancing, restorative justice, and other cultural elements. The staff team should be diverse, reflecting the ethnic and racial origins of the participants. Male and female elders should be consistently available, and paid at the same rate as other staff. Faith-based teachings can be presented as an option to young people who show interest in them.

Another lesson concerns the necessity of providing structured, intentional programming with high-quality adult supervision. By their very nature, gang programs bring high-risk and gang-involved young people in contact with each other. Friendships between program participants will develop. In the absence of highly structured programming and effective adult supervision, there is the chance that youth at risk for gang involvement will become actual gang members for no other reason than they are exposed to these new friends in the intervention.

Next, programs should include strategies to address mental health and trauma. Gang-involved young people have very complex needs. Almost all have suffered extensive trauma and many have mental health needs as a result. Services should be delivered wherever the young person is most comfortable, whether in the home, the neighbourhood, or a facility.

An additional lesson relates to the importance of providing opportunities for meaningful youth engagement. In a positive youth development model, youth are given ample opportunities to participate in the design of programs and the development of governing policies and procedures. This encourages ownership over services, and results in participants who are dedicated. Peer-to-peer mentoring programs can be effective. Many gang-involved youth are too old to qualify for many programs by their early twenties, yet they still need ongoing support and are not ready for independent living. They should be given opportunities to become mentors and youth leaders, where appropriate.

This must involve careful supervision by adult staff and life skills training, and the youth should be paid for their participation. Even a nominal honorarium payment gives participants the clear message that their input and work is valued and appreciated.

Programs should be set up with the knowledge that resisting recruitment into gangs and exiting from gangs will be uneven and difficult. Often, it seems that high-risk young people take one or two steps backward for every two steps forward. This is normal and should be expected. For young people who have grown up in gang families, not joining a gang or, once in, getting out, is incredibly hard. In many cases it means disowning biological family members. The same holds true for those youth who have been recruited into gang life by violence. Leaving, or refusing to join in the first place, can be life-threatening.

Programs should engage family members wherever possible. This is a critical area of intervention and often overlooked in gang programs. Given the fact that many parents of gang-involved youth have complex needs themselves and have survived their own traumatic experiences, there is an identifiable need for parenting classes and coaching. To interrupt cycles of ill-health, violence, and gang involvement, it is often helpful to speak with a parent or the parents either alone or together with their child. The goals of this type of intervention are to have the parents listen to their child and understand the nature of the child's issues; to have the child understand, from the parent's perspective, the causes of the parental problems; and to develop an action plan to address communication and behavioural issues.

Another key lesson is that programs should operate late evenings and weekends—in fact, at all hours. Traditional nine-to-five programs do not work with this population.

Recreational and artistic programming are particularly important to young people trying to exit gangs. Mountain climbing and canoe trips, poker nights, dances, culture camps, rapping,

painting, and beading are examples of activities that can provide opportunities for staff to initiate in-depth discussions with
their clients, giving them a better understanding of their clients'
complex needs. These activities can promote bonding between
participants, many of whom may have been sworn enemies on
the street prior to entering the project.

Staff members should be trained about maintaining appropriate boundaries with youth. This is particularly important
for paraprofessional staff, who rely on their own life experiences as past gang members, sex trade workers, or addicts as
the backbone of their interventions. Although there is nothing
inherently wrong with using this type of staff, ethical dilemmas
often arise, that can be addressed through effective training and
supervision. Typical boundary problems include associating with
gang-involved family or friends outside of work hours; having
knowledge of serious criminal activities of family or friends and
withholding such information from the police; having siblings,
nieces, or nephews involved as participants in programming; or
frequenting bars and clubs at the same time as clients.

Another key lesson relates to the necessity of developing solid
partnerships with police, corrections, schools, social welfare agencies, and cultural groups. Gang intervention and prevention projects
need support and assistance. Partnerships should be developed with
local health, counselling, shelter, recreational, artistic, employment,
and school programs. It is important that case-related information
be shared as much as possible between the individual project and
relevant professionals in these organizations, though this must be
done only with the young person's written consent.

A key dilemma in almost all gang prevention and intervention programs concerns how to involve the police in positive
ways in the lives of participants, especially those who are engaged
in serious criminal activities. Those projects that are able to
develop close working relationships with the police typically have

participants who look upon the police as mentors and counsellors. In such projects, officers spend time, often when they are off duty, with participants. Officers may engage with youth in such recreational, artistic, or employment-related activities as playing sports or cards, or constructing music studios or sweat lodges. Their primary concern is to develop trusting relationships. As the participants develop trusting relationships with the police, they are more likely to ask for support in exiting gangs and for help dealing with serious crimes. It is imperative that police not engage in intelligence-gathering when spending time with participants. A written protocol outlining the terms of the partnership is often helpful. The partnership between the Regina Anti-Gang Services Project (RAGS) and the Regina Police Gang Unit is a good example of an effective partnership.

Finally, programs should develop a plan to deal with the risk of violence to youth and staff, including weapons confiscation. Gang exit projects are fundamentally risky to operate. Gang leaders do not want their members to leave the gang and will resort to threats and violence against staff and program participants to prevent it. The risks should be mitigated through the following steps: setting up a confidential office space with appropriate security; conducting comprehensive intake assessments off-site, including an in-depth examination of the prospective participant's level of motivation; regularly conducting safety audits and discussing risks with the staff team and host agency; implementing a review process for all incidents, including "near misses" (i.e., where acts of violence have been narrowly avoided, such as by removing a loaded gun from a participant).

* * *

The best way to address the gang problem in Canada is to work to prevent high-risk children from joining gangs in the first place.

Compared to criminal justice system strategies, keeping children out of gangs is very cost effective. The second best strategy is to intervene in the lives of youth at risk of gang recruitment and to support the exit from gangs of those who already are involved. This is more expensive than prevention, but nonetheless a key ingredient of success. Failing these two strategies, policing and corrections should be used, and only as a last resort. Putting police on the street and locking up gang members costs a lot of money—although these measures do increase public safety in the short term. Unfortunately, Canada is stuck on the last strategy and puts relatively few resources into prevention and intervention.

For those who want to exit gangs, the journey is long and treacherous. Making the decision to leave is typically related to surviving a life-threatening attack at the hands of a rival gang or one's own gang, wanting to start a family, or just being tired of gang life. Committing suicide or being killed are, unfortunately, common ways to end gang involvement, as are being beaten or raped out. Sometimes geographic relocation works, provided there are high-quality programs and supports in the ex-gang member's new place of residence.

The lessons learned from Canadian initiatives have taught us that certain strategies work, and many others don't. Governments should stop funding those programs that have been proven time and again to be failures, and instead focus scarce resources on those initiatives that have sound scientific evidence demonstrating success.

✳ CHAPTER 10 ✳

SOME FINAL THOUGHTS

Gangs are a symptom, not a cause, of social ills. They grow in areas where social inequality and social injustice thrive. It is too easy to lay the blame solely on gang members for the violent crimes they perpetrate and their own ensuing misery. I am not suggesting that gang members should be let off the hook. They are and should continue to be held accountable for their crimes. Yet criminal justice approaches to gangs will not have the intended effect unless combined with adequately resourced prevention and intervention strategies. If criminal justice strategies actually worked, we should have seen a noticeable decrease in the number of gangs and gang membership in Canada over the past two decades. We should have seen a significant decrease in gang-related homicides and other serious gang crimes. But we have not. Gangs have been present in Canada for a long time. Although it is unclear whether or not the number of gang members and the number of gangs are increasing, they pose a serious risk in Canada. There is solid demographic evidence that rates of gang involvement will dramatically increase among Aboriginal and refugee young people over the next decade. A radical change in thinking is required if Canada is to avert this crisis.

Gangs offer a logical and understandable opportunity for young people whose lives are marked by entrenched poverty, school exclusion, unemployment, racism, gender inequality, emotional and behavioural disorders, imploding families, ineffective child welfare and justice systems, and psychological despair and hopelessness. Gangsters are made, not born. Tragedy defines their young lives. Unimaginable suffering transforms these children into social outcasts. This suffering is well hidden, lying behind a mask of violence or indifference. Do gang members do monstrous things? Absolutely. Were they born this way? Absolutely not. If gang activity is rooted in communities where social inequalities abound, what is to be done?

ENTRENCHED POVERTY

The vast majority of Canadian gang members come from backgrounds of severe poverty. Gangs are not found in all parts of the country, but in pockets of marginalization. These pockets are characterized by chaos and ill health, where a transient population is comprised of a disproportionate number of disenfranchised ethnic and racial minorities. Homelessness, unstable housing, deep poverty, addictions, mental health problems, and disabilities are common among the people who live in these areas. It would thus be inaccurate to characterize whole cities as being gang-infested, despite the stereotypes popularized by the news media. Cities like Toronto, Vancouver, Halifax, Winnipeg, Regina, Edmonton, and Calgary do have gang issues, but these problems are largely confined to small segments of the population living in marginalized neighbourhoods. Some First Nations reserves have serious gang activity as well, but only in a small minority of cases. The majority of First Nations communities are vibrant and healthy, and have low rates of violence and crime.

What works? The negative effects of poverty can be overcome with a positive family environment (e.g., good parenting skills, a stable family unit, and good mental health), positive community supports (e.g., regular involvement in structured, skill-building recreational activities that develop self-esteem; an adult mentor who provides unconditional support and models healthy behaviour); access to high-quality health and social services; positive school experiences (e.g., high engagement, good grades, supportive teachers, development of future academic and vocational interests); and particular individual attributes (e.g., perseverance and determination). At the policy level, concentrating poverty in social housing projects and isolating First Nations peoples on reserves have been abject failures.

SCHOOL EXCLUSION AND UNEMPLOYMENT

Increasing school bonding is an effective way to reduce drop-out and expulsion rates of high-risk students, most of whom are low-income. Staying in school and bonding with adults in schools develops the aspirations of high-risk students, leading to a successful transition into adulthood. High-risk youth who graduate from secondary school are much more likely to be employed than school drop-outs are.

Gang members often lack legitimate employment opportunities because of exclusion from school and a lack of jobs in their communities. Even if gang members can get through high school, the vast majority do not have the money to pursue post-secondary education. The lack of employment opportunities for youth in many communities goes a long way toward explaining the economic foundation of gangs.

Gangs, like legitimate businesses, provide an opportunity structure for earning a wage. Members who have been involved in a gang for a relatively long period usually have to stay in the gang for social and economic reasons. They have been out of the legitimate labour market for too long to re-enter it. But young people who have been involved for a relatively brief period have a much easier time getting legitimate jobs once they exit.

What's to be done about school exclusion and unemployment? Aboriginal and minority students need special support to have successful experiences in school. This involves cultural competence—where Aboriginal and minority children learn about and are exposed to cultural activities. It is far too easy for administrators to suspend and expel high-risk students. Instead, school boards should develop stay-in-school initiatives for them. If suspensions are warranted, the student should serve them in the school, where adequate supervision and support can be provided. The families of such students should be included in school life, particularly when it comes to celebrating their children's successes. Refugee and new-Canadian students have unique needs, including language barriers. Often they are highly traumatized from having experienced war atrocities. Parents are often afraid of school authorities, believing that they will be deported if administrators come in contact with them.

Employment initiatives are particularly important both for preventing youth from becoming involved in gangs and for supporting their exits. The vast majority of gang members come from communities where unemployment has been rampant for many years. Not only are there no jobs for them, but their parents and grandparents have not been able to secure steady employment either. Children exposed to intergenerational unemployment learn that keeping a legitimate job is virtually impossible. It is not surprising, therefore, when they turn to crime.

It should be obvious that young people need meaningful job experiences that provide adequate wages. High-risk youth need supports to find and keep jobs. This involves training and on-the-job coaching. These young people have to be shown how to turn their strengths into marketable skills and how to develop passion for a career before they will see legitimate employment as a viable alternative to gangs as work.

RACISM

Discrimination and social exclusion are parts of daily life for many youth, both those who are at high risk for gang involvement and those who are already gang members. There are many positive aspects of gang life for Aboriginal and minority young people, including a sense of family and belonging, a safe place to hang out with friends, an identity, and protection. Gangs can also provide a shelter for young people who have suffered from racism, war atrocities, and the adverse effects of colonization. Some gang members develop a sense of cultural pride and see gang crimes as a way to fight back against social injustice.

Extreme social and cultural marginalization often intersect with poverty (this is called racialized poverty). We cannot assume that gang activity is a "reserve problem," out of sight and out of mind. Many Aboriginal young people are leaving their reserves because of intolerable living conditions. Young people from sub-Saharan Africa and other war-torn countries are also highly over-represented in gangs in Canada. These war-affected young people, having experienced atrocities and having been forced into child soldiering, arrive in Canada highly trained to engage in violence and well-suited to gang life. They do not get the specialized programs they need to address educational, economic, and psychosocial challenges. Gang leaders can spot these traumatized kids a mile away.

Some people take great relief in the fact that gang members seem to like killing each other off—as if in a distorted Darwinian process. Who cares if one Aboriginal person kills another, so long as they keep it all in the family? Or so what if blacks are murdering blacks, so long as it does not impact upon "us"? What is behind this dynamic? I argue that it is a case of the Aboriginal person killing the Aboriginal within, the black killing the black part of himself. It is an extreme form of self-hatred.

In broader Canadian society, Aboriginals are relegated to

the bottom rungs of the social hierarchy. Aboriginals, ethnic minorities, and racial minorities are most likely to experience blocked opportunities in school and the labour market. Because of racism, their access to legitimate business opportunities is blocked. Aboriginal gang members are no different: racism is alive and well in the criminal underworld. In their relationships with other gangs and criminal organizations, they are left to do the less lucrative and lower status jobs.

How can racism be addressed? Immigrant and Aboriginal youth with strong academic aspirations and positive family backgrounds are unlikely to become involved in gangs. But the more that youth and their parents suffer from economic and social marginalization, the greater the risk of gang recruitment. Anti-poverty and school inclusion strategies are thus important. On the other hand, some gang members come from relatively affluent backgrounds. Their parents work long hours, often at more than one job, but when the parents are absent their children lack of supervision. It is a form of neglect, and some of these youth turn to gangs. Cultural leaders need to sensitize parents on this topic.

GENDER INEQUALITY

Gender inequalities in gangs are a reflection of gender-based discrimination in broader Canadian society. Gender-based violence does not happen only in gangs; woman abuse is widespread in Canadian families and dating relationships, and many more men kill their spouses than women kill their male partners. All that being said, gender does play a key role in gang life. The vast majority of gangs in Canada are male-dominated, and women tend to be in subservient positions. Young women in gangs face various risks at the hands of men: female members of all-women street gangs are relatively safe from male violence, but women who are affiliated with male-dominated gangs and street women in the sex trade face elevated levels of violence from gang-involved men. Although an increasing number of female gang members sexually exploit and traffic girls, male gang members are far more likely to do this. Many of the women in my studies have been trafficked. Gang members, both male and female, have made large sums of money forcing these women to work in the sex trade across the country. Each such woman I studied was forcibly taken against her will by members of a rival gang and forced to work the streets in other provinces. Each was gang raped and beaten by these men as well before they managed to escape their captors and make their way back to their home cities.

Pathways into gangs are gendered as well. Almost all female gang members have been severely sexually abused by men that they knew, long before they ever became involved in gangs. Many male gang members have likewise been sexually abused by male family members or other male acquaintances. Although male and female gang members are physically and emotionally abused by both male and female caregivers, men by far leave the most serious injuries.

The needs of gay, lesbian, bisexual, and transgender (GLBT) gang members are quite different from those of heterosexual gang members. Of all gang members, these young people likely face the highest risk of life-threatening harm. This risk is directly related to the extreme homophobia that characterizes many male-dominated, heterosexual gang activities. Sadly, these GLBT young people have turned to the streets to escape brutal maltreatment at home, which, for many, was directly related to rejection by their caregivers. They chose gangs for acceptance and belonging—where homophobic violence was likely just as harmful as what they experienced at home.

How can gender inequality be addressed? Prevention and intervention programs should employ gender-appropriate staff and the focus of programming should be on trauma, mental health, parenting, healthy relationships, life skills development, self-injurious behaviour, and a harm reduction philosophy. Gender responsiveness is founded upon specific principles rooted in developmental, psychological, and social characteristics. Programs for female gang members in particular must address their unique needs. As well, much more research is needed into the backgrounds and activities of both male and female gang members who sexually exploit and traffic young women. It is not good enough only to help the victims: high-quality prevention, intervention, and suppression strategies are required that target the persons perpetrating these crimes.

IMPLODING FAMILIES

The families of origin for almost all gang members are extremely problematic. It is hard to find a gang member who has not experienced violence and neglect at the hands of caregivers, or parental addictions, intergenerational incarceration of caregivers, absent or unhealthy fathers, or socialization into criminal and gang lifestyles. Parents have a key role to play in preventing their children from becoming gang members. They can't do it on their own, however. Families don't implode if they can get the resources and supports required to increase their health. Most of these families have problems that are so severe that either they don't get the help they need or they are constantly one step ahead of the authorities who should be supporting them (such as child welfare, police, school, and health officials).

What works? There is solid scientific evidence that epidemics are best prevented by using public health approaches. The inoculation of millions of people in Canada against the H1N1 flu virus is a recent example. Canada must confront the public health epidemic of child maltreatment and woman abuse using a similar, broad-based approach. The effects of suffering violence are so profound, and the numbers of individuals involved are so staggering, that traditional methods of intervention are inadequate.

For parents with complex needs to get help, they have to be identified when their children are young and they have to be motivated to get support. The best programs are strengths-based and family-centred. Such strategies have formal systems in place to identify needy children at a very young age. (Typically, these young children exhibit emotional and behavioural disorders involving aggression and other conduct problems.) In communities where these strategies are working well, there is a round table of various professionals that meet regularly to share information and to provide required supports. Typically, representatives from education, the police, youth justice, child welfare, recreation, social services, and public health sit on this committee. When a high-risk family is identified, a plan is developed to introduce services to the family in a positive manner that builds upon strengths and culture (which is an essential ingredient of the strategy). If families feel threatened or singled out, they will not be motivated to participate, so programs that work well usually introduce non-threatening services at the start, such as offering a single parent mother free access to children's recreational and arts programs, or giving her the option to be reimbursed for recreation-related expenses such as bikes for her children. Next, supports are offered related to daycare, social assistance, and health. Parent training is a key aspect of this approach. It is much more effective to train parents in appropriate child rearing techniques than to use the heavy hand of the child welfare system to remove children from the family home. The concept of in-home visitation by a public health nurse can also be introduced—it is the best way to prevent child maltreatment and neglect. Once trusting relationships have been built, complex issues such as healthy relationships and the impact of familial gang involvement can be addressed.

EMOTIONAL AND BEHAVIOURAL DISORDERS

Almost all gang members have had emotional and behavioural disorders, and approximately one in five children in the general population exhibit symptoms. Scientific evidence demonstrates that current services only reach 20 per cent of all young people with these disorders, to which suffering violence is a key contributor. When these children, youth, and families receive cross-sectoral coordinated services, their functioning substantially improves at school, at home, and in their community. Rates of child maltreatment and woman abuse are dramatically reduced in communities where all individuals, organizations, and sectors involved in the well-being of families and young people work in partnership to deliver a seamless and comprehensive continuum of prevention and intervention services.

INEFFECTIVE CHILD WELFARE AND JUSTICE SYSTEMS

The Canadian child welfare and youth justice systems are in deep trouble. If a child is not born into a gang family, the next best way to become gang-involved is to bounce around in multiple foster homes, group homes, and secure young offender facilities. Long-term involvement in these systems is a pipeline into gang life for far too many youth. Young people searching for an identity, a source of income, and a sense of family are placed in an environment that is a breeding-ground for gangs. Jails and prisons are no better—most are so gang-infested that administrators place gang-involved inmates on ranges with other inmates who belong to the same gang. This can reduce gang rivalry and the ensuing violence.

We need to radically reconceptualize these systems. Minor tinkering is not sufficient. Although some child welfare agencies have undergone major changes, the vast majority still rely on placement in group and foster homes as the backbone of their programs. Although external placements are sometimes needed, often these homes are overcrowded, understaffed, under-resourced, and dumping grounds for complex-need children with severe problems. Placement of high-risk young people in the same environment is a recipe for disaster; there is no better predictor of anti-social behavior than a negative peer group.

What's to be done? Instead of removing children from their families, intensive resources need to be pumped into high-risk families. Although there is a role for external placements, such options should be short-term and predicated on family reunification wherever possible. The goal is to provide supports in children's natural environment, not to extract them from the family home. Resources should focus on parenting, violence prevention, physical and mental health needs, and respite care for parents. Given the high cost of residential placements, home-based services are still much more cost-effective (even if offered on a full-time basis). In addition, the over-representation of Aboriginal and racial minority children in foster and group homes is a serious matter. Far more Aboriginal kids are in care now than at the height of the residential school system and, unfortunately, many of these children are placed in white settings, where their culture is inaccessible.

The situation in the youth and adult justice systems is no better. We can't incarcerate nor punish our way out of the gang problem. Putting more police on the street, building more prison cells, and lengthening sentences have absolutely no positive effect on crime rates, recidivism, or deterrence. In fact, there is good evidence that these strategies actually increase gang crimes and make offenders more entrenched in their gang's activities. Merely moving the bad guys off the street is a short-term solution.

Of particular concern once again is the situation of Aboriginal offenders. Despite making up a relatively small proportion of the Canadian population, Aboriginals make up a large portion of those incarcerated, in both the youth and adult systems. It seems to me that incarceration and institutionalization comprise a major plank of the federal government's policy towards Aboriginal peoples in Canada.

PSYCHOLOGICAL DESPAIR AND HOPELESSNESS

By the time gang members reach young adulthood, they are emotionally numb and resigned to getting out of their gang only if they die or spend prolonged periods of time in protective custody. Their souls are barely alive, their spirits barely ticking. Their psychic wounds are so profoundly deep, the cuts to their souls so severe, that they can communicate only through violence and intimidation. It is too painful for them to acknowledge their suffering. Heavy drug and alcohol use mask this pain, further freezing their psyches.

Many gang members have fathers and uncles who have spent decades in prison. It is seen as a legitimate option in the context of poverty: three meals a day, no rent to pay, status, and a good way to meet new associates to commit crimes once back on the outside. The case of gang-involved Aboriginal young men is particularly disturbing. Most have experienced multiple losses of family members and friends through suicide, accidental death, homicide, and illness (AIDS, diabetes, cirrhosis, etc.). Many have had close brushes with death themselves. To them, life is short and fleeting. Dying young is not such a bad thing if one can go down in a blaze of glory, as in a gang homicide, police shooting, or prison break.

How do gang members create meaning out of psychologically homeless lives? Psychological thrills are gained from committing crimes like home invasions. Engagement in violence has been shown to light up the brain like a Christmas tree in some people. This is a "power high." Young gang members with few resources find excitement and adventure in violent crime, simultaneously finding an outlet to express their anger and rage. They create their own excitement and thrills through crime, violence, and substance abuse to contrast with the boring, daily drudgery of hanging out. Gang members are able to momentarily transcend their despair, their lack of power, and the hopelessness of their daily lives at these times.

In general, gang members have been systematically excluded and devalued at every single moment in their lives. It is not only that they have suffered tremendous violence and neglect, and bounced from pillar to post; suffering has not been acknowledged, and their lives have not been valued. Their deep emotional wounds are hidden. Communities that provide young people with a voice and meaningful opportunities for engagement have lower rates of violence and anti-social behavior. When all young people are included, especially the most vulnerable, they all achieve their fullest potential.

Poverty, school exclusion and unemployment, racism, gender inequality, imploding families, ineffective child welfare and justice systems, and a lack of support for children with emotional and behavioural disorders are systemic factors that have marginalized certain groups of people within our society: the development of gangs is simply one logical response. If we as a society are not going to address the systemic problems, gangs will step in and create their own solutions. New collaboration and problem-solving partnerships are required in Canada. We must examine gangs in a broader social context by addressing the link between individual life experiences and social and economic inequalities. Community mobilization is needed, where adults, youth, community groups, leaders, and agencies engage to develop and plan opportunities and to coordinate linkages to existing organizations.

* * *

You have been introduced to many of the young adults I have interviewed and spent time with over the past seventeen years. This book is about their stories and their reflections on life. I have tried to give them a voice and to build stories around their narratives. I have listened attentively to their words and tried to accurately illustrate, from their perspectives, the complexities of gang life in Canada. What have I learned from the 519 young people in my studies? I have learned that they are much more than gang members. They are sons, daughters, nephews, nieces, and grandchildren. Many are parents, although few have access to their children. All have special talents and skills, often unrecognized because nobody has taken the time to look for them. Many have good business savvy and excellent leadership skills. When society sees them as only gangsters, their talents and skills remain hidden: the solution to the gang problem in part involves uncovering what gang members are good at, their strengths, their hopes for the future, their talents. Most gang members are remarkably resilient. They have stared down what have seemed to be insurmountable challenges and have come out as strong young people.

Carolyn's letter to her two daughters, both in the care of child welfare, is a good illustration of the resiliency and determination of the participants in my studies. It is also a poignant reminder of how gang involvement can tear families apart. Once a gang leader, addicted to hard drugs, and subjected to brutal violence from her boyfriend, Carolyn exited her gang, left her partner, stopped the drugs, and took parenting classes. She is determined to get her daughters back.

> *Hello my girls! I think of you both often and miss*
> *you very much. I wish I could be there for you both,*
> *but, I can't right now. I'm sorry I haven't written*
> *you girls for a long time, but I'll try to write more.*
> *I love you, I want you to always remember that, no*

matter what. I hope you both understand one day why I wasn't there. But don't listen to other people. Always know that I love you and I want to be a part of your lives, just that bad things happened and maybe one day I'll be able to see you both again. Please don't give up on me, because I will never give up on you both, no matter what. I love you.

We must learn from the tragic deaths of so many gang-involved young people in Canada. Ten youth involved in my studies have died over the past two years: two committed suicide, one young woman was killed by a male gang member, and another two died from an overdose. These deaths were all preventable and more will occur if we fail to act, and more gang members afflicted with AIDS and other serious illnesses will die in the near future.

Many more young people I have gotten to know have attempted suicide often, have been stabbed or shot, or have had their lives put at risk in other ways. Somehow they escaped death. A significant minority has been convicted of murder and manslaughter. Traumatic rage fuelled these killings.

Still others have had family members die violently. The mother of Kim, an ex-gang member, was murdered five years ago by Kim's father, who then killed himself. The brother of Christine was murdered last year. Jimmy witnessed the murder of his father and uncle when he was eight. He also witnessed the attempted murder of his two brothers in the same incident. While Jeremy was sitting on his father's lap at age three, his father's head was blown off by a gunshot.

Perhaps the best way to conclude this book is with a quote from fifteen-year-old Shelly, who was struggling with addictions, involvement in the sex trade, and gang life. She was a participant in a program for gang-involved youth. Despite her many challenges, she was hopeful about her future. She told me:

But now being in this program, I have…somewhere to discuss the person who I am, the person I can be, and the achievements I can make with my life. I love that I have somewhere I can come, call home, and talk to someone truthfully about how I feel and what I can do to improve myself. I learned that I have somewhere to go where people [will] support me, and [help me] be the real me. Somewhere that I feel comfortable sharing my life experiences. I learned I can be a positive person, who can be sober knowing I have my supports here to help me achieve the life I want for myself.

ENDNOTES

CHAPTER 1

1. Pseudonyms are used for all young people to ensure confidentiality.

2. Goldstein, 1991; Decker and Van Winkle, 1996.

3. Davies, 1998; Humphries, 1995.

4. LeBlanc and Lancot, 1994; Gay and Marquart, 1993; Klein, 2002; Joe and Robinson, 1980.

5. Giles, 2000.

6. My research for this book is based on a sample of 290 gang members derived from a series of six Canadian qualitative investigations on gangs over a ten-year period (1995 – 2005), as well as an additional 229 gang members who were participants in two large-scale gang program evaluation studies over the past five years. These studies took place in various geographic regions of the country. They include: *Youth Services Bureau 1999 Youth Survey* (Totten, 2000a; n = 51 gang members); 2000 *Guys, Gangs and Girlfriend Abuse* (Totten, 2000b; n = 90 gang members), 2001 *Serious Youth Violence Study* (Totten and Reid, 2002; n = 31 gang members), 2002 *When Children Kill Study* (Kelly and Totten, 2002; n = 9 gang members), 2003 *Youth Literacy and Violence Prevention Study* (Totten, 2002b; n = 84 gang members), 2005 *Gays in the Gang Study* (Totten, 2011b; n = 25 gang members), and the evaluations of two large gang projects in Western Canada (Totten and Dunn, 2011a,b).

7. Fifty-seven per cent (297) had done both youth and adult time; nine per cent (48) had done youth time only; and three per cent (15) had done adult time only.

8. Random sampling is not possible because the total number of street gang members in Canada is unknown, it is very difficult to access gangs, there is

no available list of gang member names and contact information, and not all potential participants want to participate.

9. In the fields of criminology, sociology, and anthropology, there is an established tradition of qualitative research on street gangs in naturally occurring settings using methods that capture the social meanings of the actions and ordinary activities of members. Like my research, this involves spending long periods watching members, coupled with talking to them about what they are doing, thinking, and saying. The goal is to see how they understand their world and to learn as much as possible about their lives. (For example, see Thrasher, 1927; Whyte, 1943; Spergel, 1964; Keiser, 1969; Moore,1978; Campbell, 1990; Hagedorn and Macon,1988; Sanchez-Jankowski, 1991).

10. Interviews in the two gang evaluation studies were not recorded because the evaluation measures consisted of quantitative surveys.

11. Including the conflict tactics scales (Strauss, 1990), the sexual experiences survey (Koss and Gidyzc), the Rochester Youth Development Study Depression scale, and the Rutgers Teenage Risk and Prevention Questionnaire.

12. Many of these scales can be found in the Centers for Disease Control's *Measuring Violence-related Attitudes, Behaviors, and Influences Among Youths* (2005).

13. The average structured evaluation interviews took from sixty to ninety minutes. For both studies, a baseline survey was administered at the point of intake, and follow-up interviews were conducted at six-month intervals thereafter. The follow-up surveys consisted of modified versions of the baseline surveys and were considerably shortened. Since most participants had long-term involvement in the programs, most had six-, twelve-, eighteen-, and twenty-four month follow-up measures.

14. Glaser and Straus, 1967.

15. Grounded theory provides the structure often lacking in other qualitative approaches without sacrificing flexibility or rigor. The resulting theory is an explanation of categories, their properties, and the relationships among them. The results lead to an evolutionary body of knowledge that is grounded in data. The in-depth interview data were transcriptions from the interview audio tapes and hand-written notes. The 290 qualitative interviews yielded thousands of pages of transcripts and many more pages of related documentation. The development of coding categories involves the interaction of theoretical concerns with the empirical observations contained in the data. For each qualitative study, the vast amount of data collected in the interviews was organized into analytical categories. The analytical process focused on similarities and differences among participants and attempted to understand what would account for these.

16. SPSS (Statistical Package for the Social Sciences) was this database.

17. Denzin, 1989.

18. Rabon, 1994.

CHAPTER 2

1. Totten, 2008, 2009a, b.

2. Mellor et al., 2005.

3. Young adults are defined as those between 12 and 30 years.

4. Totten, 2000b, 2001; Gordon, 2000.

5. Totten, 2008; Mellor et al., 2005.

6. Block and Block, 2001.

7. Klein, 2002.

8. Grennan et al., 2000.

9. Totten and Dunn, 2011a, 2011b.

10. Mathews, 1993, 2.

11. Totten, 2008.

12. Valdez, 2000.

13. Ibid.

14. CISS, 2005.

15. Totten and Dunn, 2011a; Totten and Dunn, 2011b.

16. Totten, 2011a, b; CSC, 2004; CISC; 2004; Knox, 2000; Leet, Rush, and Smith, 2000; Stone, 2002; Sanders, 1993.

17. Knox, 2000.

18. Ibid.

19. Totten, 2011a, 2006a; Jackson and McBride, 2000; Leet, Rush, and Smith, 2000.

20. Totten, 2008.

21. Galabuzi, 2001.

22. Ibid; Ornstein, 2006; Totten, 2005.

23. Anisef and Kilbride, 2003; Galabuzi, 2002; Noh et al., 1999; Surko et al., 2005.

24. Statistics Canada, 2004.

25. Berry et al., 2006; Anisef and Kilbride, 2003; Khanlou and Crawford, 2006; Beiser, 2005; Beiser and Hyman, 1997.

26. Beiser, 2005.

27. Kanu, 2008.

28. Ibid.

29. Wortley and Tanner, 2006.

30. Ibid.

31. Statistics Canada, 2008a.

32. Bittle et al., 2002; Dooley et al., 2005.

33. Shah 1990; York 1990; Statistics Canada 2001; Chandler et al. 2003.

34. Meaning overrepresentation at all stages of the criminal justice system (Statistics Canada 2006a, 2008b).

35. Statistics Canada 2006a, 2008b; Canada, 1990; RCAP 1996.

36. NWAC, 2010.

37. Farley and Lynne, 2005; Lynne, 2005; Farley, Lynne and Cotton, 2005.

38. RCAP, 1996; Statistics Canada, 2001.

39. This includes institutionalization in child welfare, justice and mental health facilities (Grekul and LaBoucane-Benson, 2006; Trevethan et al., 2002; Blackstock et al., 2004).

40. Including the Astwood survey, which asked police officers to estimate the number of youth gangs in their jurisdiction (2004).

41. Totten, 2003; Gordon, 2000; CISC, 2004; Astwood Strategy Corp., 2004; Gordon and Foley, 1998; Hamel et al., 1998; Craig et al., 2002.

42. Nafekh and Stys, 2004; Nafekh, 2002.

43. Totten, 2008.

44. RCMP, 1997.

45. Group of Ten, 2004.

46. Astwood Strategy Corp., 2004.

47. Young and Craig, 1997.

48. Hamm, 2001.

CHAPTER 3

1. For example, see Gordon, 2000; Nimmo, 2001; Totten, 2009a, 2008, 2000b.

2. CISC, 2010.

3. These data on gang activity come from a number of sources, including interviews conducted by Mark Totten with gang members across Canada; CISC and RCMP reports; and confidential interviews with municipal, provincial, and federal law enforcement organizations.

4. RCMP, 2010.

5. Based on data from the Canadian Centre for Justice Statistics, Statistics Canada.

6. The VVT is a Tamil gang in Toronto founded in the early 1990s by Tamil

immigrants. It has been engaged in a rivalry with another Tamil gang, the AK Kannan. They are involved in drug trafficking, human smuggling, fraud, weapons trafficking, counterfeiting, and extortion.

7. These gangs include the Southside Crips, Cedarwood Crips, H-Block Crips, Hells Angels, Asian Boyz, Viet Boyz, Overbrook Bloods, Baycrest Crips, Eastside Mafia Crips, D Block Mobstaz, Sandlewood Crips, Huntclub Crips , Russel Ridas, Russel Crips, Overbrook Crips, Donald Project Gangstas, and Double R Bloods.

CHAPTER 4

1. Totten, 2012, 2002a, c.

2. Totten, 2009b, 2004b; Miller, 2001; Chesney-Lind and Hagedorn, 1999.

3. Moore, 2007.

4. Ibid.

5. Totten, 2009b.

6. Campbell, 1990; Curry, 1998.

7. Totten, 2009b.

8. Campbell, 1987, pp. 463-464.

9. Nimmo, 2001.

10. Brotherton, 1996; Deschenes and Esbenson, 1999

11. Chesney-Lind et al., 1996; Miller, 1998; Lurigio, Swartz, and Chang, 1998

12. Miller, 2001.

13. Fishman, 1999.

14. See Totten, 2011b.

15. On Feb 3, 2009, twenty-two year-old Brianna Kinnear was shot to death in Coquitlam. She was known to police as a crack cocaine dealer. Police reported that the shooting was gang related. A couple of weeks after Kinnear's murder, twenty-three year-old Nikkie Alemy, mother to a young child and also known to be associated with the United Nations gang, was also shot dead in Surrey. In March 2009, Laura Lamoureux, aged thirty-six, was also shot dead in Langley. Police reported it to be related to her involvement in the street-level drug trade.

CHAPTER 5

1. This term was first coined by Athens in 2003.

2. Totten, 2012 .

3. Hardy and Laszloffy, 2005.

4. Howard et al., 1999; Luthar et al., 2000; Smokowski et al., 1999.

5. Dekovic, 1999; Gutman and Midgley, 2000; Smokowski et al., 1999; Voydanoff and Donnelly, 1999.

6. McCreary Center Society, 1999a.

7. Totten 2012, 2009a.

8. MacMillan et al., 1997; Macmillan, 2000.

9. Trocme et al., 2001; Totten, 2000b; MacMillan et al., 1997; MacMillan, 2000.

10. Perry, 1995; Sappington et al, 1997.

11. MacMillan, 2000.

12. Sudermann and Jaffe, 1999; Peled, 1997.

13. Jaffe and Reitzel, 1990; Johnson, 1996; Sappington et al, 1997.

14. Totten, 2002c.

15. Totten, 2012, 2008, 2000b.

16. Totten 2009a, 2009b; Totten and Dunn, 2011a,b.

17. Trocme et al 2004; Blackstock et al. 2004.

18. Trocme et al., 2005.

19. Thobani, 2007; Child Welfare Anti-Oppression Roundtable, 2009.

20. Chapter 6 discusses attachment disorders in detail.

21. McCreary Center Society, 1999a.

22. Kelly and Totten, 2002.

23. Plomin and Crabbe, 2000.

24. Moffitt et al., 2001.

25. Buxton, 2004; Kyskan and Moore, 2005

26. Stark, 2004.

27. Rhee and Waldman, 2002; Moffitt, 2005.

28. Shaw, 2001; Sprott, Doob and Jenkins, 2001.

29. Offord and Lipman, 1996.

30. Offord, Boyle and Racine, 1990; Offord, Lipman and Duka, 1998; Offord et al., 1998.

31. FAS diagnosis requires a confirmed history of maternal alcohol consumption, evidence of facial dysmorphology, growth retardation, and central nervous system dysfunction. It is the most severe developmental impairment on the spectrum.

32. Currently, FAE and ARBD are understood to fall within the broader term ARND. Individuals with ARND are unlikely to have the facial malformations but have central nervous system impairment.

33. Chavez, Cordero and Becerra 1988; Sokol and Clarren, 1989; Sampson et al., 1997, 1994.

34. Roberts and Nanson, 2000; Health Canada, 2003.

35. Prevalence rates for FASD in these studies range widely from 7.2 to 190 per thousand live births (Robinson, Conry and Conry, 1987; Williams, Odaibo, and McGee, 1999). Fetal Alcohol Syndrome prevalence ranges from 0.515 to 101 per thousand live births (Square, 1997; Asante and Nelms-Maztke, 1985; Habbick et al., 1996).

36. Tait, 2003.

37. For example, Tait (2003) argues that the behavioural and cognitive effects of suffering physical and sexual abuse in residential schools are comparable to the behavioural and cognitive effects of FASD—and in the absence of concrete evidence of a mother's alcohol abuse during pregnancy, it is entirely plausible that the trauma suffered in residential schools (and not prenatal alcohol abuse) is the root cause of developmental delays and other disabilities.

38. Masotti et al., 2006.

39. Sokol, Delaney-Black, and Nordstrom, 2003.

40. Durst and Bluechardt, 2001; OFIFC, 2000.

41. Totten, Dunn, and NWAC, 2011c.

42. Ibid; Murphy, Chittenden, and The McCreary Centre Society, 2005.

43. Durst and Bluechardt, 2001.

44. Pardini and Loeber, 2008; May et al., 2006; Fast and Conry, 2004.

45. Grant et al., 2006.

46. The issue of ""inappropriate" sexual behavior is addressed in the section on FASD and Sexual Exploitation.

47. Streissguth et al., 2004, 1997, 1996; Brown and Fudge Schormans, 2004.

48. Totten, 2012.

49. Such as withdrawal, anxiety, eating disorders, and suicidal behavior.

50. Such as hyperactivity, concentration problems, and aggression.

51. Webster-Stratton and Lindsay, 1999; Crick and Werner, 1998; Wyatt and Haskett, 2001; Coie and Dodge, 1998

52. Brown et al., 2000, 2001.

53. Offord and Lipman, 1996; Offord, Lipman and Duka, 1998; Totten and Quigley, 2003.

54. Kelly and Totten, 2002.

55. Skiba and Peterson, 1999; Sprott, Jenkins, and Doob, 2000.

56. Totten and Quigley, 2003; Sprott, Doob, and Jenkins, 2001; Sprott,

Jenkins, and Doob, 2000; Mahoney, 2000; The President and Fellows of Harvard College, 2002; Munn, Lloyd, and Cullen, 2002.

57. Totten and Quigley, 2003.

58. Totten, 2000b.

59. Ibid.

60. Examples include Michael Le and Konaam Shirzad (Red Scorpions), Clayton Roueche, Jing Bon Chan, Evan Appell (UN gang), and Tyshan Riley, Jason Atkins and Jason Wisdom (Galloway Boys).

61. Jackson et al., 2001.

62. Totten, 2008.

63. For example, see Strohschein, 2005.

64. See Sampson, 1993. In New Zealand, for example, most adolescents who exhibit several behavioural problems come from very poor and dysfunctional families. Only one out of every 400 – 500 children from economically advantaged homes becomes a multi-problem adolescent, and 80 percent have no problems at all (Fergusson et al, 1994).

65. Gutman et al., 2005

66. Statistics Canada, 2002.

CHAPTER 6

1. MacMillan, 2000.

2. Young and Klosko, 1994.

3. Bettelheim, 1974; Crenshaw and Garbarino, 2007.

4. Young and Klosko, 1994.

5. Ibid.

6. www.knowledge.offordcentre.com

7. Ibid.

8. Statistics Canada, 2006a, 2006b, 2006c.

9. Ontario Native Women's Association, 1989.

10. Amnesty International, 2004.

11. Statistics Canada, 2006a.

12. CAEFS and NWAC, 2006.

13. NWAC, 2010.

14. Examples of these families include the Wolfes, Raphaels, Bacons, Worms, Sangheras, Singhs, and Buttars.

15. Examples of brothers in arms include:

• Bobby, Navdip, and Savdip Sanghera (the Sanghera crime family)

• Amandeep and Sonny Manj
• Sukhveer and Gurmit Dhak
• Sandup, Balraj and Paul Duhre
• Sukvinder (Bicky) Singh Dosanjh (killed in a car accident), Gerpal (Paul Singh Dosanjh (killed), and their cousins Ron and Jimmy Dosanjh (both killed).
• Peter and Mike Adiwal (Peter was shot dead)
• Tommy and Sammy Chan (Tommy was killed)
• Bal (blind and paralyzed after being shot), Kelly (murdered) and Manny Buttar
• Jamie, Jerrod, and Jonathan Bacon (Jonathan was murdered)
• Jacob, Richard, and Tyrone Worm
• Richard Daniel and Daniel Richard Wolf (Richard was murdered)
• Roland and Roger Chin (FOB)
• Timothy and Nicholas Chan (FOB)
• Half brothers Tyshan Riley and Courtney Francis (Galloway Boys)
• Cody, Willie, Bruce, and Russell Knife (NS)
• Pierre Antoine, Miguel, Philistin, Gregoire and Jocelyn Paul (Blood Mafia Family, Montreal)
• Jermaine and Kevin Ebanks (Versace Crew, Toronto)
• Raphael brothers

CHAPTER 7

1. Totten and Dunn, 2011a; Totten and Dunn, 2011b; Totten, 2012, Totten and NWAC, 2010.

2. Totten and NWAC, 2010; Totten, Dunn and NWAC, 2011; Sikka, 2009; Sethi, 2007.

3. Totten, 2009b; Totten and NWAC, 2010.

4. This definition is based on the United Nations Protocol to Prevent, Suppress and Punish Trafficking in Persons, Especially Women and Children, Article 3.

5. Amnesty International 2004.

6. Totten, 2009b; Totten and NWAC, 2010.

7. Totten and Dunn, 2011b.

8. NWAC, 2008; Amnesty International, 2004.

9. Such as the family, school, peer group, media, religion, professional sports, and the military.

10. Totten, 2000b.

11. See Totten, 2000b, for an in-depth discussion on this.

12. Totten 2012, 2000b.

13. Blagg 2000.

14. For example, see Whitbeck et al., 2004; Kitts, 2005.

15. Hagedorn, 1994; Harry, 1992; Weissman, 1992; Katz, 1988.

16. Victims include Larry King, Scott Joe Weaver, Arthur Warren, Billy Jack Gaither, Matthew Shepard, Barry Winchell, and Scott Amedure among others.

17. For example, see Chambliss, 1973; Spergel and Curry, 1988; Curry and Spergel, 1991; Sullivan, 1989.

18. Sex is used here to mean the biological status of being male or female. Sexual orientation refers to the direction of sexual, emotional, and physical attraction (heterosexual, lesbian, gay). Gender refers to the social beliefs, meanings and behaviour ascribed to masculinity and femininity. Whereas sex is physiological, gender is socially constructed and learned (Herek, 1992).

19. Totten, 2011b.

20. Questions on sexual orientation were not included on the questionnaires but were used on participants in the two gang studies conducted by Sharon Dunn and myself (229 gang members).

21. Transsexuals are transgender people who live or wish to live full-time as members opposite to their birth sex. This definition is found in the American Psychological Association (2006), *Answers to Your Questions About Transgender Individuals and Gender Identity.*

22. Homophobia is likely a result of repressed same-sex urges or a form of latent homosexuality. Latent homosexuality is the term used to denote homosexual arousal that the individual is either unaware of or denies (Adams et al., 1996). The concept of repressed or latent homosexuality is useful to explain the emotional malaise and irrational attitudes displayed by some individuals who feel guilty about their erotic interests and struggle to deny and repress homosexual impulses (Herek 1984). Homophobic men show more sexual arousal to homosexual cues than non-homophobic men. Those with the most homophobic attitudes tend to be repressed homosexuals (Adams et al., 1996).

23. Rich, 1980.

24. Campbell, 1987.

CHAPTER 8
1. Merton, 1938; Cloward and Ohlin, 1960.

2. Spergel, 1995.

3. Levitt and Venkatesh, 2000.

4. Hagedorn, 1994.

5. For example, vitamins or skin care products.

6. Levitt and Venkatesh, 2000.

CHAPTER 9

1. Office of the Parliamentary Budget Officer, 2010.

2. Statistics Canada, 2010.

3. MacMillan, 2000; MacMillan, Fleming and Trocme, 1997.

4. Totten, 2009a.

5. Totten, 2008.

6. "Getting down with my gang" means hanging out with the gang. "Getting rushed" means getting attacked by a group of gang members. "Repping myself" means being alone, no longer involved in gangs.

7. Offord, Boyle, and Racine 1990.

8. Burchard et al., 2002; Duchnowski et al, 1998.

9. Aos, Miller, and Drake, 2006.

10. Greenwood, 2006.

11. Caputo, Kelly, and Totten, 2006; Shaw and Jane, 1998; Stuart, 1997; Shaw, 2001.

12. Mahoney, Stattin, and Magnusson, 2001; Jones and Offord, 1989; ICPC, 1999.

13. US Dept. Ed., 2000; Gottfredson, Wilson, and Najaka, 2002; Gottfredson et al., 2004.

14. Burrows, 2003.

15. For example, some communities in BC and Ontario have done this.

16. WSIPP, 2004; Jacobsen et al., 2002; Kalil, 2003; Lynch, 2004.

17. Totten, 2005; Totten, 2007; Brown, 2003; Browne et al, 2000, 2001.

18. Offord, Lipman, and Duku, 1998; Offord and Lipman, 1996.

19. In the *Families First* program, for example, when parents apply for social assistance they are also introduced to day care, recreation, and public health staff. Families are provided with a yearly stipend of approximately $250 per child for recreation expenses, which parents can use in a variety of ways to access recreation services and equipment. The Peel program is being replicated in Edmonton with a $10 million evaluation study.

20. Offord and Bennett, 2002.

21. Spergel and Curry, 1991; Spergel, 1995.

22. Stinchcomb, 2002.

23. Howell, 2000.

24. Cultural schools for Aboriginal students are founded upon traditional practices and teachings. Elders are involved on a full-time basis and staff at the school are primarily Aboriginal.

25. Huff, 1990.

26. OJJDP, 2006.

27. Burch and Kane, 1999.

28. Spergel, 2006; Spergel et al., 2003.

29. Spergel et al., 2003.

30. Braga and Kennedy, 2002.

31. Henggeler, 1997.

32. Henggeler et al., 1992.

33. For example, the Second Chance program in Galveston, TX, which targets gang-involved youth. See Thomas, 1996.

34. Portland State University Research and Training Center, 2003.

35. Burchard et al., 2002.

36. VandenBerg and Grealish, 1996; Totten, 2011c; Kamradt, 2000; Milwaukee County Behavioural Health Division, 2003; Walker and Schutte, 2004.

37. The US Congress established Integrated Systems of Care in 1992 and there are more than sixty Integrated Systems of Care communities across the country. They are funded through cooperative agreements with states, communities, territories, and tribal nations, and administered by the Center for Mental Health Services, Substance Abuse and Mental Health Services Administration, and the US Department of Health and Human Services.

38. State of California Board of Corrections, 2002.

39. Zhang and Zhang, 2005; Schumacher and Kurz, 2000; State of California Board of Corrections, 2002.

40. Fight Crime: Invest in Kids, 2004; McClanahan, 2004.

41. Totten and Dunn, 2011a.

42. Totten and Dunn, 2011b.

43. Heney and Kristiansen, 1998.

44. Bloom, 2003; Bloom and Covington, 2001; Freitas and Chesney-Lind, 2001.

45. Including post-traumatic stress disorder, bipolar disorder, depression, and borderline personality disorder.

46. O'Malley, 2007.

47. Totten, 2011c.

48. The First Nations and Inuit Fetal Alcohol Syndrome/Fetal Alcohol Effects Initiative is delivered through the First Nations and Inuit Health Branch and the Population and Public Health Branch. The First Nations and Inuit Health Branch is responsible for delivering First Nations and Inuit component programs to First Nations (on-reserve) and Inuit communities.

49. Aos, Miller, and Drake, 2006.

50. Benda and Tollet, 1999; Olson, Dooley, and Kane, 2004; Nafekh, 2002; Nafekh and Stys, 2004.

51. Nafekh, 2002; Nafekh and Stys, 2004.

52. Totten, 2004a.

53. Esbensen and Osgoode, 1999; Esbensen et al., 2001; DHHS, 2001; NIJ, 1998.

54. Klein, 1995.

55. Poulin, Dishion, and Burraston, 2001.*and Prevention.* Seattle: University of Washington School of Medicine, Department of Psychiatry and Behavioral Sciences. Report No.: R04/CCR008515.Washington State

BIBLIOGRAPHY

Adams, H., L. Wright, and B. Lohr. (1996). Is homophobia associated with homosexual arousal? *Journal of Abnormal Psychology, 105* (3), 440-445.

Amnesty International. (2004). *Stolen Sisters: A Human Rights Response to Discrimination and Violence Against Indigenous Women in Canada.* Retrieved from www.amnesty.ca/stolensisters/amr2000304.pdf

Anisef, P., and M. Killbride. (2000). *The Needs of Newcomer Youth and Emerging "Best Practices" to Meet Those Needs: Final Report.* http://www.ceris.metropolis.net/ Virtual%20Library/other/anisefl.html

Aos, S., M. Miller, and E. Drake. (2006). *Evidence-Based Public Policy Options to Reduce Future Prison Construction, Criminal Justice Costs, and Crime Rates.* Olympia: Washington State Institute for Public Policy.

Asante, K., and J. Nelms-Maztke. (1985). *Report on the Survey of Children with Chronic Handicaps and Fetal Alcohol Syndrome in the Yukon and Northwest British Columbia.* Whitehorse: Council for Yukon Indians.

Astwood Strategy Corporation (2004). *2002 Canadian Police Survey on Youth Gangs.* Ottawa: Public Safety and Emergency Preparedness Canada.

Athens, L. (2003). Violentization in larger social context. In L. Athens and J. Ulmer (Eds.), *Violent Acts and Violentization: Assessing, Applying, and Developing Lonnie Athens' Theories* (pp. 1-42). Oxford, UK: Elsevier Science.

Beiser, M., and I. Hyman. (1997). Refugees' time perspective and mental health. *American Journal of Psychiatry, 154,* 996-1002.

Beiser, M. (2005). Health of Immigrants and Refugees in Canada. *Canadian Journal of Public Health, 96,* 30-44.

Benda, B., and C. Tollett. (1999). A Study of Recidivism of Serious and Persistent Offenders Among Adolescents. *Journal of Criminal Justice, 27* (2), 111-126.

Berry, J., J. Phinney, D. Sam, and P. Vedder. (2006). *Immigrant Youth in Cultural*

Transition: Acculturation, Identity and Adaptation Across National Contexts. New Jersey: Lawrence Erlbaum Associates, Inc.

Bettelheim, B. (1974). *A Home for the Heart.* New York: Knopf.

Bittle, S., N. Hattem, T. Quann, T., and D. Muise (2002). *A One-day Snapshot of Aboriginal Youth in Custody across Canada.* Department of Justice Canada.

Blackstock, C., N. Trocme, and M. Bennett. (2004). Child Maltreatment Investigations Among Aboriginal and Non-Aboriginal Families in Canada. *Violence Against Women, 10* (8), 1-16.

Blagg, H. (2000). *Crisis Intervention in Aboriginal Family Violence: Summary Report.* Commonwealth of Australia: Crime Research Centre, University of Western Australia.

Block, C., and R. Block. (2001). Street Gang Crime in Chicago. In Miller, Maxson, and Klein (Eds.), *The Modern Gang Reader* Los Angeles, CA: Roxbury.

Bloom, B., B. Owen, and S. Covington. (2003). *Gender Responsive Strategies: Research, Practice and Guiding Principles for Women Offenders.* U.S. Department of Corrections, National Institute of Corrections.

Bloom, B., and S. Covington. (2001). *Effective Gender-Responsive Interventions in Juvenile Justice: Addressing the Lives of Delinquent Girls.* Paper presented at the 2001 Annual Meeting of the American Society of Criminology, Atlanta, Georgia. Retrieved from centerforgenderandjustice.org/girls/html

Box, S. (1981). *Deviance, Reality and Society.* London: Holt, Rinehart and Winston.

Braga, A., and D. Kennedy. (2002). Reducing Gang Violence in Boston. In Reed and Decker (Eds.), *Responding to Gangs: Evaluation and Research.* Washington, DC: National Institute of Justice.

Brotherton, D. (1996). 'Smartness,' 'Toughness,' and 'Autonomy': Drug Use in the Context of Gang Female Delinquency. *Journal of Drug Issues, 26* (1), 261-277.

Browne, G. (2003). Making the case for youth recreation: Integrated service delivery: More effective and less expensive. *Ideas that Matter, 2* (3).

Browne, G., Roulston, J., B. Ewart, M. Schuster, J. Edward, and L. Boily. (2000). Investments in comprehensive programming: Services for children and single-parent mothers on welfare pay for themselves within one year. In *Our Children's Future: Child Care Policy in Canada* (pp. 334-346). Toronto: University of Toronto Press.

Browne, G., J. Roberts, C. Byrne, A. Gafni, R. Weir, and B. Majumdar. (2001). *More Effective and Less Expensive Community Approaches to Care of Vulnerable Populations: Lessons from 12 Studies in Ontario.* Hamilton: Working Paper Series, System-Linked Research Unit, Health and Social Service Utilization, McMaster University.

Brown, I., and A. Fudge Schormans. (2004). *Maltreatment Rates in Children with Developmental Delay. CECW Information Sheet #9E.* Toronto: Faculty of Social Work, University of Toronto.

Burchard, J., E. Bruns, and S. Burchard. (2002). *The Wraparound Process: Community-based Treatment for Youth.* Oxford: Oxford University Press.

Burch, J., and C. Kane. (1999). *Implementing the OJJDP Comprehensive Gang Model.* Fact Sheet. Washington, DC: U.S. Department of Justice, Office of Justice Programs, Office of Juvenile Justice and Delinquency Prevention.

Burrows, M. (2003). *Evaluation of the Youth Inclusion Programme: End of phase one report.* London: Youth Justice Board. Retrieved from www.youth-justice-board.gov.uk

Buxton, B. (2004). *Damaged Angels.* Toronto: Knopf Canada.

Campbell, A. (1990). *The Girls in the Gang* (2nd ed.). New Brunswick: Rutgers University Press.

Campbell, A. (1987). Self-definition by rejection: The case of gang girls. *Social Problems, 34,* 451-466.

Canada House of Commons Standing Committee on Aboriginal Affairs. (1990). *Unfinished Business: An Agenda for all Canadians in the 1990s.* Queen's Printer.

Canadian Association of Elizabeth Fry Societies and Native Women's Association of Canada. (2006). *Bill C-9 Act to Amend the Criminal Code.* Submission to the Standing Committee on Justice, Human Rights, Public Safety and Emergency Preparedness.

Caputo, T., K. Kelly, and M. Totten. (2006). Evaluating the Move Towards the Community: Experiences from a Community-based Restorative Justice Project. *Canadian Review of Social Policy, 56:* 85-103.

Chambliss, W. (1973). The Saints and the Roughnecks. *Society, 11* (1), 24-31.

Chandler, M., C. Lalonde, B. Sokol, and D. Hallett. (2003). Personal Persistence, Identity Development, and Suicide: A Study of Native and Non-Native North American Adolescents. *Monographs of the Society for Research in Child Development, Serial No. 273,* 68 (2).

Chavez, G., J. Cordero, and J. Becerra. (1988). Leading major congenital malformations among minority groups in the United States, 1981–1986. *Morb Mortal Wkly Rep, 37* (3), 17-24.

Chesney-Lind, M., and J. Hagedorn. (1999). *Female Gangs in America: Essays on Girls, Gangs, and Gender.* Chicago: Lake View Press.

Chesney-Lind, M., G. Randall, and K. Joe. (1996). Girls, Delinquency and Gang Membership. In R. Huff (Ed.) *Gangs in America* (pp. 185-204). Thousand Oaks, CA: Sage Publications.

Child Welfare Anti-Oppression Roundtable. (2009). *Anti-Oppression in Child Welfare: Laying the Foundation for Change. A Discussion Paper.* Toronto: The Child Welfare Anti-Oppression Roundtable.

Cloward, R., and L. Ohlin. (1960). *Delinquency and Opportunity: A Theory of Delinquent Gangs.* Glencoe, IL: Free Press.

Coie, J., and K. Dodge. (1998). Aggression and antisocial behaviour. In N. Eisenberg and W.

Damon (Eds.), *Handbook of Child Psychology: Social, Emotional, and Personality*

Development (5th ed., Vol. 3, pp. 779-862). New York: Wiley.

Correctional Service Canada. (2008). *Backgrounder Managing the Inter-connectivity of Gangs and Drugs in Federal Penitentiaries.* Ottawa: Correctional Service Canada.

Correctional Service Canada. (2004). *A Profile and Examination of Gang affiliation within the Federally Sentenced Offender Population.* Ottawa: Correctional Service Canada.

Craig, W., R. Vitaro, C. Gagnon, and R. Trembly. (2002). The road to gang membership: Characteristics of male gang and non-gang members from ages 10 to 14. *Social Development, 11,* 53-68.

Crenshaw, D., and J. Garbarino. (2007). The Hidden Dimensions: Profound Sorrow and Buried Potential in Violent Youth. *Journal of Humanistic Psychology, 47* (2), 160-174.

Crick, N., and N. Werner. (1998). Response decision processes in relational and overt aggression. *Child Development, 69,* 1630-1639.

Criminal Intelligence Services Canada. (2010). *Annual Report on Organized Crime.* Ottawa.

Criminal Intelligence Service Canada. (2004). *Annual Report on Organized Crime.* Ottawa.

Criminal Intelligence Service Saskatchewan. (2005). *2005 Intelligence Trends: Aboriginal-Based Gangs in Saskatchewan.* Regina, SK.

Curry, D. (1998). Female Gang Involvement. *Journal of Research in Crime and Delinquency, 35* (1), 100-118.

Curry, D., and I. Spergel. (1991). *Youth Gang Involvement and Delinquency: A Report to the National Youth Gang Intervention and Suppression Research and Development Project.* Washington: Office of Juvenile Justice and Delinquency Prevention.

Dahlberg, L., S. Toal, M. Swahyn, and C. Behrens. (2005). *Measuring Violence-related Attitudes, Behaviors, and Influences Among Youths: A Compendium of Assessment Tools* (2nd ed.). Atlanta: Centers for Disease Control and Prevention, National Center for Injury Prevention and Control.

Davies, A. (1998) Youth gangs, masculinity and violence in late Victorian Manchester and Salford. *Journal of Social History, 32* (2), 349-369.

DeCecco, J. and D. Parker. (1995). The biology of homosexuality: sexual orientation or sexual preference? *Journal of Homosexuality, 28* (1/2, 1-28.

Decker, S., and B. Van Winkle. (1996). *Life in the Gang, Friends, and Violence.* Cambridge, MA: Cambridge University Press.

Dekovic, M. (1999). Risk and protective factors in the development of problem behavior during adolescence. *Journal of Youth and Adolescence, 28* (6), 667-685.

Denzin, N. (1989). *Interpretive Biography.* Newbury Park, CA: Sage.

Department of Health and Human Services. (2001). *Youth Violence: A Report of the Surgeon General.* Surgeon General of the United States.

Deschenes, E., and F. Esbensen. (1999). Violence and Gangs: Gender Differences in Perceptions and Behavior. *Journal of Quantitative Criminology, 15* (1), 63-96.

Dickson-Gilmore, J., and C. Laprairie. (2005). *Will the Circle be Unbroken? Aboriginal Communities, Restorative Justice, and the Challenges of Conflict and Change.* Toronto: University of Toronto Press.

Dishion, T., F. Poulin, and B. Burraston. (2001). Peer group dynamics associated with iatrogenic effects in group interventions with high-risk young adolescents. In D. Nangle and C. Erdley (Eds.), *New Directions for Child and Adolescent Development: Friendship and Psychological Adjustment* (pp. 79-92). San Francisco: Jossey-Bass.

Dooley, S., A. Welsh, R. Floyd, S. Macdonald, and T. Fenning. (2005). *Aboriginal Youth Justice: Emerging Strategies for Program Development.* Vancouver Police Department. Surrey, BC: Kwantlen University College.

Durst, D., and M. Bluechardt. (2001). *Urban Aboriginal Persons with Disabilities: Triple Jeopardy.* Retrieved from http://www.uregina.ca/spru/spruweb/durst.html

Esbensen, F., and D. Osgood. (1999). Gang Resistance Education and Training (G.R.E.A.T.): Results from the National Evaluation. *Journal of Research in Crime and Delinquency, 36* (2), 194-225. Retrieved from http://www.promisingpractices.net/

Esbensen, F., D. Osgood, T. Taylor, D. Peterson, and A. Freng. (2001). How Great is G.R.E.A.T.? Results from a Longitudinal Quasi-Experimental Design. *Criminology and Public Policy, 1* (1), 87-118.

Farley, M., and J. Lynne. (2005). Prostitution of Indigenous Women: Sexual Inequality and the Colonization of Canada's First Nations Women. *Fourth World Journal, 6* (12), 1-29.

Farley, M., J. Lynne, and A. Cotton. (2005). Prostitution in Vancouver: Violence and the colonization of First Nations women. *Transcultural Psychiatry, 42* (2), 242-271.

Fast , D., and J. Conry. (2004). The challenge of fetal alcohol syndrome in the criminal legal system. *Addiction Biology, 9,* 161-166.

Fergusson, D., L. Horwood, and M. Lynskey. (1994). Culture makes a difference...or does it? A comparison of adolescents in Hong Kong, Australia, and the United States. In R. Silbereisen and E. Todt (Eds.), *Adolescence in Context* (pp. 99-113). New York: Springer-Verlag.

Fight Crime: Invest in Kids. (2004). *Caught in the Crossfire: Arresting Gang Violence by Investing in Kids.* Washington, DC.

Fishman, L. (1999). Black female gang behavior. In M. Chesney-Lind and J. Hagedorn (Eds.), *Female Gangs in America: Essays on Girls, Gangs and Gender* (pp. 64 -84). Chicago: Lake View Press.

Freitas, K., and M. Chesney-Lind. (2001, August/September). Difference doesn't mean difficult: Practitioners talk about working with girls. *Women, Girls & Criminal Justice, 2* (5): 65 - 78.

Galabuzi, G. (2001). *Canada's Creeping Economic Apartheid: The Economic Segregation and Social Marginalization of Racialized Groups.* Toronto: Center for Social Justice Foundation for Research and Education.

Gay, B., and J. Marquart. (1993). Jamaican Posse: A new form of organized crime. *Journal of Crime and Justice, 16* (2), 139-170.

Giles, C. (2000). History of Street Gangs in Winnipeg 1945–1997: A Qualitative Newspaper Analysis of Gang Activity. (Unpublished master's thesis.) Department of Criminology, Simon Fraser University.

Glaser, B., and A. Straus. (1967). *The Discovery of Grounded Theory.* Chicago: Aldine.

Goldstein, A. (1991). *Delinquent Gangs: A Psychological Perspective.* Champaign, IL: Research Press.

Gordon, R. (2000). Criminal business organizations, street gangs and 'wanna-be' groups: A Vancouver perspective. *Canadian Journal of Criminology 42(1): 39–60.*

Gordon, R., and S. Foley. (1998). *Criminal Business Organizations, Street Gangs and Related Groups in Vancouver: The Report of the Greater Vancouver Gang Study.* Ministry of Attorney-General, British Columbia.

Gottfredson, D., D.Wilson, and S. Najaka. (2002). School-based crime prevention. In L. Sherman et al. (Eds.), *Evidence-based Crime Prevention* (pp. 56-164). New York: Routledge.

Gottfredson, D., S. Gerstenblith, D. Soule, S. Womer, and S. Lu (2004). Do after school programs reduce delinquency? *Prevention Science, 5* (4), 253–266.

Grant, B., P. MacPherson, and A. Chudley. (2006). *Update on Research in a Federal Prison on FASD.* Unpublished Paper.

Greenwood, P. (2006). *Changing Lives: Delinquency Prevention as Crime-Control Policy.* Chicago: University of Chicago Press.

Grekul, J., and P. LaBoucane-Benson. (2006). *When You Have Nothing to Live For, You Have Nothing to Die For: An Investigation into the Formation and Recruitment Processes of Aboriginal Gangs in Western Canada.* Ottawa: Public Safety Canada.

Grennan, S., M. Britz, J. Rush, and T. Barker. (2000). *Gangs: An International Approach.* Upper Saddle River, NJ: Prentice Hall.

Group of Ten. (2004). *South Asian-Based Group Crime in British Columbia: 1993–2000. Ottawa:* Heritage Canada.

Gubrium, J. and J. Holstein (1997). *The New Language of Qualitative Method.* New York: Oxford University Press.

Gutman, L., V. McLoyd, and T. Tokoyama. (2005). Financial strain, neighborhood stress, parenting behaviours, and adolescent adjustment in urban African American families. *Journal of Research on Adolescence, 15*, 425-449.

Gutman, L., and C. Midgley (2000). The role of protective factors in supporting the academic achievement of poor African American students during the middles school transition. *Journal of Youth and Adolescence 29* (2), 223-248.

Habbick B., J. Nanson, R. Snyder, R. Casey, and A. Schulman (1996). Foetal alcohol syndrome in Saskatchewan: Unchanged incidence in a 20-year period. *Can J Pub Health, 87* (3), 204-207.

Hagedorn, J. (1994). Homeboys, Dope Fiends, Straights, and New Jacks. *Criminology 32*, 197-219.

Hagedorn, J., and P. Macon. (1988). *People and Folks: Gangs, Crime and the Underclass in a Rustbelt City.* Chicago: Lakeview Press.

Hamel, S., C. Fredette, M. Blais, and J. Bertot. (1998). *Youth and Street Gangs, Phase II: Field Research Results.* Montréal, QC: l'Institute de recherche pour le développement social des jeune (IRDS).

Hamm, M. (2001) The Differences Between Street Gangs and Neo-Nazi Skinheads. In J. Miller, C. Maxson, and M. Klein (Eds.), *The Modern Gang Reader* (2nd ed., pp. 157-161). Los Angeles, CA: Roxbury.

Hardy, K., and T. Laszloffy. (2005). *Teens Who Hurt: Clinical Interventions to Break the Cycle of Adolescent Violence.* New York: Guilford Press.

Health Canada. (2003). *Fetal Alcohol Spectrum Disorder: A Framework for Action.* Ottawa: Minister of Public Works and Government Services Canada.

Heney, J., and C. Kristiansen. (1998). An analysis of the impact of prison on women survivors of childhood sexual abuse. *Women and Therapy, 20* (4), 13.

Henggeler, S. (1997). The development of effective drug abuse services for youth. In J. Egertson, D. Fox, and A. Leshner (Eds.), *Treating Drug Abusers Effectively* (pp. 253-279). New York: Blackwell Publishers.

Henggeler, S., G. Melton, and L. Smith. (1992). Family preservation using multisystemic

therapy: An effective alternative to incarcerating serious juvenile offenders. *Journal of Consulting and Clinical Psychology, 60*, 953–961.

Herek, G. (1992). The social context of hate crimes: Notes on cultural heterosexism. In G. Herek and K. Berrill (Eds.), *Hate Crimes: Confronting Violence Against Lesbians and Gay Men* (pp. 89-104). Newbury Park, CA: Sage.

Herek, G. (1984). Beyond 'homophobia': A social psychological perspective on attitudes toward lesbians and gay men. *Journal of Homosexuality, 10* (1/2), 1-15.

Herek, G., J. Cogan, J. Gillis, and E. Glunt. (1998). Correlates of internalized homophobia in a community sample of lesbians and gay men. *Journal of the Gay and Lesbian Medical Association, 2*, 17-25.

Howard, S., J. Dryden, and B. Johnson. (1999). Childhood resilience: Review and critique of the literature. *Oxford Review of Education 25* (3), 307-323.

Howell, J. (2000). *Youth Gang Programs and Strategies.* Washington, DC: US Department of Justice, Office of Justice Programs, Office of Juvenile and Delinquency Prevention.

Huff, C. (1990). Denial, overreaction and misidentification. In C. Huff (Ed.), *Gangs in America* (pp. 263-287). New York: Sage.

Humphries, S. (1981). *Hooligans or Rebels? An Oral History of Working-Class Childhood and Youth 1889–1939.* Oxford: Blackwell, 1995.

International Centre for the Prevention of Crime. (1999). *100 Programs to Inspire Action Across the World.* Montreal: ICPC.

Jackson, A., L. Hanvey, S. Tsoukalas, L. Buckland, E. Roberts, and N. Perkins. (2001). *Recreation and Children and Youth Living in Poverty: Barriers, Benefits and Success Stories.* Ottawa: CCSD.

Jackson, R., and W. McBride. (2000). *Understanding Street Gangs.* Cincinnati: Copperhouse.

Jacobsen, V., N. Mays, R. Crawford, B. Annesley, P. Christoffel, G. Johnston, et al. (2002). *Investing in Well-being: an Analytical Framework.* Wellington: New Zealand Treasury.

Jaffe, P., and D. Reitzel. (1990). Adolescents' views on how to reduce family violence. In R. Roesch, D. Dutton, and V. Sacco (Eds.), *Family Violence: Perspectives on Treatment, Research and Policy* (pp. 51-66). Burnaby, BC: Simon Fraser University.

Joe, D., and N. Robinson. (1980). Chinatown's immigrant gangs. *Criminology, 18* (3), 337-345.

Johnson, H. (1996). *Dangerous Domains: Violence Against Women in Canada.* Toronto: Nelson Canada.

Jones, M., and D. Offord. (1989). Reduction of anti-social behaviour in poor children by non-school skill development. *Journal of Child Psychology and Psychiatry, 30,* 737-750

Kalil, A. (2003). *Family Resilience and Good Child Outcomes: A Review of the Literature.* Wellington: Centre for Social Research and Evaluation, Ministry of Social Development.

Kamradt, B. (2000). Wraparound Milwaukee: Aiding Youth With Mental Health Needs. *Juvenile Justice Journal, 7* (1), 14-23.

Katz, J. (1988). *Seductions of Crime: Moral and Sensual Attractions in Doing Evil.* New York: Basic Books.

Kelly, K., and M. Totten. (2002). *When Children Kill: A Social Psychological Study of Youth Homicide.* Peterborough, ON: Broadview.

Kanu, Y. (2008). Educational needs and barriers for African refugee students in Manitoba. *Canadian Journal of Education, 31* (4): 915-940.Khanlou, N., and C. Crawford. (2006). Post-migratory experiences of newcomer female youth: Self-esteem and identity development. *Journal of Immigrant and Minority Health, 8* (1), 45-56.

Kitts, R. (2005). Gay adolescents and suicide: Understanding the association. *Adolescence, 40* (159), 621-628.

Klein, M. (2002). Street Gangs: A Cross-National Perspective. In C. Huff (Ed.) *Gangs in America III* (pp. 237-254). Thousand Oaks, CA: Sage.

Klein, M. (1995). *The American Street Gang.* New York: Oxford University Press.

Knox, G. (2000). *An Introduction to Gangs* (5th ed.). Chicago: New Chicago School Press.

Koss, M., and C. Gidycz. (1985). Sexual experiences survey: reliability and validity. *Journal of Consulting and Clinical Psychology, 53,* 422-423.

Kyskan, C., and T. Moore. (2005). Global perspectives on fetal alcohol syndrome (FAS): Assessing practices, policies, and campaigns in four English-speaking countries. *Canadian Psychology, 46,* 153-165.

LeBlanc, M., and N. Lanctôt. (1994). *Adolescent gang members social and psychological characteristics, gang participation: A selection or activation process?* Paper presented at the Annual Meeting of the American Society of Criminology, Miami, FL.

Leet, D., G. Rush, and A. Smith. (2000). *Gangs, Graffiti and Violence* (2nd ed.). Nevada: Copperhouse.

Levitt, S., and S. Venkatesh. (2000). An economic analysis of a drug selling gang's finances. *Quarterly Journal of Economics 115* (3), 755-789.

Lurigio, A., J. Swartz, and J. Chang. (1998). A Descriptive and Comparative Analysis of Female Gang Members. *Journal of Gang Research, 5* (4), 23-33.

Luthar, S., D. Cicchetti, and B. Becker. (2000). The construct of resilience: A critical evaluation and guidelines for future work. *Child Development 72* (3), 543-562.

Lynch, R. (2004). *Exceptional Returns: Economic, Fiscal, and Social Benefits of Investment in Early Childhood Development.* Washington, DC: Economic Policy Institute.

Lynne, J. (2005). *Prostitution of First Nations Women in Canada.* Audience of the Sub-committee on Solicitation Laws. Retrieved from http://sisyphe.org/article. php3?id_article=1803

MacMillan, H. (2000). Child maltreatment: What we know in the year 2000. *Canadian Journal of Psychiatry 45,* 702-709.

MacMillan, H., J. Fleming, N. Trocme, et al. (1997). Prevalence of child physical and sexual abuse in the community: Results from the Ontario Health Supplement. *Journal of the American Medical Association, 278* (2), 131-135.

Mahoney, J. (2000). School extracurricular activity participation as a moderator in the development of anti-social patterns. *Child Development, 71* (2), 502-516.

Mahoney, J., H. Stattin, and D. Magnusson. (2001). Youth recreation center participation and criminal offending: A 20-year longitudinal study of Swedish boys. *International Journal of Behavioral Development, 25* (6), 509-552.

Masotti, P., et al. (2006). Preventing Fetal Alcohol Spectrum Disorder in Aboriginal Communities: A Methods Development Project. *PLoS Medicine, 3* (1).

Mathews, F. (1993). *Youth Gangs on Youth Gangs.* Ottawa: Solicitor General of Canada.

Matza, D. (1964). *Delinquency and Drift.* New York: Wiley.

McCreary Centre Society. (1999a). *Healthy Connections: Listening to BC Youth. Highlights from the Adolescent Health Survey II.* Burnaby: The McCreary Centre Society.

McCreary Centre Society. (1999b). *Being Out: Lesbian, Gay, Bisexual and Transgender Youth in BC: An Adolescent Health Survey.* Burnaby: The McCreary Centre Society.

McClanahan, W. (2004). *Alive at 25: Reducing Youth Violence Through Monitoring and Support.* Philadelphia: Public/Private Ventures.

Mellor, B., L. MacRae, M. Pauls, and J. Hornick(2005). *Youth Gangs in Canada: A Preliminary Review of Programs and Services.* Prepared for Public Safety and Emergency Preparedness Canada. Calgary: Canadian Research Institute for Law and the Family.

Merton, R. (1938). Social Structure and Anomie, *American Sociological Review, 3,* 672-682.

Miller, J. (2001). *One of the Guys: Girls, Gangs and Gender.* New York: Oxford University Press.

Miller, J. (1998). Gender and Victimization Risk Among Young Women in Gangs. *Journal of Research in Crime and Delinquency, 35* (4), 429-453.

Milwaukee County Behavioral Health Division. (2003). *Wraparound Milwaukee: 2002 Annual Report.* Milwaukee, WI: Milwaukee County Behavioral Health Division, Department of Health and Human Services.

Moffitt, T. (2005). The new look of behaviour genetics in developmental pathology: Gene-environment interplay in antisocial behaviour. *Psychological Bulletin, 131,* 533-554.

Moffitt, T., et al. (2001). *Sex Differences in Antisocial Behaviour.* Cambridge, UK: Cambridge University Press.

Moore, J. (1978). *Homeboys: Gangs, Drugs, and Prisons in the Barrios of Los Angeles.* Philadelphia: Temple University Press.

Moore, J. (2007). Female Gangs. In J. Hagedorn (Ed.), *Gangs in the Global City: Alternatives to Traditional Criminology* (pp.). Champaign, IL: University of Illinois Press.

Munn, P., G. Lloyd, and M. Cullen. (2000). *Alternatives to Exclusion from School.* London: Sage.

Murphy, A., M. Chittenden, and The McCreary Centre Society. (2005). *Time Out II: A Profile of BC Youth in Custody.* Vancouver, BC: The McCreary Centre Society.

Nafekh, M. (2002). *An Examination of Youth and Gang Association Within the Federally Sentenced Aboriginal Population.* Ottawa: Correctional Services Canada.

Nafekh, M., and Y. Steys. (2004). *A Profile and Examination of Gang Affiliation within Federally Sentenced Inmates.* Ottawa: Correctional Services Canada.

National Institute of Justice. (1998). *Research in Brief, Preventing Crime: What Works, What Doesn't, What's Promising.* Washington: US Department of Justice, Office of Justice Programs..

Native Women's Association of Canada. (2010). *Sisters in Spirit 2010 Research Findings.* Ottawa: NWAC.

Nimmo, M. (2001). *The Invisible Gang Members: A Report on Female Gang Association in Winnipeg.* Winnipeg: Canadian Centre for Policy Alternatives.

Noh, S., M. Beiser, V. Kaspar, F. Hou and J. Rummens (1999). Perceived racial discrimination, depression, and coping: A study of Southeast Asian refugees in Canada. *Journal of Health and Social Behavior, 40,* 193-207.

Office of the Parliamentary Budget Officer. (2010). *Fiscal Sustainability Report.* Ottawa.

Offord Centre. (2009). *The Importance of Attachment.* Retrieved from www.knowledge.offordcentre.com

Offord, D., et al. (1998). Lowering the burden of suffering from child psychiatric disorder: trade-offs among clinical, targeted and universal interventions. *Journal of the American Academy of Child and Adolescent Psychiatry 37,* 686-694.

Offord, D., and E. Lipman. (1996). Emotional and behavioural problems. In *Growing Up in Canada: National Longitudinal Survey on Children and Youth.* Ottawa: HRDC and Statistics Canada.

Offord, D., E. Lipman, and E. Duku. (1998). *Which Children don't Participate in Sports, the Arts, and Community Programs?* Ottawa: Human Resources Development Canada.

Offord, D., and K. Bennett. (2002). Prevention. In M. Rutter and E. Taylor (Eds.), *Child and Adolescent Psychiatry* (4th ed., pp. 881-899). Oxford, UK: Blackwell Science.

Offord, D., M. Boyle, and Y. Racine. (1990). *Ontario Child Health Study.* Toronto: Queen's Printer.

Office of Juvenile Justice and Delinquency Prevention. (2006). *Juvenile Offenders and Victims: 2006 National Report.* Washington, DC: Office of Juvenile Justice and Delinquency Prevention.

Olson, D., B. Dooley, and C. Kane. (2004). The Relationship Between Gang Membership and Inmate Recidivism. *Research Bulletin, 2* (12). Chicago, IL: Illinois Criminal Justice Research Authority.

O'Malley, K. (2007). Fetal Alcohol Syndrome Disorders: An overview. *ADHD and Fetal Alcohol Spectrum Disorders.* New York: Nova Science Publishers.

Ontario Federation of Indian Friendship Centres (2000). *Urban Aboriginal Child Poverty: A Status Report on Aboriginal Children and their Families in Ontario.* Toronto: OFIFC.

Ontario Native Women's Association. (1989). *Breaking Free: A Proposal for Change to Aboriginal Family Violence.* Thunder Bay: Ontario Native Women's Association.

Ornstein, M. (2006). *Ethno-racial Groups in Toronto, 1971–2001: A Demographic and Socio-economic Profile.* Toronto: Institute for Social Research, York University.

Page, K. (2001). Fetal alcohol spectrum: The hidden epidemic in our courts. *Juvenile and Family Court Journal, 52,* 21-31.

Pardini, D., and R. Loeber. (2008). Interpersonal Callousness Trajectories Across Adolescence: Early Social Influences. *Criminal Justice and Behavior, 35,* 173-196

Parker, P., and J. DeCecco. (1995). Sexual expression: A global perspective. *Journal of Homosexuality, 28* (3/4), 427-430.

Peet, W., B. Vogelsang, and D. Wiks. (2008). *Regina Provincial Correctional Centre Escape Report.*

Peled, E. (1997). Intervention with children of battered women: A review of current literature. *Children and Youth Services Review (UK), 19* (4), 277-299.

Perry, B. (1995). Incubated terror: Neurodevelopmental factors in the cycle of violence. In J. Osofsky (Ed.), *Children, Youth and Violence: Searching for Solutions.* New York: Guilford Press.

Plomin, R., and J. Crabbe. (2000). DNA. *Psychological Bulletin, 126,* 806-828.

Portland State University Research and Training Center. (2003). Quality and Fidelity in Wraparound. *Focal Point 17(2).*

Rabon, D. (1994). *Investigative Discourse Analysis.* Durham, NC: Carolina Academic Press.

Rhee, S., and I. Waldman. (2002) Genetic and environmental influences on antisocial behavior: A meta-analysis of twin and adoption studies. *Psychological Bulletin, 128* (3), 490-529.

Rich, A. (1980). Compulsory heterosexuality and lesbian existence. *Signs, 5,* 631-660.

Roberts, G., and J. Nanson. (2000). *Best Practices. Fetal Alcohol Syndrome/Fetal Alcohol Effects and the Effects of Other Substance Use During Pregnancy.* Ottawa: Government of Canada.

Robinson G., J. Conry, and R. Conry. (1987). Clinical profile and prevalence of fetal alcohol syndrome in an isolated community in British Columbia. *Canadian Medical Association Journal, 137,* 203-207.

RCMP. (2010). *Briefing Note Public Safety and Emergency Preparedness Canada: Organized Crime and Gangs and Violence.* CACP Organized Crime Committee.

RCMP. (1997). *Understanding Asian Organized Crime. Pony Express,* 26-31 (December).

Royal Commission on Aboriginal Peoples. (1996). *Looking Forward Looking Back. Report of the Royal Commission on Aboriginal Peoples.* Ottawa: Minister of Supply and Services Canada.

Sampson, R. (1993). The community context of violent crime. In W. Wilson (Ed.), *Sociology and the Public Agenda* (pp. 259-286). Newbury Park, CA: Sage.

Sampson, P., et al. (1997). Incidence of fetal alcohol syndrome and prevalence of alcohol-related neurodevelopmental disorder. *Teratology, 56* (5), 317-326.

Sampson P., et al. (1994). Prenatal alcohol exposure, birthweight, and measures of child size from birth to age 14 years. *Am J Public Health, 84* (9),1421-1428.

Sanchez-Jankowski, M. (1991). *Islands in the Street: Gangs in American Urban Society.* Berkeley: University of California Press.

Sanders, W. (1993). *Drive-Bys and Gang Bangs: Gangs and Grounded Culture.* Chicago: Aldine.

Sappington, A., R. Pharr, A. Tunstall, and R. Edward R. (1997). Relationships between child abuse, date abuse, and psychological problems. *Journal of Clinical Psychology, 53* (4), 319-329.

Schumacher, M., and G. Kurz. (2000). The 8% Solution—Preventing Serious Repeat Juvenile Crime. Thousand Oaks, CA: Sage.

Scott, M., and S. Lyman. (1968). Accounts. *American Sociological Review, 33,* 46-62.

Sethi, A. (2007). Domestic trafficking of Aboriginal girls in Canada: Issues and implications. *First Peoples Child and Family Review, 3* (3): 57-71

Shah, C. (1990). *Public Health and Preventive Medicine in Canada.* Toronto: University of Toronto Press

Shaw, M., and F. Jane. (1998). *Restorative Justice and Policing in Canada: Bringing the Community into Focus.* Monograph. Montreal: Concordia University, Department of Sociology and Anthropology.

Shaw, M. (2001). *Investing in Youth 12–18: International Approaches to Preventing Crime and Victimization.* Montreal, QC: ICPC.

Sikka, A. (2009). *Trafficking of Aboriginal Women and Girls in Canada.* Aboriginal Policy Research Series. Ottawa: Institute on Governance.

Silverman, D. (1993). *Interpreting Qualitative Data.* London: Sage.

Skiba, R., and R. Petersen. (1999). The dark side of zero tolerance: Can punishment lead to sage schools? *Phi Delta Kappan, 80* (5), 381-382.

Smokowski, P., A. Reynolds, and N. Brezruczko. (1999). Resilience and protective factors in adolescence: An autobiographical perspective from disadvantaged youth. *Journal of School Psychology 37* (4), 425-448.

Sokol R., V. Delaney-Black, and B. Nordstrom. (2003). Fetal alcohol spectrum disorder. *Journal of the American Medical Association 290* (22), 2996-2999.

Sokol, R., and S. Clarren. (1989). Guidelines for use of terminology describing the impact of prenatal alcohol on the offspring. *Alcohol Clin Exp Res, 13* (4), 597-598. Retrieved from http://www.cmaj.ca/cgi/external_ref?access_

num=10.1111/j.1530-0277.1989.tb00384.x&link_type=DOI

Spergel, I. (2006). *Reducing Youth Gang Violence: The Little Village Gang Project in Chicago.* Violence Prevention and Policy Series. Lanham, MD: Altamira Press.

Spergel, I. (1995). *The Youth Gang Problem: A Community Approach.* New York: Oxford University Press.

Spergel, I. (1964). *Racketville, Slumtown, Haulburg: An Exploratory Study of Delinquent Subcultures.* Chicago: University of Chicago Press.

Spergel, I., and D. Curry. (1988). *Socialization into Gangs: Preliminary Baseline Report.* Chicago: University of Chicago, School of Social Service Administration.

Spergel, I., and D. Curry. (1991). *The National Youth Gang Survey: A Research and Development Process.* Chicago: University of Chicago and Office of Juvenile Justice and Delinquency Prevention.

Spergel, I., K. Wa, S. Grossman, A. Jacob, S. Choi, R. Sosa, E. Barrios, and A. Spergel. (2003). *The Little Village Gang Violence Reduction Project in Chicago.* Chicago: University of Chicago, School of Social Service Administration.

Sprott, J., A. Doob, and J. Jenkins. (2001). Problem behaviour and delinquency in children and youth. *Juristat 21* (4). Catalogue 85-002-XPE.

Sprott, J., J. Jenkins, and A. Doob. (2000). *Early Offending: Understanding the Risk and Protective Factors of Delinquency.* Ottawa: Applied Research Branch, Strategic Policy, Human Resources Development Canada.

Square, D. (1997). Fetal alcohol syndrome epidemic on Manitoba reserve. *Canadian Medical Association Journal, 157* (1), 59-60.

Stark, J. (2004). Breaking the cycle: A community approach to prevention of low-birth weight babies. *Leadership in Health Services, 17* (4), 1-8.

State of California Board of Corrections. (2002). *Repeat Offender Prevention Program.* California: State of California Board of Corrections.

Statistics Canada. (2010). Police Resources in Canada 2010. *Juristat.* Catalogue No. 85-225-X

Statistics Canada. (2008a). *Aboriginal Peoples, 2006 Census.* Catalogue No. 97-558-XWE2006002.

Statistics Canada. (2008b). Crime Statistics in Canada, 2007. *Juristat 28* (7). 85-002-XWE

Statistics Canada. (2006a). Victimization and Offending Among the Aboriginal Population in Canada. *Juristat 26* (3).

Statistics Canada. (2006b). *Aboriginal People as Victims and Offenders. The Daily,* June 6 2006.

Statistics Canada. (2006c). *Family Violence in Canada: A Statistical Profile 2006.* Statistics Canada Catalogue No. 85-224-XIE.

Statistics Canada. (2004). *2001 CensusAnalysis Series: Canada's Ethnocultural*

Portrait: The Changing Mosaic.

Statistics Canada. (2002, December 17). Child-friendly neighbourhoods. *The Daily.*

Stinchcomb, J. (2002). Promising (and not so promising) gang prevention and intervention strategies: A comprehensive literature review. *Journal of Gang Research, 10* (1), 27-45.

Stone, S. (2002). *Contemporary Gang Issues: An Inside View.* Chicago: New Chicago School Press.

Strauss, M. (1990). Ordinary violence, child abuse, and wife-beating: What do they have in common? In M. Straus and R. Gelles (Eds.), *Physical Violence in American Families* (pp. 403 - 424). New Brunswick: Transaction.

Streissguth, A., H. Barr, J. Kogan, and F. Bookstein . (1997). Primary and secondary disabilities in fetal alcohol syndrome. In A. Streissguth and J. Kanter (Eds.), *The Challenge of Fetal Alcohol Syndrome: Overcoming Secondary Disabilities* (pp. 25-39). Seattle: University of Washington Press.

Streissguth, A., et al. (1996). *Understanding the Occurrence of Secondary Disabilities in Clients with Fetal Alcohol Syndrome (FAS) and Fetal Alcohol Effects (FAE): Final Report for Centers for Disease Control and Prevention.* Seattle: University of Washington School of Medicine, Department of Psychiatry and Behavioral Sciences. Report No.: R04/CCR008515.

Streissguth, A., et al. (2004). Risk factors for adverse life outcomes in fetal alcohol syndrome and fetal alcohol effects. *Journal of Developmental and Behavioral Pediatrics, 25,* 228-238.

Strohschein, L. (2005). Household income histories and child mental health trajectories. *Journal of Health and Social Behaviour, 46,* 359-375.

Stuart, B. (1997). *Building Community Partnerships: Community Peacemaking Circles.* Ottawa: Minister of Public Works and Government Services, Canada.

Sudermann, M., and P. Jaffe. (1999). *A Handbook for Health and Social Service Providers and Educators on Children Exposed to Woman Abuse/Family Violence.* Ottawa: Minister of Public Works and Government Services, Canada.

Suicide Prevention Resource Center. (2008). *Suicide Risk and Prevention for Lesbian, Gay, Bisexual, and Transgender Youth.* Newton, MA: Education Development Center, Inc.

Sullivan, M. (1989). *"Getting Paid": Youth Crime and Work in the Inner City.* Ithica: Cornell University Press.

Surko, M., D. Ciro, C. Blackwood, M. Nembhard and K. Peake (2005). Experience of racism as a correlate of developmental and health outcomes among urban adolescent mental health clients. *Social Work in Mental Health, 3* (3), 235-260.

Tait, C. (2003). *Fetal Alcohol Syndrome Among Aboriginal People in Canada: Review and Analysis of the Intergenerational Links to Residential Schools.* Ottawa: Aboriginal Healing Foundation.

The President and Fellows of Harvard College. (2002). *Opportunities Suspended: The Devastating Consequences of Zero Tolerance and School Discipline Policies.* Boston: The Civil Rights Project and the Advancement Project, Harvard University.

Thobani, S. (2007). *Exalted Subjects: Studies in Making of Race and Nation in Canada.* Toronto: University of Toronto Press.

Thomas, C. (1996, June). *The Second Chance program.* Unpublished paper presented at the National Youth Gang Symposium in Dallas, TX.

Thrasher, F. (1927). *The Gang: A Study of 1,313 Gangs in Chicago.* Chicago: University of Chicago Press.

Totten, M. (2012). An Overview of Gang-Involved Youth in Canada. In J. Winterdyke and R. Smandych (Eds.), *Youth at Risk and Youth Justice: A Canadian Overview.* Don Mills, ON: Oxford University Press.

Totten, M. (2011a). Use of the Tear Drop Tattoo by Young Canadian Street Gang Members. *Journal of Gang Research, 19(1).*

Totten, M. (2011b). Gays in the Gang. Forthcoming in *Journal of Gang Research, Winter 2012.*

Totten, M., and S. Dunn. (2011a). *Final Evaluation Report for the Prince Albert Outreach Program Inc. Warrior Spirit Walking Gang Project.* Gatineau, QC: Totten and Associates.

Totten, M., and S. Dunn. (2011b). *Final Evaluation Report for the North Central Community Association Regina Anti-gang Services Project.* Gatineau, QC: Totten and Associates.

Totten, M., S. Dunn, and NWAC. (2011c). FASD, Gangs, Sexual Exploitation and Woman Abuse in the Canadian Aboriginal Population: An Environmental Scan of Programs. Ottawa: NWAC.

Totten, M., and NWAC. (2010). Investigating the Linkages Between FASD, Gangs, Sexual Exploitation, and Woman Abuse in the Canadian Aboriginal Population: A Preliminary Study. *First Peoples Child and Family Review,* 5 (2): 9-Totten, M. (2009a). Aboriginal Youth and Violent Gang Involvement in Canada: *Quality Prevention Strategies.* Institute for the Prevention of Crime Review, 3:135- 156.

Totten, M. (2009b). Preventing Aboriginal Youth Gang Involvement in Canada: A Gendered Approach. In J. White and J. Bruhn (Eds.), *Aboriginal Policy Research: Exploring the Urban Landscape* (Vol. 8, pp. 255 - 279). Toronto: Thompson.

Totten, M. (2008). *Promising Practices for Addressing Youth Involvement in Gangs.* British Columbia Ministry of Public Safety and Solicitor General End Youth Gang Violence Strategy. Vancouver: BCMPSS General.

Totten, M. (2007). *The Health, Social and Economic Benefits of Increasing Access to Recreation for Low-income Families.* Toronto: Parks and Recreation Ontario.

Totten, M. (2006). *Street Gang Research Methodology and Implications for R. v. Abbey: Report prepared for the Honourable Justice Mr. Archibald.* Gatineau, QC: Totten and Associates.

Totten, M., and K. Kelly. (2006). Conducting Field Research with Young Offenders Convicted of Murder and Manslaughter: Gaining Access, Risks, and 'Truth Status.' In D. Pawluch, W. Shaffir, and Charlene Miall (Eds), *Studying Social Life: Substance and Method* (pp. 77 - 89). Toronto: CSPI/Women's Press.

Totten, M. (2005). *The Cost of Excluding Ontario's Youth from Play.* Toronto: Play Works Partnership of Ontario.

Totten, M. (2004a). *M.A.R.S. Literature and Best Practices Review: Summarising the Risk and Protective Factors Related to the Harassment and Abuse of Young People in Recreation Settings.* Ottawa: Canadian Parks and Recreation Association.

Totten, M. (2004b). *Gender Responsive Youth Justice Services and the Need for Female Staff.* Ottawa: Youth Services Bureau.

Totten, M. (2003). Girlfriend abuse as a form of masculinity construction among violent, marginal male youth. *Men and Masculinities, 6* (1), 70-92.

Totten, M., and P. Quigley. (2003). *Bullying, School Exclusion and Literacy.* Ottawa: Human Resources Development Canada and Canadian Public Health Association.

Totten, M. (2002a). *The Special Needs of Young Women in Canada's Youth Justice System.* Report prepared for Department of Justice Canada. Ottawa: Department of Justice Canada.

Totten, M. (2002b). *Youth Literacy and Violence Prevention Research Report.* Ottawa: Canadian Public Health Association.

Totten, M. (2002c). *Maltreated Kids, Violence Adolescents: Is There a Link?* Report prepared for Health Canada.

Totten, M., and P. Reid. (2002). *Understanding Serious Youth Violence.* Ottawa: YSB.

Totten, M. (2001). Legal, Ethical and Clinical Implications of Doing Field Research with Youth Gang Members who Engage in Serious Violence, *Journal of Gang Research, 8* (4): 35 - 56.

Totten, M. (2000a). *YSB May 1999 Youth Survey: Summary of Findings.* Ottawa: YSB.

Totten, M. (2000b). *Guys, Gangs and Girlfriend Abuse.* Peterborough, ON: Broadview.

Trevethan, S., S. Auger, J. Moore, M. MacDonald, and J. Sinclair (2002). *The Effect of Family Disruption on Aboriginal and Non-Aboriginal inmates.* Ottawa: Research Report R-113, Correctional Service of Canada.

Trocmé, N., D. Knoke, and C. Blackstock. (2004). Pathways to the Overrepresentation of Aboriginal Children in Canada's Child Welfare System. *Social Service Review, 78* (4), 577-601. Retrieved from http://www.journals.uchicago.edu/doi/abs/10.1086/424545 - fn1

Trocmé, N. (2005). *Canadian Incidence Study of Child Abuse and Neglect—2003: Major Findings.* Ottawa: Minister of Public Works and Government Services Canada.

Trocmé, N., B. MacLaurin, B. Fallon, et al. (2001). *The Canadian Incidence Study of*

Reported Child Abuse and Neglect: Final Report. Ottawa: Minister of Public Works and Government Services Canada.

U.S. Department of Education. (2000). *After-School Programs: Keeping Children Safe and Smart.* Washington, DC.

U.S. Department of Health and Human Services. (2001). *Youth Violence: A Report of the Surgeon General.*

Valdez, A. (2000). *A Guide to Understanding Gangs.* San Clemente, CA: LawTech Publishing.

VanDenBerg, J., and E. Grealish. (1996). Individualized services and supports through the wraparound process: Philosophy and procedures. *Journal of Child and Family Studies, 5 (1)*:7-21.

Voydanoff, P., and B. Donnelly. (1999). Multiple roles and psychological distress: The intersection of the paid worker, spouse, and parent roles with the adult child role. *Journal of Marriage and the Family, 61,* 725-738.

Walker, J., and K. Schutte. (2004). Practice and process in wraparound teamwork. *Journal of Emotional and Behavioral Disorders, 12,* 182-192.

Washington State Institute for Public Policy. (2004). *Benefits and Costs of Prevention and Early Intervention Programs for Youth.*

Weatherburn, D., J. Fitzgerald, and J. Hua. (2003). Reducing Aboriginal overrepresentation in prison. *Australian Journal of Public Administration, 62* (3), 65-73.

Webster-Stratton, C., and D. Lindsay. (1999). Social competence and conduct problems in young children: Issues and assessment. *Journal of Clinical Child Psychology, 28,* 25-43.

Weissman, E. (1992). Kids who attack gays. In G. Herek and K. Berrill (Eds.), *Hate Crimes: Confronting Violence Against Lesbians and Gays* (pp. 170-178). Newbury Park, CA: Sage.

Whitbeck, L., X. Chen, D. Lloyt, K. Tyler and K. Johnson (2004). Mental disorder: Subsistence strategies and victimization among lesbian, gay and bisexual homeless and runaway adolescents. *Journal of Sex Research, 41:* 329 - 342.

Whyte, W. (1943). *Street Corner Society.* Chicago: University of Chicago Press.

Williams, R., F. Odaibo, and J. McGee. (1999). Incidence of fetal alcohol syndrome in northeastern Manitoba. *Canadian Journal of Public Health, 90,* 192-194.

Wolfe, D.,, C. Wekerle, D. Reitzel-Jaffe, and R. Gough (1995). Strategies to address violence in the lives of high-risk youth. In E. Paled, P. Jaffe, and J. Edelson (Eds.), *Ending the Cycle of Violence* (pp. 255-274). Thousand Oaks, CA: Sage.

Wortley, S., and J. Tanner. (2006). Immigration, social disadvantage and urban youth gangs: Results from a Toronto-area survey. *Community Journal of Urban Research, 15* (2), 18-37.

Wyatt, L., and M. Haskett. (2001). Aggressive and nonaggressive young adolescents' attributions of intent in teacher/student interactions. *Journal of Early Adolescence, 21,* 425-446.

Wyles, P. (2007). Success with Wraparound. *Youth Studies Australia, 26* (4), 45-53.

Young, J., and J. Klosko. (1994). *Reinventing Your Life: The Breakthrough Program to Reinventing Your Life and Feeling Great Again.* New York: Plume.

Young, K., and L. Craig. (1997). Beyond White Pride: Identity, Meaning and Contradiction in the Canadian Skinhead Subculture. *Canadian Review of Sociology and Anthropology 34* (2): 175 – 206.

York, G. (1990). *The Dispossessed: Life and Death in Native Canada.* London: Vintage UK.

Zhang, S., and L. Zhang. (2005). An Experimental Study of the Los Angeles Repeat Offender Prevention Program: Its Implementation and Evaluation. *Criminology and Public Policy, 4,* 205–36.

INDEX